Light in the Labyrinth

Constantino V. Riccardi

Contra Mundum Productions
Redlands, California

 Inquiries should be sent to: Contra Mundum Productions, 25 South 6th Street, #102, Redlands, CA 92373.
Cover design and layout by Angie Biesterfeld, abiest@inland.net.

The light shines on
in the darkness, and
the darkness has
never mastered it.

The Gospel of John
Chapter 1, Verse 5

CONTENTS.

INTRODUCTION.

LIGHT IN THE LABYRINTH attempts to chart the path of the spiritual truth seeker in the labyrinth of this world.
It begins with the story of the labyrinth at Crete as described by classical Greek and Roman authors. The story of Minos, the Minotaur, Theseus, and Ariadne are recreated for the modern reader.

The philosophical and theological implications of the spiritual maze are then analyzed through John Calvin's 16th century references to the labyrinthine image. The humanistic side of Calvin becomes apparent as well as his insights concerning radical evil.

Finally, dramatic dialogues present the struggle for the light in the lives and thoughts of Doubting Thomas, Soren Kierkegaard, Dietrich Bonhoeffer, and Camilio Torres.

Thomas, an Apostle, found it hard to believe.
Soren Kierkegaard, a famous thinker, thought that belief in the light overcomes despair and anxiety.
Dietrich Bonhoeffer, a German theologian who was hanged by the Nazis, felt that the light demands that we expose the depraved darkness of an Adolf Hitler.
Camilio Torres, a Colombian priest turned freedom fighter, believed that the light requires us to feed the hungry and clothe the naked.

PART I

CHAPTER ONE
The Labyrinth at Crete

In discovering the story of the labyrinth at Crete as based in classical Greek and Roman sources, it would be most advantageous to understand that one now enters a realm divided between fiction and fact, exaggeration and history, and myth and reality. In this realm scenes are enacted which range from the pornographic to the sublime. This being the case, it is best at present to hold theory at bay and let the scenes present themselves. This is most easily done by beginning with the person of Daedalus.

A. Daedalus

With respect to the actual historical existence and mythical influence of the person of Daedalus, the classical Greek and Roman sources offer only a possible reconstructive sketch of his origin, his abilities, his character, and his role in the story of the labyrinth at Crete. Plato speculates that Daedalus lived "some one thousand or two thousand years" prior to the writing of the Platonic dialogue The Laws.[1] This would mean that Daedalus lived between the years 2350 B.C. and 1250 B.C. His place of birth was Athens.[2] His name was

---

[1] Plato Laws 3. 677d.
[2] Pausanias Guide to Greece 9. 3, 2. Diodorus Siculus The Library of History 4. 76, 1.

derived from the festival or the wooden figures.[3] The origin of this festival was as follows:

> They say Hera was angry with Zeus over something or other, and withdrew to Euboia, and Zeus, not being able to win her round, went to Kithairon who at that time was ruling Plataia. Now no wiser creature existed than Kithairon. He told Zeus to make a wooden statue, wrap it up in veils, and put it in an ox-wagon: and then to say he (Zeus) was marrying Plataia, daughter of Asopos. Zeus did what Kithairon suggested: Hera knew at once she was on the spot. When she came up close and ripped the clothes off the statue, she was delighted with the trick, seeing it was a wooden woman and not a bride, and she was reconciled with Zeus. They hold the Daidala as the festival of that reconciliation, because the ancients called wooden figures daidala.[4]

Another account of the origin of this festival concludes that Hera, being reconciled to Zeus,

> herself led the bridal procession with joy and laughter; she gave honour to the wooden image, by naming the festival Daidala, but for all that she burnt it up, lifeless though it was, in her jealousy.[5]

This etymological analysis of the name "Daedalus" further indicates and outlines those legends which surround Daedalus himself. Apollodorus describes him as "an excellent architect and the first inventor of images."[6] According to Pliny "Daedalus was the first person who worked in wood; it was he

---

[3] Pausanias Guide to Greece 9. 3, 2-4.
[4] Pausanias Guide to Greece 9. 3,1-2.
[5] Plutarch On the Festival of Images at Plataea fragment 157. 6.
[6] Apollodorus The Library 3. 15, 8.

who invented the saw, the axe, the plummet, the gimlet, glue, and isinglass."[7] For Pliny Daedalus was also the inventor of sailing ships.[8]

Commenting on the overall quality of his art Diodorus Siculus states:

> In natural ability he towered far above all other men and cultivated the building art, the making of statues, and the working of stone. He was also the inventor of many devices which contributed to the advancement of his art and built works in many regions of the inhabited world which arouse the wonder of men. In the carving of his statues he so far excelled all other men that later generations invented the story about him that the statues of his making were quite like their living models; they could see, they said, and walk and, in a word, preserved so well the characteristics of the entire body that the beholder thought that the image made by him was a being endowed with life. And since he was the first to represent the open eye and to fashion the legs separated in a stride and the arms and hands as extended, it was a natural thing that he should have received the admiration of mankind for the artists before his time had carved their statues with the eyes closed and the arms and hands hanging and attached to the sides.[9]

This description at Daedalus' artistic ability is also affirmed by other classical sources. According to Athenaeus of Naucratis all beautiful works of art were ascribed to Daedalus.[10] Although Pausanias contends that "the works of

---

[7] Pliny Natural History 7. 57.
[8] Pliny Natural History 19. 1.
[9] Diodorus Siculus The Library of History 4. 76, 1-3.
[10] Athenaeus of Naucratis The Deipnosophists 7. 301b.

Daidalus are rather clumsy to look at,"[11] he also asserts that "they have a strong sense of something divine."[12] Apollodorus records that Daedalus' statue of Hercules was so realistic that Hercules mistook it "at night for living and threw a stone and hit it."[13] Lucian comments that one of his statues was actually capable of "playing truant" from its pedestal.[14] Socrates, claiming Daedalus as his first ancestor, refers to him as the "founder of my line."[15] Socrates not only refers to Daedalus' works as ideal models,[16] but also wishes to use the legend of the moving statues to help illustrate the necessity of correct thinking and right reason. Socrates argued that many statements and thoughts were analogous to Daedalus' statues in that they were not fully "tied down" through proper reasoning. Popular opinion, human traditions, and fluctuating biases all aid in forming unsubstantial definitions, statements, and thoughts. These insubstantial definitions, statements, and thoughts are prone to augment confusion and frustrate the human person's search for an abiding clarity about the real nature of knowledge.[17] For Socrates real knowledge is to be worked out and "tethered" through the dialectical reasoning process of recollection.[18]

Perhaps the final summation concerning Daedalus' ability as an artist comes from Hyginus' Fabulae. Hyginus simply states that Daedalus' talents were so great that he "is said to have received the art of craftsmanship from Athena,"[19] the Greek goddess who was the patroness of arts and crafts. However, despite this aesthetic reputation, Hyginus goes on

---

[11] Pausanias Guide to Greece 2. 4, 5.
[12] Pausanias Guide to Greece 2. 4, 5.
[13] Apollodorus The Library 2. 6, 3.
[14] Lucian The Lover of Lies 19.
[15] Plato Euthyphro 11c.
[16] Plato Ion 533b. Plato Republic 7. 529e. Plato Greater Hipppias 282a.
[17] Plato Euthyphro 11c, d, e; 15b-c. Plato Meno 97d,e.
[18] Plato Meno 97e-98a.
[19] Hyginus Fabulae 39.

to say that Daedalus "threw down from the roof Perdix, son of his sister, envying his skill, because he first invented the saw."[20] Despite Pliny's report that Daedalus was the inventor of the saw,[21] there is much evidence which sides with Hyginus' account. Although there is some disagreement as to the name of Daedalus' nephew (variously called Kalos,[22] Talos[23] and Perdix[24]), there is a decided agreement that this nephew did invent the saw.[25] According to Diodorus Siculus and Apollodorus, the nephew of Daedalus invented the saw by improvising on the jawbone of a snake.[26] According to Ovid, the same nephew "observed the backbone of a fish and, taking it as a model, cut a row of teeth in a thin strip of iron and thus invented the saw."[27] In addition to the invention of he saw this pupil of Daedalus has also been credited with the invention of the compasses[28] and the potter's wheel.[29] All of these accomplishments help to explain why "Daedalus, becoming jealous of the youth and feeling that his fame was going to rise far above that of his teacher, treacherously slew the youth."[30]

For the murder of his nephew and pupil, Daedalus was brought to trial in Athens and found guilty.[31] From Athens he fled to Attica and then to the island of Crete.[32]

---

[20] Hyginus Fabulae 39.
[21] See footnote 9, Chapter One.
[22] Pausanias Guide to Greece 1. 21, 6.
[23] Apollodorus The Library 3. 15, 8. Diodorus Siculus The Library of History 4. 76, 4-5.
[24] Hyginus Fabulae 39.
[25] Apollodorus The Library 3. 15, 8. Diodorus Siculus The Library of History 4. 76, 5. Ovid Metamorphoses 8. 235-250.
[26] Diodorus Siculus The Library of History 4. 76, 5. Apollodorus The Library 3. 15, 8.
[27] Ovid Metamorphoses 8. 244-246.
[28] Ovid Metamorphoses 8. 247-249. Diodorus Siculus The Library of History 4. 76, 5.
[29] Diodorus Siculus The Library of History 4. 76, 5.
[30] Diodorus Siculus The Library of History 4. 76, 6.
[31] Ibid., 4. 76, 7.
[32] Ibid., 4. 76, 7-4. 77, 1.

B. The Labyrinth at Crete and the Minotaur

At the time of Daedalus' arrival in Crete, King Minos was the ruler of the island. Minos' laws were considered to be a paradigm of justice delivered to him every nine years by Zeus himself.[33] Minos had also increased the fortune and security of Crete by establishing a strong navy.[34] The prosperity of Minos' realm at the time of Daedalus' arrival is well attested to by Minos' desire to become a patron of the arts. Daedalus was commissioned to design a dancing floor for Ariadne, one of Minos' daughters.[35] He was also commissioned to undertake the sculpting of various wooden idols.[36] Pasiphae, the wife of Minos and sister of Circe,[37] also desired that Daedalus design a particular invention which was to be completely hidden from the public.

In explaining the need for this invention, it is necessary to briefly note a few historical-mythological incidents which pertain to the kingdom of Minos. Minos was reputed to be the son of Zeus and Europa. A brief account of this courtship is that Zeus loved Europa "and turning himself into a tame bull, he mounted her on his back and conveyed her through the sea to Crete. There Zeus bedded with her, and she bore Minos, Sarpedon, and Rhadamanthys...."[38]

This image of the beast, beginning with Zeus' seduction of Europa and the birth of Minos, have extended meanings. It seems that although Mino's ability as a legislator and ruler was of high repute, there was some doubt

---

[33] Plato The Laws 624b. Homer The Odyssey 19. 178-179.
[34] Callimachus Aetia 4. Diodorus Siculus The Library of History 5. 78, 3.
[35] Homer The Iliad 18. 590-592.
[36] Pausanias Guide to Greece 8. 53, 8.
[37] Apollodorus The Library 1. 9, 1.
[38] Ibid., 3. 1, 1.

concerning his own private morality and feigned religious devotion.

> Now if any woman had intercourse with Minos, it was impossible for her to escape with life; for because Minos cohabited with many women, Pasiphae bewitched him, and whenever he took another woman to his bed, he discharged wild beasts at her joints, and so the women perished.[39]

The "wild beasts" which Minos emitted from his body were "snakes, scorpions, and millipeds."[40]

It should not be inferred that Pasiphae, in her desire to curb her husband's appetitive nature with an early form of venereal disease, remained a devoted yet vengeful spouse. Apparently

> it had been the custom of Minos annually to dedicate to Poseidon the fairest bull born in his herds and to sacrifice it to the god; but at the time in question there was born a bull of extraordinary beauty and he sacrificed another from among those which were inferior, whereupon Poseidon, becoming angry at Minos, caused his wife Pasiphae to become enamoured of the bull.[41]
>
> In her love for the bull she (Pasiphae) found an accomplice in Daedalus, an architect, who had been banished from Athens for murder. He constructed a wooden cow on wheels, took it, hollowed it out in the inside, sewed it up in the hide of a cow which he had skinned, and set it in the meadow in which the bull used to

---

[39] Ibid., 3. 15, 1.

[40] This is Sir James George Frazier's citation of Antoninus Liberalis (Transform. 41) in Apollodorus, The Library, vol. 1, p. 105, n. 1 of The Loeb Classical Library.

[41] Diodorus Siculus The Library of History 4. 77, 2-3.

> graze. Then he introduced Pasiphae into it; and the bull came and coupled with it, as if it were a real cow. And she gave birth to Asterius, who was called the Minotaur.[42]
>
> This creature, they say, was of double form, the upper parts of the body as far as the shoulders being those of a bull and the remaining parts those of a man.[43]

Once the Minotaur had been born, Minos was then forced to find some means for hiding it and its implied shame and disgrace.[44] The ingenuity of Daedalus was again called upon. Daedalus was aware of an Egyptian tomb known as the Labyrinth which the Egyptian king Mendes (whom some called Marrus) had had constructed for his own burial.[45] This Egyptian labyrinth was of enormous size possessing three thousand rooms above and below ground, courts, sculptures, galleries, and an almost infinite number of winding passages.[46] The labyrinth which Daedalus designed and constructed at Crete "was only the hundredth part of it, that portion namely, which encloses circuitous passages, windings, and inextricable galleries which lead to and fro."[47] The design and intricacy of the labyrinth at Crete was so complex that, once Daedalus had completed its construction, he was "himself scarce able to find his way back to the place of entry...."[48] The Minotaur, Pasiphae's "hybrid monster-child"[49] and "the monster of the bull-man form,"[50] was then hidden in the inextricable windings of the Cretan labyrinth.

---

[42] Apollodorus The Library 3. 1, 4.
[43] Diodorus Siculus The Library of History 4. 77, 3.
[44] Ovid Metamorphoses 8. 152-158.
[45] Diodorus Siculus The Library of History 1. 61, 1-2.
[46] Herodotus 2. 148.
[47] Pliny Natural History 36. 19.
[48] Ovid Metamorphoses 8. 166-170.
[49] Ibid., 8. 156.
[50] Ibid., 8. 169.

C. Human Sacrifice, Theseus, and Ariadne's Thread.

Coinciding with the scandal caused by the birth of the Minotaur, there occurred another incident which totally inflamed the wrath of Minos. Androgeos, a son of Minos, had been slain in Athens during the reign of the Athenian king Aegeus.[51] One account contends that Aegeus killed Androgeous because the latter had attempted to gain control of the city for his father.[52] Another version states that Androgeous was killed by the Marathon Bull (a monster sent by the gods to punish the human race by ravaging the countryside "killing whomever it met"[53]) while he was visiting Athens.[54] Regardless of which account is accepted, Minos sought to avenge the death of his son through war and the intervention of Zeus. Zeus, granting his request, plagued the Athenians with draught and famine.[55] The Athenians at first attempted to appease the wrath of the god by sacrificing the daughters of Hyacinth in obedience to an ancient oracle.[56] When the girls' deaths failed to change anything,

> they inquired of the oracle how they should be delivered; and the god answered them that they should give Minos whatever satisfaction he might choose. So they sent to Minos and left it to him to claim satisfaction. And Minos ordered them to send seven youths and the

---

[51] Diodorus Siculus The Library of History 4. 60, 5-4. 61, 2.
[52] Diodorus Siculus The Library of History 4. 60, 4-5.
[53] Pausanias Guide to Greece 1. 27, 9.
[54] Ibid.
[55] Pausanias (Guide to Greece 1. 27, 9) states that the Athenians were defeated by Minos' navy and then capitulated to his will. However Apollodorus (The Library 3. 15, 8) reports that the war ended inconclusively. Minos then sought the intervention of Zeus. The intervention of Zeus is also recorded by Diodorus Siculus The Library of History 4. 61, 1.
[56] Apollodorus The Library 3. 15, 8.

> same number of damsels without weapons to be fodder for the Minotaur.[57]

This sacrifice of seven youths and seven maidens was to be given "every nine years to the Minotaur for him to devour, for as long a time as the monster should live."[58] When the Athenians complied with Minos' requests, the famine, draught, and warfare with Crete ended.[59]

The sources are in agreement that the Minotaur fed upon the flesh and blood of the young Atheninas at least once.[60] After nine years, Minos again returned to Athens for the required number of youths and maidens.[61]

At this time Theseus, son of the Athenian king Aegeus, was present to listen to the demands of Crete. Theseus had already distinguished himself by a series of heroic deeds. At the age of seven this son of Aegeus had attended a dinner where Hercules himself was present. Hercules had taken off the lion-skin he was known to wear and laid it aside. The other children present with Theseus saw the lion-skin and, thinking it to be a real lion, fled. Theseus also believed it was a real lion; however, he "grabbed an axe from the attendants, and made a fierce attack on it...."[62] As Theseus grew up he became notorious for his battles with more animate monsters. With the demise of Hercules, robber-barons began to plague the Athenian

---

[57] Ibid., c.f. also Pausanias Guide to Greece 1. 27, 9; Hyginus Fabulae 41; Plutarch Theseus 15. 1-2; Ovid Heroides epistle 10.
[58] Diodorus Siculus The Library of History 4. 61, 3.
[59] Ibid.
[60] Diodorus Siculus The Library of History 4. 61, 4. Ovid (Metamorphoses 8. 169-171) states that the Minotaur fed twice on Athenian blood.
[61] Diodorus Siculus The Library of History 4. 61, 4. This account may throw some light on Ovid's contention that the youths were sacrificed twice. That there was to be a second sacrifice is beyond dispute. Their having actually been sacrificed a second time remains a debatable issue.
[62] Pausanias Guide to Greece 1. 27, 8.

countryside. One such hoodlum named Sciron lived among the cliffs and would

> Wantonly thrust out his feet to strangers and bid them wash them, and then, while they were washing them, kick them off into the sea.[63]

Theseus killed him.

Another villain Phaeu,

> a female robber, a woman of murderous and unbridled spirit who dwelt in Crommyon, was called Sow because of her life and manners....[64]

Theseus also killed her.

After destroying these and other monsters[65] and/or robber-miscreants,[66] Theseus then did battle with the Marathon Bull.[67] He mastered the beast and, driving it through the city of Athens, killed and sacrificed it to the gods on the Acropolis.[68] By the time of Theseus' encounter with Minos, his legend had so begun to flourish that the invention of the art of wrestling[69] was attributed to him as well as descent from the god Poseidon.[70]

---

[63] Plutarch Theseus 10. 1-2. Pausanias Guide to Greece 1. 44, 12.
[64] Plutarch Theseus 9.
[65] Plutarch Theseus 6. 6-14.
[66] Ibid.
[67] Callimachus Hecale.
[68] Plutarch Theseus 14. 1. Pausanias Guide to Greece 1. 27, 9. Plutarch has Theseus sacrificing the Marathon Bull to the Delphinian Apollo while Pausanias has him sacrificing it "to the goddess."
[69] Pausanias Guide to Greece 1. 139, 3.
[70] Plutarch (Theseus 6. 1-2) gives a more rational origin of his descent from Poseidon. The more mythological interpretation can be found in Plato The Republic 3. 391c-d; Statius Thebaid 665; and Cicero De Natura Deorum 3. 18, 45.

When Minos again demanded the human sacrifice for the beast-man, Theseus "of his own accord"[71] and boasting loudly[72] "promised to go against the Minotaur"[73] and master it.[74] Minos assured him that if he could kill the monster without using any warlike weapons the penalty would cease.[75] Theseus was then charged by his father Aegeus "to have white sails for his ships if he came back the victor; those who were sent to the Minotaur journeyed with black sails."[76] After the sacrificial victims were chosen by lot and Theseus had offered his prayers and vows to the gods; the victims, Theseus, and Minos sailed to Crete.[77]

It appears that at first Minos simply desired the demise of Theseus to complete the vendetta begun with the death of his own son Androgeos. This is not only plausible because of Minos' readiness to accept Theseus' offer to fight the Minotaur unarmed, but also because of an incident which occurred when they first arrived at Crete. Minos questioned Theseus' legendary descent from Poseidon. He contended that if Theseus was really a son of Poseidon he would be able to recover Minos' signet ring if it were thrown into the sea. Minos then dropped his ring into the sea, perhaps desiring that Theseus would drown. However, Theseus not only recovered the ring, but also surfaced wearing a golden wreath presented to him by Amphitrite, the wife of Poseidon.[78]

After this occurrence Minos' attitude began to change. Combined with the gods marked favor for Theseus was the

---

[71]Hyginus Fabulae 41.
[72] Plutarch Theseus 17. 4
[73] Hyginus Fabulae 41.
[74] Plutarch Theseus 17. 4.
[75] Plutarch Theseus 17. 3
[76] Hyginus Fabulae 41. Compare also Plutarch Theseus 17. 4; Diodorus Siculus The Library of History 4. 61, 4; and Apollodorus Epitome 1. 7-8.
[77] Plutarch Theseus 18.
[78] Pausanias Guide to Greece 1. 17, 3; cf. also Hyginus Poetica Atronomica 2. 5.

actual strength of the man himself. This attribute was to become useful to Minos. Taurus, a general of Minos, had recently become a powerful threat to the Cretan king. This same general was also accused "of too great intimacy with Pasiphae."[79] Upon the return of Minos, funeral games were scheduled in which Taurus was expected to be the undisputed victor. However, Theseus was permitted to enter the games as a competitor against Taurus. Minos was delighted with the outcome in that Taurus was defeated and disgraced.[80]

At these same games Ariadne, the daughter of Minos, was present. She became infatuated with the appearance of Theseus and admired his athletic abilities.[81] The infatuation quickly led to a deeply passionate love. Ariadne then offered her assistance to Theseus if he would agree to take her to Athens and marry her.[82] He vowed to do as she requested.[83] Ariadne then consulted with Daedalus with respect to the best means for escaping the labyrinth.[84] Upon the artist's advice to Ariadne, Theseus took a ball of thread from her and, tying it to the door of the labyrinth, unwound it as he made his way through the numerous circuits and passages.[85]

As Theseus began to wander through the innumerable and confusing passage-ways, he was forced to move ever so cautiously in order that the delicate thread would not snap. In the darkness he had to be alert, to listen for any other noise or

---

[79] Plutarch Theseus 19. 1-3.
[80] Ibid. Plutarch quotes Philochorus as the source. According to Philochorus, Minos was so delighted that he gave the youths and maidens back to Theseus and remitted the tribute. However, as will be seen, the majority of sources (including Plutarch himself Theseus 19. 1) report that Theseus did battle with the Minotaur.
[81] Plutarch Theseus 19. 3.
[82] Apollodorus Epitome 1. 8. Cf. also Catullus 64.
[83] Ibid.
[84] Apollodorus Epitome 1. 8.
[85] Ibid. 1. 9. Cf. also Ovid Metamorphoses 8. 170-175; Plutarch Theseus 19. 1; Catullus 64.

movement. Cautious, waiting, stepping through innumerable outward and inward mists, he knew that any darkened, winding tunnel could produce the sudden vicious onslaught of an inhuman monster. Unarmed, unknowing but listening, he was forced to distinguish his own movement and breathing from that of an unseen yet real threat of certain destruction.

Exactly where in the last section of the labyrinth Theseus met the Minotaur is unknown. There is no chart and there is no map. Theseus himself would be unable to say. What is known is that in some darkened cave an unearthly bellow was heard and, against the tossing horns of the man-bull, Theseus was forced to fight.[86] In an extremely close and darkened arena the Athenian wrestler was able to grab one of the horns with a single hand. With his free fist he began smashing at the forehead of the beast.[87]

It is not known how long it took to defeat the monster. How many times the Minotaur broke loose and attacked again is also unknown. What is known is that Theseus finally succeeded in killing the man-beast with his fists.[88]

Rewinding the unbroken thread, the suitor of Ariadne returned to her. On the same day Theseus, Ariadne, and the sacrificial youths and maidens sailed for Athens stopping the first night on the island of Naxos.[89]

D. The Fall of Icarus, Ariadne's Abandonment, and Theseus' Return to Athens.

a. The Fall of Icarus

---

[86] Apollodorus Epitome 1. 9; Catullus 64.
[87] Statius Thebaid 12. 668-671.
[88] Apollodorus Epitome 1. 9; Catullus 64.
[89] Apollodorus Epitome 19. 1. Cf. also Plutarch Theseus 19. 1.

After Theseus, Ariadne, and the intended sacrificial victims had departed, Minos' wrath became enkindled against Daedalus. There are varied reasons why this occurred. Although Daedalus had constructed the labyrinth to hide the recriminating presence of the Minotaur, he had also been instrumental in the monster's birth. Furthermore, without Minos' permission, the sculptor-architect had plotted with Ariadne to save Theseus. Perhaps the hot flames of vendetta had not yet been stamped out within Minos' breast. Androgeos had died in Athens, and he had had the Athenian prince under his power. Despite his admiration for Theseus, Minos had still demanded that he confront the Minotaur. With Theseus free, the intended victims liberated, and his daughter gone, Minos must have felt a definite resentment with respect to the present order of things. Who could be a better victim for his vengeance than Daedalus?

In venting his rage Minos ordered that Daedalus and his son Icarus, "who had been born to Daedalus by Naucrate, a female slave of Minos,"[90] be shut up in the labyrinth.[91]

> But Daedalus constructed wings for himself and his son, and enjoined his son, when he took to flight, neither to fly high, lest the glue should melt in the sun and the wings should drop off, nor to fly near the sea, lest the pinions should be detached by the damp.[92]

A more detailed account is as follows:

> Ills often stir the wits; who would e'er have believed that man could sail the paths of air? He arranges in order feathers, the oarage of the birds, and interweaves the frail fabric with

---

[90] Apollodorus Epitome 1. 12.
[91] Ibid.
[92] Ibid.

linen fastenings; the base is bound with wax softened in the fire, and already the toil of the wondrous work was over. With beaming face the boy handled the feathers and the wax, not knowing that the harness was prepared for his own shoulders. "These are the ships," said his father, "whereon we must sail home; by their aid must we flee from Minos. The air Minos could not close, though he had closed all else; break through the air (for there thou canst) by my device. But not on the Tegean maid nor on sword-bearing Orion, comrade of Bootes, must thou fix thy gaze: me do thou follow on the wings that I shall give thee; I will lead the way, let it be thine to follow; under my leadership thou wilt be safe. For if we go nigh the sun through the upper air, the wax will be impatient of the heat; or if we beat our low-flying wings too near the sea, the nimble feathers will be wet with watery spray. Fly between the two; and the winds also hold in awe, my son, and where the breezes carry thee, spread thy sails to the breeze." While he counsels, he fits his handiwork on the boy, and shows him how to move, as their mother instructs the tender fledglings. Then he fastens on his shoulders the wings he has made for himself, and cautiously poises his body for its new journey. And now on the verge of flight he kissed his little son, nor could the father's eyes restrain the tears. There was a hill smaller than a mountain, but rising above the level plains; from this the bodies of the twain were launched on their hapless flight. Daedalus, while he plies his own, looks back at his son's wings, and ever keeps on his own course. And now the wondrous voyage delights them and forgetting his fear Icarus flies more courageously with daring skill. One who was angling for fish with tremulous line beheld them, and his right hand left the task he had begun. Already

> was Samos on their left, (Naxos and Paros had been passed, and Delos loved by the Clarian god): on their right was Lebynthos and Calymne shady with forests, and Astypallaea girt with fish-haunted seas; when the boy, too bold in his youthful daring, deserted his sire and winged his way too high. The fastenings give way, and the wax, too near the god, is melted; nor do his moving arms keep their hold on the frail air. Terrified, he gazed down at the water from the height of heaven; in his panic fear darkness came flooding upon his eyes. The wax had melted: bare are the arms he shakes; he shudders, nor has he aught that may sustain him. Down he falls, and falling cries, "Father, O father, I am borne away"; the green waters choked the words upon his lips. But his hapless sire, a sire no longer, calls, "Icarus!" "Icarus!" he cries, "where art thou? Where beneath heaven art thou flying?" "Icarus!" he was crying--he saw the feathers in the water.[93]

"Yielding to his sudden grief, Daedalus smote his breast, and his blows steered his flight though he knew it not."[94] The momentum of his arms caused him to continue flying until he safely reached Sicily.[95] The area of the Aegean Sea where his son fell came to be known as the Icarian Sea.[96]

b. Ariadne's Abandonment.

---

[93] Ovid The Art of Love 2. 43-95. Cf. also Ovid Fasti 4. 283-284; Ovid Metamorphoses 8. 183-235; Lucian Icaromenippus, or The Sky-Man 2-3; Silius Italicus Punica 12. 91-101; and Diodorus Siculus The Library of History 4. 77, 8-9.

[94] Silius Italicus Punica 12. 99-101.

[95] Apollodorus Epitome 1. 13. Cf. also Diodorus Siculus The Library of History 4. 77, 9.

[96] Pliny Natural History 4. 23; Ovid The Art of Love 2. 96; Apollodorus Epitome 1. 13; Strabo Geography 14. 1, 19.

There are varied accounts which attempt to describe Theseus' attitude towards Ariadne on the island of Naxos.[97] Some sources state that Theseus was guilty of intentionally abandoning her.[98] Another account declares that his ship was swept out to sea by a sudden storm and, against his will, he was forced to leave her.[99] Whatever may have been his intentions, there is little doubt that Ariadne held him culpable for deserting her.[100]

Listening to her own solitary lamentations on the island of Naxos, Ariadne discovers herself surrounded by wild beasts. Still, even wild beasts are more merciful than Theseus who abandoned her.[101]

In desperation she runs to a high cliff and calls to the sea for Theseus to return. Recognizing herself as a woman half-dead with despair, Ariadne feels the South wind attempting to refresh her. But now this wind only brings to bitter recognition the filled sails of Theseus' ship freely gliding on the wine-blue water.[102]

Ariadne then begins to regret all that she has done for Theseus. She mocks the tales that he will tell of his heroic deeds, unless he will also relate the deed of betraying her. More and more the daughter of Minos feels the heavy longing for home. But deserted, a prey to wild beasts, and a defenceless wretch for sailors who might land on the island, Ariadne can only say, "A thousand shapes of destruction suggest themselves to my mind; and death is a less punishment than the delay of death."[103]

---

[97] Plutarch Theseus 20.
[98] Ibid., 20. 1; Ovid The Epistles of the Heroines 10; Ovid Metamorphoses 8. 176-179; Apollonius Rhodius The Argonautica 4. 433-434.
[99] Plutarch Theseus 20. 3
[100] Ovid The Epistles of the Heroines 10.
[101] Ibid.
[102] Ibid.
[103] Ibid.

c. Theseus' Return to Athens.

Ariadne's abandonment was finally soothed by the appearance of Dionysos. Apparently, until the time of her death, she was comforted and refreshed by those gifts personified in the god of eros and wine.[104] At her death the gods took the wreath which Theseus had obtained in his diving for Minos' ring and had given to her.[105] Transforming it into a constellation of stars, they placed it in the heavens.[106] In ancient astrological descriptions, the same constellation was known as "The Crown of Ariadne."[107]

Little remains to be done in relating the story of the labyrinth at Crete. However one final episode should be recorded which pertains to Theseus' journey from the island of Naxos to Athens. This journey admits of at least two different interpretations. These two interpretations can best be presented by describing Theseus' attitude to a statue of Aphrodite made by Daedalus for Ariadne. Ariadne had given it to Theseus as a symbol of her love.[108] If Theseus' willful abandoning of Ariadne is accepted, then one can well agree with that account which has him stopping at the island of Delos, dedicating the idol of Aphrodite to Apollo and, exuberantly rejoicing in his freedom from the shackles of marriage vows, dancing with the liberated youths and maidens a dance imitating "the circling passages in the

---

[104] Ovid Metamorphoses 8. 176-179. In Pausanias Guide to Greece 1. 20, 2; 9. 40, 2; and 10. 29, 2; Dionysos, through varied machinations, took Ariadne from Theseus. Pausanias' account is also affirmed by Diodorus Siculus The Library of History 4. 61, 5 and Apollodorus The Library 1. 9.

[105] Hyginus Poetica Astronomica 2. 5.

[106] Apollonius Rhodius The Argonautica 3. 1000-1004.

[107] Ibid., cf. also Hyginus Poetica Astronomica 2. 5; Ovid Metamorphoses 8. 178-181; Callimachus Aetia 110. 58-59; Diodorus Siculus The Library of History 4. 61, 5-6.

[108] Plutarch Theseus 21. 1; Pausanias Guide to Greece 9. 40, 2.

labyrinth, and consisting of certain rhythmic involutions and evolutions."[109] On the other hand, if it is accepted that Theseus was in any manner taken from Ariadne against his will, then, the following account would be more appropriate.

> The Delians say when Theseus was torn away from her, he dedicated the goddess's wooden idol to the Delian Apollo, to avoid being reminded of Ariadne if he took it home, and perpetually renewing the sufferings of love.[110]

This same twofold possibility of interpretation is significant in analyzing Theseus' negligence upon his arrival in Athens. It should be remembered that Aegeus, king of Athens and the father of Theseus, had instructed his son to sail home with white sales if the Minotaur was conquered.[111] Either because of joy[112] or because of grief,[113] Theseus forgot his father's words. Consequently when the king saw his son's ship sailing into the harbor, the unchanged black sails proclaimed the death of his son as well as the destruction of the Athenian youths and maidens. In despair Aegeus "threw himself down from the rocks and was dashed to pieces."[114]

Immediately upon anchoring in Athens, Theseus dispatched a herald to announce the good fortune of his return. Then, before all else, the conqueror of the Minotaur made his sacrifices to the gods.[115] The shrine to which he initially went contained the statues of "Saviour Artemis."[116]

---

[109] Plutarch Theseus 21. 1.
[110] Pausanias Guide to Greece 9. 40, 2.
[111] Cf. p. 16, n. 76.
[112] Plutarch Theseus 22. 1.
[113] Pausanias Guide to Greece 1. 22, 5.
[114] Plutarch Theseus 22. 1. Cf. also Apollodorus Epitome 1. 10-11; Pausanias Guide to Greece 1. 22. 5; Diodorus Siculus The Library of History 4. 61, 6-8.
[115] Plutarch Theseus 22. 1.
[116] Pausanias Guide to Greece 2. 31, 1.

Theseus believed that through her, divine providence had favored his wanderings in the labyrinth.[117]

Meanwhile,

> the messenger found many of the people bewailing the death of their king, and others full of joy at his tidings, as was natural, and eager to welcome him and crown him with garlands for his good news. The garlands, then, he accepted, and twined them about his herald's staff, and on returning to the seashore, finding that Theseus had not yet made his libations to the gods, remained outside the sacred precincts, not wishing to disturb the sacrifice. But when the libations were made, he announced the death of Aegeus. Thereupon, with tumultuous lamentation, they went up in haste to the city. Whence it is, they say, that to this day, at the festival of the Oschophoria, it is not the herald that is crowned, but the herald's staff, and those who are present at the libations cry out: "Eleleu! Iou! Iou!" the first of which cries is the exclamation of eager haste and triumph, the second of consternation and confusion.[118]

[117] Ibid.

[118] Plutarch Theseus 22. 2-3.

CHAPTER TWO
THE LABYRINTH OF HUMAN DECISION

Commenting on the human predicament, John Calvin[1] said:

> Our condition in this world, I acknowledge, is entangled in so many miseries and is tormented by such a diversity of afflictions that scarcely a single day goes by without disgust and pain. Consequently, amidst so many uncertain occurrences, it cannot be otherwise than that we constantly perceive ourselves in a state of distress and alarm. Therefore, in whichever direction men turn themselves, a labyrinth of evils encloses them....[2]

---

[1] The story of the labyrinth at Crete may at first appear to be irrelevant in relation to the person and work of John Calvin (1509-1564). There are of course those historically nebulous yet persistently popular portraits of Calvin as the iron-fisted disciplinarian of Geneva, the ice-hearted dogmatician of stale reason, the father of Puritanism, and the murderer of Servetus. These same portraits would only be able to identify Calvin with Minos and leave it at that. However, there is indeed another picture of Calvin which might reverse common opinion of only for a moment.

In attempting to discover this latter picture, I have found it necessary to leap over the multitude of commentaries on intellectual history and current magazine articles. That is, I have found it necessary to read Calvin himself.

Such an unpopular pastime as first reading some of Calvin's works and then reflecting about them has disclosed certain phenomena which may yet be of importance to the seeker of eternal truth. Through Calvin's own use of the image of the labyrinth there has arisen the possibility of describing the maze into which we are born.

[2] "Conditio nostra, fateor, tot miseriis in hoc mundo implicita est, tantaque varietate agitatur, ut nullus fere dies sine molestia et dolore praeteereat, deinde inter tot dubios eventus fieri non potest quin assidue anxii simus ac trepidi. Quocunque igitur se vertant homines labyrinthus malorum eos circumdat." (Commentary on Psalm 30: 5-6; CO 31:294-295.)

How does one enter this "labyrinth of evils"? What does one discover within the maze? What is the quality of life lived down in the gloomy recesses of its darkened, subterranean passageways?

Initially it is to be discovered how one enters the labyrinth. For Calvin a person enters the labyrinth when he wishes to make decisions "above God."[3] Now two things have been said. First, it is the human person who is in this case making decisions. Second, he is making decisions "above God," that is, decisions which do not find their center in God or are not properly related to God. This posits that there is something definitely erratic about human decisions in relation to God. It also posits that man's knowledge of God, without God's aid, is also extremely erratic.

In further explaining these statements, it will be necessary to examine the elements contained within human decision, and what would explain the impetus of these elements to err. In this way it will be discovered how such elements of decision lead "above God" and into the labyrinth.

A. Human Decision and the Knowledge of Ourselves.

What is contained within every human decision? A brief self-examination would bring to light a highly complex amalgam composed of physical processes. In conjunction with

---

The following abbreviations will be used throughout this discussion:

CO Baum, Wilhelm, Cunitz, Edward, and Reuss, Edward (ed.), Ioannis Calvini Opera quae supersunt omnia. Braunschweig (and later Berlin): C.A. Schwetschke & Sons, 1865 ff.

OS Barth, Peter, and Niesel, Wilhelm (ed.), Johannis Calvini Opera Selecta. 5 vols. München: Chr. Kaiser Verlag, 1926-36.

such physical processes there is also a highly complex amalgam composed of such powers as reason, will, imagination, emotion, and conscience. Both the physical amalgam of complex processes and the complex amalgam composed of the human powers of reason, will, imagination, emotion, and conscience attempt to unify at the time of decision-making. However, it is often discovered that this attempt of the self to obtain unity is frustrated. The mind wishes to oversee and to possess all knowledge, but the eyes blink in exhaustion. The will wants to devour the world, but the body needs a laxative. The imagination envisions a billion years of life, but the arteries seldom allow a hundred.

Confronting this discordant wrenching of the self in opposite directions, the human person perpetually strives to make decisions concerning the most effective course of action. What is right? What is wrong? How much am I deceiving myself? Who is deceiving me? Who is getting what out of the deal? Who is dealing from the bottom of the deck? Thus the self attempts to reach a type of clarity about itself, about its world, and about the end of its world.

It is needless to comment that confronting such questions a multitude of philosophies, theologies, and opinions offer explanations and answers. Since this multitude is ever on the increase, I can find no reason to exclude any theory which may offer a plausible explanation of the dichotomy found within human decision making. One such explanation is discoverable in John Calvin's comments on the knowledge of ourselves. According to Calvin the knowledge of ourselves

---

[3] "Ainsi donc tu vois maintenant ta folie, et comme tu es du tout hors du sens, quand tu entre en un tel labyrinthine de vouloir iujer par dessus luy." (Sermons on Job 36: 25-33; CO 35:305.)

> is twofold: namely, that we know the nature of our condition in which we were at the first beginning, and the nature of our condition which commenced with the fall of Adam....[4]

In further describing the first part to of this twofold knowledge, Calvin described the life of Adam before the fall. For Calvin, Adam

> was happy in every way. Consequently in his life he esteemed equally both his body and his soul. While he lived with correct judgment in his soul and the proper moderation of affections, life also reigned. In his body there was no defect. Therefore he was completely free from death. His life on earth was indeed temporal, however he would have departed into heaven without pain and without death.[5]

Such a paradisaical state of happiness, sound judgment, and freedom from pain and death could of course be cynically mocked as some type of colossal joke perpetrated by a wanton buffoon. Misery, disease, suicide, murder, war, and cemeteries are all witnesses to the fact that Adam's Eden is indeed a lost world. However, the capacity of envisioning and striving for this paradise is not totally lost to our self-knowledge. Some parents still plan a better life for their children. Some scientists still struggle to cure disease. Some politicians still attempt universal peace. Some poets describe human wretchedness yet lament the fact that their

---

[4] "Etsi autem ea duplex est: nempe ut sciamus quales nos prima origine simus conditi, et quails nostra conditio esse coeperit post Adae lapsum...." (Institutes I, 15, 1; OS III, p. 173.)

[5] "Erat omni ex parte beatus: ideo eius vita ad corpus et animam pariter spectabat: Quum in eius anima vigeret rectum iudicium, et iusta affectuum moderatio, illic quoque vita regnabat: in corpore nullum erat vitium: quare totus a morte erat immunis. Terrena quidem vita illi fuisset temporalis: in coelum tamen sine interitu, et illaesus migrasset." (Commentary on Genesis 2:16; CO 23:45.)

descriptions are true. Thus, the vision of the paradisaical life is not totally absent from the human person. However, the total realization of such a life remains imaginary.

An explanation of why such a life remains imaginary can be found in some of Calvin's statements pertaining to the second part of twofold knowledge of ourselves which is the knowledge of the human condition after the fall of Adam. But before this second part of the knowledge of ourselves can be examined, it is necessary to have one more assertion from Calvin concerning Adam's primal human perfection. Although happiness, sound judgment, freedom from pain, and freedom from death are inordinately valuable characteristics, Calvin would not agree that they were the most fundamental and significant characteristics of the first Adam. Rather, the essence of the first Adam was the image of God.

> Indeed, God could not have acted more generously towards man than by engraving His glory upon him, in order that man might exist as the living image of the divine wisdom and justice.[6]

In further describing the image of God as well as its subsequent condition, Calvin states:

> Now the image of God is the unimpaired excellence of human nature which shined brightly in Adam before his defection. But this same image was subsequently so violated and almost destroyed that nothing remains from its ruin except confusion, imperfection, destruction, and corruption....[7]

---

[6] "Nec vero liberalius cum eo agere Deus poterat quam illi gloriam suam imprimendo, ut esset quasi viva divinae sapientiae et iustitiae effigies." (Commentary on Genesis 5:1; CO 23:105.)

[7] "Ergo quum Dei imago sit integra naturae humanae preaestantia, quae refulsit in Adam ante defectionem, postea sic vitiata et prope deleta, ut nihil ex ruina nisi

The consequences of Adam's defection are still to be apprehended:

> Therefore, after the image of heaven was obliterated in him, he was not the only one to suffer this punishment—that in the place of wisdom, excellence, sanctity, truthfulness, and justice (with which he had been arrayed), there now came forth hideous plagues, blindness, violence, infamy, emptiness and injustice – but he also entangled and immersed his descendents in the same miseries.
>
> This is the inherited corruption which the church fathers termed "original sin" meaning by the term "sin" a corruption of a nature formerly good and pure.[8]

A more detailed description of original sin is as follows:

> Moreover, we hold that original sin is a corruption spread throughout our consciousness and affections in such a manner that correct intelligence and reason is perverted in us, and we are like poor blind people in the dark. The will is also subjugated to every sinister desire, full of rebellion, and addicted to evil. In short, we are wretched prisoners confined under the tyranny of sin.

---

confusum, mutilum, labeque infectum supersit...." (Institutes I, 15, 4; OS III, p. 180.)

[8] Postquam ergo in eo obliterata fuit caelestis imago, non solus sustinuit hanc poenam, ut in locum sapientiae, virtutis, sanctitatis, veritatis, iustitiae (quibus ornamentis vestitus fuerat) teterrimae cederent pestes, caecitas, impotentia, impuritas, vanitas, iniustitia: sed iisdem quoque miseriis implicuit suam progeniem ac immersit. Haec est haereditaria corruptio, quam peccatum originale veteres nuncuparunt, Peccati voce intelligentes naturae antea bonae puraeque depravationem. (Institutes II, 1, 5; OS III, pp. 232-233.)

> Not because in doing evil we are not pushed by our own will in such a way that we do not know how to throw elsewhere the fault of all our vices, but because having issued from the cursed race of Adam, we do not have a single drop of ability to do good, and all our powers are defective.[9]

The knowledge of our condition which commenced with the fall of Adam is for Calvin the knowledge of the effects of original sin. This knowledge of original sin primarily concerns itself with the vitiated condition of the image of God. In one quotation Calvin states that "the image of God" (Dei imago) was "almost destroyed" (prope deleta).[10] In another quotation Calvin states that "the image of heaven" (caelestis imago) "was obliterated" (obliterata fuit).[11] These two quotations indicate two things. If the "image of God" was "almost destroyed" there could still be some remnant though defective traces of the image of God in the human person. But if the "image of heaven" "was obliterated" it would mean that there are no remnant traces of Adam's primal perfection. As the following pages will prove, Calvin did indeed maintain that remnant traces of the image of God are still found in the human person. However, these remnant traces in and of themselves are totally unable to again attain primal

---

[9] D'avantage nous tenons que le peché originel est une corruption espandue par nos sens et affections, en sorte que le droite intelligence et raison est pervertie en nous, et sommes comme povres aveugles en tenebres, et la volonté est subiette a toutes mauvaises cupiditez, pleine de rebellion et adonnee à mal. Bref, que nous sommes povres captifs detenus sous la tyrannie de peché: non pas qu'en mal faisant nous ne soyons poussez par nostre volonté propre, tellement que nous ne sçaurions reietter ailleurs la faute de tous nos vices, mais pource qu'estans issue de la race maudite d'Adam, nous n'avons pas une seule goutte de vertu à bien faire, et toutes nos facultez sont vicieuses." (Confession de foy au nom des Eglises reformees du royaume de France faito durant la guerre pour presenter a l'Empereur, aux Princes et Estats d'Allemagne en la journee de Francfort [1562]; CO 9:756.)

[10] See footnote 7, this chapter.

[11] See footnote 8, this chapter.

perfection. On the contrary, these remnant traces of the image of God in the human person, because they are contaminated by original sin, may tend to obliterate totally the image of God. This latter contention will be partially analyzed in this chapter; however, a full analysis will be undertaken in Chapter III.

The present primary task is to discover which remnant traces of the image of God remain in the human person, how they are influenced by original sin, and how they are dialectically interrelated to each other. With respect to the knowledge of ourselves it should be clear that the remnant traces are indications of the nature of our condition at the first beginning as well as the subsequent condition after the fall. An effective means of uncovering this self-knowledge lies in investigating the human soul and its capacities.

B. The Human Soul and Its Capacities.

The following words of Calvin will offer an all-embracing introduction to his concept of the human soul and/or the human spirit:

> Moreover, that man consists of body and soul ought to be beyond controversy. Now by the term "soul" I understand an immortal yet created essence which is his nobler part. Sometimes it is called "spirit." Although these terms are associated with each other, they differ from one another in meaning. Yet when the term "spirit" is used by itself, it means the same thing as "soul"....[12]

[12] "Porro hominem constare anima et corpore, extra controversiam esse debet: atque animae nomine essentiam immortalem, creatam tamen intelligo, quae nobilior eius pars est. Interdum spiritus vocatur; etsi enim dum simul iunguntur haec nomina, significatione inter se differunt: ubi tamen seorsum ponitur spiritus, tantundem valet atque anima..." (Institutes I, 15, 2; OS III, p. 174.)

After positing that there is a soul or spirit Calvin then wishes to show that the soul does in fact exist, that it exists as an immortal essence, that it is the nobler part of man, and that the immortality of the soul is a created immortality. He attempts to establish the contention that the soul does in fact exist through the experiential phenomena of conscience and the gifts of the human mind.

> Surely conscience, which, distinguishing between good and evil, responds to the judgment of God, is a certain sign of the immortal spirit. For how could a motion without essence penetrate into the tribunal of God and inflict itself with terror at its own guilt? Certainly the body is not affected by the fear of spiritual punishment, but it falls heavily on the soul alone. From this it follows that the soul is endowed with essence.[13]

Conscience's indication that the soul is immortal and an essence should not be separated from these same indications as experienced through the gifts of the human mind.

> In short, the great number of noble gifts for which the human mind is esteemed reveals that something divine has been engraved on it; all these are testimonies of an immortal essence. For that sense perception which is in brute animals does not go beyond the body, or at least it does not extend itself farther than to the material things presented to it. But the

[13] "Certe conscientia, quae inter bonum et malum discernens, Dei judicio respondet, indubium est immortalis spiritus signum. Quomodo enim ad Dei tribunal penetraret motus sine essentia, et terrorem sibi ex reatu incuteret? Neque enim spiritualis poenae metu afficitur corpus, sed in solam animam cadit; unde sequitur, essentia praeditam esse." (Institutes I, 15, 2; OS III, p. 175.)

> nimbleness of the human mind in examining heaven and earth and the secrets of nature, and when all ages have been comprehended by the intellect's and the memory's arranging each thing in sequence inferring future events from past ones, it clearly demonstrates that there is something in man separate from the body.[14]

The human mind's gifts also help to distinguish the human soul from the soul of beasts.

> I admit that a living soul is often attributed to beasts because they have their own form of life. But it is beyond doubt that the beasts live in one way and man in another. Accordingly there is within the human soul reason, intelligence and will. These powers of reason, intelligence and will are not bound to the body. There is nothing astonishing if this same human soul subsists without the body and does not perish like the similar soul of brutes. Brutes have nothing other than bodily senses.[15]

That the soul is the nobler part of man is for Calvin a fact derivable from its being "the seat" of the image of God.

---

[14] "Denique quum tot praeclarae dotes quibus humana mens pollet, divinum aliquid insculptum ei esse clamitent, totidem sunt immortalis essentiae testimonia. Nam qui brutis animalibus inest sensus, extra corpus non egreditur: vel saltem non longius se extendit quam ad res sibi obiectas. Mentis vero humanae agilitas caelum et terram, naturaeque arcane perlustrans, et ubi secula omnia intellectu et memoria complexa est, singula digerens sua serie, futuraque ex praeteritis colligens, clare demonstrat latere in homine aliquid a corpore separatum." (Institutes I, 15, 2; OS III, p. 175.)

[15] "Fateor animam viventem non semel attributam bestiis, quia et ipsae vitam suam degunt: verum aliter vivunt, aliter vivit homo. Anima vivens est homini, qua sapit et intelligit: anima illis vivens est, quae motum et sensum dat corpori, Quum igitur animae hominis insit ratio, intellectus, voluntas, quae virtutes non sunt corpori adnexae: nihil mirum, si sine corpore subsistat, nec pereat instar brutarum, quae nihil aliud habent, quam sensus corporeos." (Psychopannychia; CO 5:201-202.)

"Although the glory of God certainly shines brightly in the outward man, it is still not to be doubted that the proper seat of His image is in the soul."[16]

Calvin's description of the soul as an immortal essence and the nobler part of man could lead the reader to an inference which would posit an essential divinity within the soul's own nature. That is, it could be inferred that such a high entity as the human soul is an eternal particle of God. At this point not only Calvin's concept of the soul as a created image of God comes forth, but also his doctrine of original sin.

For Calvin creation is not "a pouring out" (transfusio) of the Divine Essence into the human being, "but the beginning of essence from nothing" (sed essentiae ex nihilo exordium).[17]

Calvin's doctrine of original sin helps to establish the created nature of the human soul:

> Before I proceed further, it is necessary to oppose the delirium of the Manichees, which Servetus has attempted to introduce again in this age. Because it is said that God breathed the breath of life upon man's external form (Genes. 2:7), they think the soul to be a derivative particle of God's substance, as if some portion of boundless divinity had overflowed into man. Yet it is easy to quickly show what gross and detestable absurdities this diabolical error drags along with itself. For if the soul of man is from the essence of God through derivation, it would follow that the nature of God is not only subject to change and to the passions, but also to ignorance, depraved desires, feebleness, and every

[16] "Quanvis enim in homine externo refulgeat Dei gloria, propriam tamen imaginis sedem in anima esse dubium non est." (Institutes I, 15, 3; OS III, p. 176.)
[17] "Creatio autem non transfusio est, sed essentiae ex nihilo exordium." (Institutes I, 15, 5; OS III, p. 181.)

> description of vices. Nothing is more inconstant than man. Contrary motions stir up and variously perplex his soul. Continually he wanders because of ignorance. He yields, overcome by the slightest temptations. We know his soul to be a chasm and a lurking place for every sort of filth. All these things would have to be attributed to God's nature, if we allow that the soul is from the essence of God, or that it is a hidden inflowing of divinity. Who would not shudder at this monstrosity?[18]

The difficulties of human decision-making are posited in Calvin's concept of soul. The soul exists as a created immortal essence and the seat of the image of God, yet the soul is not essentially divine in its own nature. Although the soul is the nobler part of man, it is not free in itself from confusion, darkness and depravity. The human soul is higher than the soul of brutes, yet there is nothing more inconstant than man.

Although this brief analysis of the soul again indicates the twofold knowledge of ourselves, it is still necessary to develop a more thorough investigation into how the capacities or powers of the soul operate. In accomplishing this, it should be remembered that all the capacities or powers of the human

[18] "Caeterum antequam longius progrediar, Manichaeorum delirio occurrere necesse est, quod rursus hac aetate invehere tentavit Servetus. Quod dicitur inspirasse Deus in faciem hominis spiraculum vitae (Genes. 2. b. 7), putarunt animam traducem esse substantiae Dei: quasi aliqua immensae divinitatis portio in hominem fluxisset. Atqui hic diabolicus error quam crassas et foedas absurditates secum trahat, breviter ostendere facile est. Nam si ex Dei essentia per traducem sit anima hominis, sequetur, Dei naturam non solum mutationi esse obnoxiam et passionibus, sed ignorantiae quoque, pravis cupiditatibus, infirmitati et omne genus vitiis. Nihil homine inconstantius, quia eius animam exagitant et varie distrahunt contratii motus: subinde per inscitiam hallucinatur: minimis quibusque tentationibus victus succumbit: animam ipsam scimus sordium omnium lacunam ac receptaculum esse; quae omnia Dei naturae ascribere conveniet, si recipimus animam esse ex Dei essentia, vell arcanum

soul are active at the time of decision-making and are therefore instrumental in leading the human person into the labyrinth. These capacities or powers are reason, will, imagination, emotion, and conscience.

(a) Reason and (b) Will

Although Calvin was aware of those formulations of the soul's capacities found in Plato and Aristotle,[19] he contended that the soul basically consists of two faculties, intellect (intellectum) and will (voluntatem).[20] Calvin's basic definitions of the intellect and the will, as well as the basic interrelationship between them, are:

> the intellect is as it were the leader and ruler of the soul. The will always considers the command of the intellect, and in its own desires awaits the decision of the intellect.[21]
>
> Moreover, the function of the intellect is to distinguish between objects according to the value or worthlessness of each object. However, the will chooses and conforms to that which the intellect has declared good, and rejects and flees that which the intellect disapproves.[22]

---

divinitatis influxum. Quis ad hoc portentum non exhorreat?" (Institutes I, 15, 5; OS III, p. 181.)

[19] Institutes I, 15, 6-7; OS III, pp. 182-185.

[20] "Sic ergo habeamus, subesse duas humanae animae partes, quae quidem praesenti instituto conveniant, intellectum et volutatem." (Institutes I, 15, 7; OS III, pp. 184-185.)

[21] "...intellectum esse quasi animae ducem et gubernatorem: voluntatem in illius nutum semper respicere, et iudicium in suis desideriis expectare." (Institutes I, 15, 7; OS III, p. 185.)

[22] "Sit autem officium intellectus, inter obiecta discernere, prout unumquodque probandum aut improbandum visum fuerit: voluntatis autem, eligere et sequi quod bonum intellectus dictaverit: aspernari ac fugere quod improbarit." (Institutes I, 15, 7; OS III, p. 185.)

The significance of intellect and will cannot be overestimated in any discussion of Calvin's anthropology because "no faculty can be found in the soul which does not duly refer to one or the other of these parts."[23] Within this context Calvin subsumes the faculty of sense perception (sensum) under intellect.[24]He also subsumes the faculty of desire (appetitus) under will.[25]

From Calvin's statements that the will awaits and conforms to the decision of the intellect, it might be inferred that Calvin was simply another descendent from the halcyon days of Greek philosophy who wished to reiterate the primacy of intellect as the ruling faculty in man. Such an inference would be quite incorrect. It would be incorrect because of a question Calvin asks the reader. The question is: "From whence come so many labyrinths of errors in the world but because men are led by their own understanding only into vanity and untruth?"[26] He rejects the philosophical formulation which propounds that reason, suffused with divine light, illumines all decisions; while the senses, entangled in baser things, never attains true discernment.[27]

For Calvin, reason disagrees with itself and is at cross purposes with itself.[28] He compares the disharmonies within

---

[23] "...nullam reperiri posse in anima potentiam, quae non rite ad alterutrum istorum membrorum referatur." (Institutes I, 15, 7; OS III, p. 185.)

[24] "Atque hoc modo sensum sub intellectu comprehendimus..." (Institutes I, 15, 7; OS III, p. 185.)

[25] "Rursum pro apetitus nomine, quod illi malunt, voluntatis nomen, quod usitatius est, usurpo." (Institutes I, 15, 7; OS III, p. 185.)

[26] "Unde enim tot errorum labyrinthi in mundo, nisi quod homines proprio sensu nonnisi ad vanitatem et mendaciam feruntur?" (Commentary on the Gospel of John 1:5; CO 47:5.) I have translated "sensu" as "understanding" not only because in this context of The Commentary on the Gospel of John Calvin is discussing questions pretainng to the human mind, but also because "sensum" has alredy been shown (cf. n. 24, this chapter) to be subsumed under the faculty of intellect.

[27] Institutes II, 2, 2; OS III, pp. 242-243.

[28] "Quasi no ipsa quoque ratio secum dissideat, et eius consilia alia cum aliis non secus ac hostiles exercitus confligant." (Institutes I, 15, 6; OS III, p. 183.)

reason to armies at war.[29] Contrary to the philosophical proposition that reason is the capacity by which man may govern himself correctly,[30] Calvin perceives that:

> Our reason is overwhelmed by so many forms of reveries, is subject to so many wanderings, dashes against so many obstacles, is entangled in so many difficulties, that it is very far from directing us with certainty.[31]

This description of reason substantiates Calvin's former description of original sin in that:

> original sin is a corruption spread throughout our consciousness and affections in such a manner that correct intelligence and reason is perverted in us and we are like poor blind people in the dark.[32]

However, to say that reason is perverted by original sin, is not the same thing as saying that there is no reason remaining or that all reason is entirely useless. Just as Calvin will argue that reason is insufficient for directing our lives with certainty, so he will also argue that:

> there is reason naturally implanted within us which cannot be condemned without injustice to God. But this reason has its limits. If reason exceeds these limits, reason vanishes.[33]

---

[29] Ibid.

[30] Institutes I, 15, 6. OS III, p. 184.

[31] "Tot obruitur hallucinationum formis nostra ratio, tot erroribus est obnoxia, in tot impedimenta impingit, tot angustiis irretitur, ut plurimum a certa directione absit." (Institutes II, 2, 25; OS III, p. 267.)

[32] See footnote 9, this chapter.

[33] "Nobis ingenita est naturaliter ratio, quae sine Dei iniuria damnari non potest: sed ea suos habet fines, quos si exsuperat, evanescit." (Dilucida Explicatio Sanae Doctrinae de Vera Participatione Carnis et Sanguinis Christi in Sacra Coena ad Discutiendas Heshusii Nebulas 1561; CO 9:474.)

In explaining the limits of reason, there is substantial evidence in Calvin's writings to support his assertion that:

> We know that this is the principal difference between men and brute animals – men understand and decide, but brute animals are carried away by their senses.[34]

Thus the vitiation of reason due to original sin does not mean that there is no longer reason operative in the human person. Not only do beasts by their lack of this capacity indicate that there is something distinctive in human nature, but also other human beings in whom reason is either undeveloped or absent indicate reason's reality. By this is meant that undeveloped reason in infants and the lack of reason in the mentally incapacitated are still testimonies to us of our own reason as a definite capacity.[35]

Consequently Calvin in no way wishes to deny the manifestations of the rational capacity of those under the dominion of original sin. However, in enumerating these manifestations he also establishes the definite limits of reason:

> Therefore this distinction is to be made: there is one kind of intelligence pertaining to earthly things, and another pertaining to heavenly things. I call "earthly things" those which are not related to God or His kingdom,

---

[34] "Scimus autem hoc esse praecipuum discrimen inter homines et bruta animalia, quod homines intelligunt et judicant: bruta autem animalia suo sensu rapiuntur." (Commentary on Daniel 5:21; CO 40:715.) Cf. also: Institutes II, 2, 12; OS III, p. 255. Institutes II, 2, 17; OS III, p. 260. Commentary on Psalms 119:69; CO 32:291. Commentary on the Gospel of John 1:9; CO 47:9. Sermons on Job 28: 10-28; CO 34:523. Sermons on Job 31:9-15; CO 43:659. Sermons on Job 35:8-11; CO 35:239-240.

[35] Sermons on Job 29:8-13; CO 34:553. With respect to the mentally incapacitated proving to us our reason see: Sermons on Job 27:19-23 to 28:1-9; CO 34:503. Institutes II, 2, 14; OS III, pp. 257-258. Institutes II, 2, 17; OS III, p. 259.

> to true righteousness, or to the blessedness of the future life; but which have their calculation and relation to the present life, and which are, in a certain sense, enclosed within its ends. I call "heavenly things" the pure knowledge of God, the consideration of true righteousness, and the mysteries of the celestial kingdom. In the first category are government, the management of household affairs, all the mechanical skills, and the liberal arts. In the second category are the knowledge of God and of the Divine Will, and the rules by which we conform our life to the Divine Will.[36]

With respect to "earthly things" Calvin does not deny that rational processes are effective despite the reality of original sin. The human being, inclined to society, forms and enforces laws to preserve that society.[37] Medicine, mathematics, science, the liberal arts,[38] and all the abilities experientially discoverable in the human being's capacity to transform and appreciate the world are for Calvin surviving marks within the human person of God's image.[39]

Thus a definite competence is discernible in the human person with respect to "earthly things." However, "when the mind is elevated above the measure of the present

---

[36] "Sit ergo haec distinctio, esse aliam quidem rerum terrenarum intelligentiam, aliam vero caelestium. Res terrenas voco, quae ad Deum regnumque eius, ad veram iustitiam, ad futurae vitae beatitudinem non pertingunt: sed cum vita praesenti rationem relationemque habent, et quodammodo intra eius fines continentur. Res caelestes, puram Dei notitiam, verae iustitiae rationem, ac regni caelestis mysteria. In priore genere sunt politia, oeconomia, artes omnes mechanicae, disciplinaeque liberales. In secundo, Dei ac divinae voluntatis cognitio, et vitae secundum eam formandae regula." (Institutes II, 2, 13; OS III, p. 256.)

[37] Institutes II, 2, 13; OS III, pp. 256-257.

[38] Institutes II, 2, 14-16; OS III, pp. 257-259.

[39] "Caeterum in hac diversitate conspicimus tamen aliquas imaginis Dei superstites notas, quae totum humanum genus ab aliis creaturis distinguant." (Institutes, II, 2, 17; OS III, p. 260.) Cf. also Sermons on Job 31: 9-15; CO 34: 659-660. Sermons on Job 35:8-11; CO 35:240. Institutes I, 3, 3; OS III, p. 39.

life, it is especially convinced of its own feebleness."[40] For Calvin human reason corrupted by original sin fails in discerning those matters pertaining to "heavenly things." That is, such reason lacks spiritual insight (spiritualem perspicientiam).[41] This spiritual insight

> consists chiefly of three things: (1) knowing God; (2) knowing His Fatherly good-will towards us, in which our deliverance consists; (3) knowing how to form the structure of life according to the rule of His law. In the first two points – and especially the second – the greatest human geniuses are blinder than moles! Certainly I do not deny that one can read here and there some acute and proper statements about God in the philosophers; but such statements always savor of a certain giddy imagination. As was stated above, the Lord did indeed offer to them a slight taste of His Divinity in order that they would not pretend ignorance in disrespect. And occasionally God impelled them to say somethings which, once acknowledged, caused the philosophers to be refuted to themselves. But their discerning of that which they saw hardly led them to the smallest consideration of the truth much less the attainment of it. They are like a traveler in the middle of a field at night. A flash of lightning enables him to see far and wide for a moment. But the visibility vanishes so quickly that he is swallowed up in the darkness of night before he can take a step much less be led on his way by such assistance. Besides those droplets of truth with which they by chance (so to speak) sprinkle their books, how many and what monstrous lies have defiled them? In short,

---

[40] "Nam quum supra vitae praesentis spatium evehitur, tum praecipue demum convincitur suae imbecillitatis." (Institutes II, 2, 13; OS III, p. 256.)
[41] Institutes II, 2, 18; OS III, p. 260.

> they never sensed that assurance of the Divine good-will towards us (without which man's understanding can only be filled with immense confusion). Human reason, therefore, neither approaches, nor strives towards, nor takes proper aim at this truth: to understand who is the true God or what He wills to be towards us.[42]

This long quotation needs further interpretation. First, as with "earthly things" so with "heavenly things" there is some remnant of reason remaining. However, Calvin's attitude to the processes of reason with respect to "earthly things" is quite different than his attitude to rational processes with respect to "heavenly things." Reason in fallen man can lead to civic order and the development of the arts and sciences. Thus in relation to earthly things reason is effective. But reason in fallen man *cannot* lead him to a definite and substantial knowledge of the true God. This is not to say that there is no reason operative in relation to heavenly things. This should be noted because in the last quotation Calvin made this remark with respect to the

---

[42] "... quae tribus potissimum rebus constat, Deum nosse, paternum erga nos eius favorem, in quo salus nostra consistit: et formandae secundum legis regulam vitae reationem. Cum in primis duobus, tum vero in secundo proprie, qui sunt hominum ingeniosissimi, talpis sunt caeciores. Equidem non inficior, sparsim quaedam apud philsophos de Deo legi scite et apposite dicta: sed quae vertiginosam quandam imaginationem semper resipiant. Praebuit quidem illis Dominus, ut supra dictum est, exiguum divinitatis suae gustum, ne ignorantiam impietati obtenderent: et eos interdum ad dicenda nonnulla impulit, quorum confessione ipsi convincerentur: sed ita viderunt quae videbant, ut tali intuitu minime ad veritatem dirigerentur, nedum pertingerent; qualiter nocturni fulgetri coruscationem, qui in medio agro est viator, longe lateque ad momentum videt: sed adeo evanido aspectu, ut ante noctis caligine resorbeatur, quam pedem movere queat: tantum abest ut in viam tali subsidio deducatur. Praeterea illae veritatis guttulae, quibus libros tanquam fortuito aspergunt, quot et quam portentosis mendaciis sunt inquinatae? Denique illam divinae erga nos benevolentiae certitudinem (sine qua hominis ingenium immensa confusione repleri necesse est) ne olfecerunt quidem unquam. Ad hanc ergo veritatem nec appropinquat, nec contendit, nec collimat humana ratio, ut intelligat quis sit verus Deus, qualisve erga nos esse velit. (Institutes II, 2, 18; OS III, pp. 260-261.)

philosophers: "As was stated above, the Lord did indeed offer to them a slight taste of His Divinity in order that they would not pretend ignorance in disrespect." This comes from The Institutes of the Christian Religion Book II, Chapter 2, Section 18. Prior to this statement there can be found the following remarks in The Institutes of the Christian Religion:

> We assert it to be beyond controversy that there is within the human mind, and indeed by natural impulse, an awareness of divinity. In order that no one would take refuge in the excuse of ignorance, God has Himself implanted a certain comprehension of His Will within everyone. Constantly renewing its memory, He repeatedly pours in fresh drops.[43]

> It will always be plainly manifest to people of sound judgment that an awareness of divinity which can never be effaced is engraved upon the human mind.[44]

The same contention of the awareness of Divinity within the human mind which does not allow anyone the excuse of ignorance before God can also be found in another work of Calvin. In his Commentary on the Prophet Ezekiel, Calvin speaks of the "sparks" (scintillae) of reason:

> What then? Certainly these very sparks of reason shine forth in the darkness in order that we be rendered without excuse. Consequently what man's reason does is make

[43] "Quendam inesse humanae menti, et quidem naturali instinctu, divinitatis sensum, extra controversiam ponimus: siquidem, nequis ad ignorantiae praetextum confugeret, quandam sui numinis intelligentiam universis Deus ipse indidit, cuius memoriam assidue renovans, novas subinde guttas instillat..." (Institutes I, 3, 1; OS III, p. 37.)

[44] "Hoc quidem recte iudicantibus semper constabit, insculptum mentibus humanis esse divinitatis sensum, qui deleri nunquam potest." (Institutes I, 3, 3; OS III, p. 39.)

> man feel convicted before himself so that he does not hold out to himself any pretext of ignorance or error.[45]

With respect to such sparks of reason convicting man, certain implications can be drawn from the preceding statements of Calvin. To be convicted before one's self is of course the knowledge of one's self convicted. That is all it is. For Calvin such knowledge of one's self convicted cannot be construed as the complete knowledge of the true God. Rather, it is a true knowledge of ourselves that in and of ourselves we have a brief taste periodically of something or someone transcendent to ourselves. What or who this something or someone is cannot be fully known or investigated by the power of reason. Indeed Calvin's conclusion that "Human reason, therefore, neither approaches, nor strives towards, nor takes proper aim at this truth: to understand who is the true God or what He wills to be towards us"[46] can in no way imply that any spark of reason can fan itself into a roaring blaze of divine truth. Reason as reason can only intimate to any person (be he or be he not a blind-mole genius) that there is a deity. At this point the efficacy of the powers of reason, with respect to discerning the true God, stops. Reason has only become aware of its own limitations. It cannot in and of itself overcome those limitations.

But who wants to boast of his or her limitations? Can we go to the market place and find someone carrying a sign saying: "I AND MY MERCHANDISE ARE LIMITED"? Can we go to the cemetery and find the epitaph: "HERE LIES THE LIMITED"? Can we go to the library and find a notice

[45] "Quid igitur? nempe ideo scintillae emicant in tenebris, ut reddamur inexcusabiles. En igitur quid valeat hominis ratio, ut convictus apud se sentiat non restare sibi ullum ignorantiae vel erroris praetextum." (Commentary on Ezekiel 11:20; CO 40:246.)

[46] See the concluding sentence of footnote 42, this chapter.

reading: "SILENCE! THE LIMITED ARE STUDYING"? Of course not. The human person wants something more. To say he "wants" means that sooner or later he will "will" something more. At this point the basic interconnection between reason and will in Calvin's anthropology presents itself. As was previously stated:

> the intellect is as it were the leader and ruler of the soul. The will always considers he command of the intellect, and in the will's own desires it awaits the decision of the intellect.[47]

Coupled with the former statement was the following:

> Moreover, the function of the intellect is to distinguish between objects according to the value or worthlessness of each object. However, the will chooses and conforms to that which the intellect has declared good, and rejects and flees that which the intellect disapproves.[48]

It was also previously remarked that reason was at cross purposes with itself comparable to armies at war.[49] There is little wonder why reason is in conflict with itself if it apprehends the human soul to contain sparks of a divine image yet is unable to actualize the fulfillment of that image. Frustrated by the vitiation caused by original sin, reason stands only to immediately collapse in its own impotence. Reason impels itself to seek something more yet cannot take the first step in the right direction. Convicted by the apprehension of the Deity yet ignorant of the true nature of the Deity, reason (whose nature is, after all, to know) turns

---

[47] See footnote 21, this chapter.
[48] See footnote 22, this chapter.
[49] See footnotes 28 and 29, this chapter.

against itself. It cannot find the right Reality to investigate, yet it strives to investigate, to know, to analyze. It is true that reason can investigate itself through the means of art, dialectics, and other varied forms of culture. It is also true that reason can form laws regulating the power of government and the rights of individuals. It can scan the pages of history and science making rational deductions. However, for reason to know itself in relation to the intuited apprehension of Divinity and then to pursue and develop the meaning and consequences of such an apprehension, this reason cannot do. For reason to be forced to constantly control itself in such ignorance, to perpetually say to itself, "You have only the spark, forget about the fire" is not at all easy. Reason now frustrated and anxious will manufacture any form of ultimate goal which will give it some comfort. Yet reason's own tendency to again analyze and investigate will put such a manufactured ultimate goal in jeopardy. That is, reason facing itself will realize that the ultimate goal is not ultimate at all but merely a product of reason. Reason caused the would-be ultimate goal. The psuedo ultimate goal did not cause reason. Reason is therefore alone again with its apprehension of Divinity while at the same time reason is constantly desiring to know more but is at war with itself because it cannot know more.

But if reason is frustrated and at war with itself, what are the possibilities of willing? If the will waits upon the decision of the intellect then the will must also be frustrated and at war with itself since reason is the will's guide. It is true that in relation to earthly things the will can follow those distinctions of the intellect and pursue the arts, science, politics, etc. But the will, like the intellect, cannot always be satisfied within the limits of earthly things. Just as an individual attempts to know the ultimate source of his being through reason, so he attempts to pursue such knowledge to its ultimate source through will. Real freedom of the will would not be vapidly concerned with the flavor of ice cream any person "x" might choose in any ice cream parlor "y".[50] Rather real freedom of the will would be the possibility of pursuing the ultimate source of human existence. The pursuit would end with the unification of the human person with the ultimate source of human life.

For Calvin, Adam, prior to the fall, had the capacity for such a pursuit. That is, "the individual parts of his soul were formed to uprightness, the soundness of his mind stood firm, and his will was free to choose the good."[51] Had Adam consistently pursued the good as it was manifested through the Will of God, Adam would "have departed into heaven without pain and without death."[52] His time spent on earth would have then been a testimony that he had lived "as the living image of the divine wisdom and justice."[53] For Calvin such a testimony would have been actualized through a truly "free-will." Thus, Adam's reason would have disclosed to him the true God, and Adam's will would have pursued and finally joined him to the true God.

However, Calvin's question still remains before us: "From whence come so many labyrinths of errors in the world but because men are led by their own understanding only into

---

[50] The illustrious paradigm of the ice cream parlor is often used in many academic philosophical debates to prove or disprove the freedom of the will. The determinists predicate a forced flavor choice because of environmental and socioeconomic factors originating from birth. The more "existential" proponents of the will's freedom predicate the "freedom" to choose a flavor. (The most existential of proponents of the will's freedom would even permit the possibility of "making oneself" a sundae.) I contend that the context of discussion pertaining to the will's freedom must soon take place in relation to a more profound question than a soda jerk's asking: "Chocolate or vanilla?"

[51] "Nam ad rectitudinem formatae erant singulae animae partes, et constabat mentis sanitas, et voluntas ad bonum eligendum libera." (Institutes I, 15, 8; OS III, p. 186)

[52] See footnote 5, this chapter.

[53] See footnote 6, this chapter.

vanity and untruth?"[54] As can now be seen, the vitiation of the human soul which is a product of original sin does not stop with reason. What effects the reasoning capacity must also effect the will. If the understanding cannot determine the ultimate source of existence in such a way that the will can pursue that ultimate source, the will must will inadequately. This means that the will must be constantly dissatisfied with the feigned ultimate source which reason attempts to specify.

Just as it is difficult if not impossible for reason to remain within the limits of its vitiated nature, so it is difficult if not impossible for the will to contain itself without a proper ultimate goal. Despite the fact that reason cannot disclose to the will the true Deity, the will continues in its energy. Original sin has taken away the possibility of willing correctly in relation to the true Deity. It has not removed the will from the human person.[55] However, what the will must now pursue are the dissatisfactions of reason, the specters of psuedo-gods, the "earthly-things" which reason transforms into "gods." That is, the will begins to force each human person down into the unmarked channels of the mind's devising – down into the labyrinth of errors.

(c) Imagination

In discussing the nature and function of reason and will in Calvin's theology it is necessary to again reiterate that reason and will are central to Calvin's anthropology in such a manner that "no faculty can be found in the soul which does

---

[54] See footnote 26, this chapter.

[55] With respect to the assertion that the will continues in its energy but cannot pursue by its own power the true Deity (i.e., that the will continues, but the soundness of the will is removed) see the following: Institutes II, 2, 12; OS III; p. 255. Institutes II, 3, 5; OS III, p. 277.

not duly refer to one or the other of these parts."[56] This means two things. One, reason and will are always in a dialectical relationship with any and all other faculties of the soul. Two, other faculties of the soul exist. One of the most important faculties pertaining to the image of the labyrinth is the faculty of imagination. As a faculty of the soul it was in the first Adam created good and part of the image of God in man. But like reason and will, imagination became corrupted through the fall of the first Adam. That imagination is corrupt may at first cause excessive offense to those who extol imaginative production. It seems that immediately legions of poets, novelists, painters, musicians and sculptors come forth to defend the good of imagination by the very fact of their artistic achievements. Calvin in a very definite way would not only praise these achievements, he would also go so far as to describe the ability for such achievements as a sign of divinity in the human person. This is affirmed by Calvin's statement that "sculpture and painting are the gifts of God."[57] It is also affirmed by the following words of Calvin:

> Manifold indeed is the agility of the soul with which it surveys heaven and earth, joins past to future, retains by personal recollection what it has heard long ago, and what is more, even pictures to itself whatever it pleases. Manifold also is the ingenuity which devises incredible things and which is the mother of so many admirable arts. Certainly these are marks of Divinity in man.[58]

[56] See footnote 23, this chapter.
[57] "...scupltura et pictura Dei dona sunt..." (Institutes I, 11, 12; OS III, p. 100.)
[58] "Multiplex sane animae agilitas qua caelum et terram perlustrat: praeterita futuris coniungit: retinet memoriter quae pridem audivit: imo quidlibet sibi figurat: solertia etiam qua res incredibiles excogitat, et quae tot mirabilium artium mater est, certa sunt divinitatis insignia in homine." (Institutes I, 5, 5; OS III, p. 49.)

However, this same "agility of the soul" or "ingenuity" has in no way escaped the vitiation of the soul which is the product of original sin:

> But because sculpture and painting are gifts of God, I seek a pure and legitimate use of each, lest those things which the Lord has conferred upon us for His glory and for our good are not only contaminated by absurd waste but are also turned to our destruction.[59]

Calvin's remarks in this last quotation apply not only to sculpture and painting but to all the products of the imagination. These same remarks in turn apply to the imagination itself. Despite the fact that the imagination's abilities indicate marks of Divinity in the human person, these abilities do not in and of themselves make the human person divine. Calvin seeks the proper use of imagination in order to avoid (1) absurd waste and (2) the possible destruction of the human person. But is not Calvin being arrogant? Who is Calvin to indicate to anyone how he or she should use imagination? Does not the modern world proclaim a type of justification by imagination? How often are the faults of the "great creators" of culture dismissed by the words: "So what if he murdered and raped a few people? After all, he was a 'creative' genius?" But if a dull and unimaginative criminal faces the judgment of the populace, he is either trampled to death by the crowd rushing to sharpen the blade on the guillotine or, what may be worse, he is ignored.

---

[59] "Sed quia sculptura et pictura Dei dona sunt, purum et legitimum utriusque usum requiro: ne quae Dominus in suam gloriam et bonum nostrum nobis contulit, ea non tantum polluantur praepostero abusu, sed in nostram quoque perniciem convertantur." (Institutes I, 11, 12; OS III, p. 100.)

Whatever the world has come to, justification by imagination would be antithetical to Calvin's thought. It would be antithetical to his thought because although Calvin has an appreciation of imagination as a mark of Divinity in the human person, Calvin refers to imagination as an agency of idolatry.[60] To say that imagination is an agency of idolatry does not mean that idolatry's sole source stems from the imagination. Specifically idolatry's source can be found in one of Calvin's questions: "But from whence is the origin of idolatry if not from the decision of men?"[61] Human decision of course also posits the activities of reason and will. But human decisions do not take place solely by the agencies of reason and will. Myriad images, recollections and projections come into play at the time of decision making. Thus imagination remains active and in dialectical tension with reason and will. Therefore if the source of idolatry arises from human decision, it must also in some way arise from the imagination.

How the imagination functions in relation to idolatry will become apparent through an analysis of idolatry. However, before such an analysis is begun, some statements of Calvin should be reflected upon. At the beginning of this chapter Calvin was cited as saying that a person enters the labyrinth when he wishes to make decisions "above God."[62] It has recently been established that idolatry has its origin from the decisions of men.[63] There is then a definite interrelationship between entering the labyrinth and idolatry.

---

[60] "Hac etiam ratione confirmat propheta quod prius dixit, nimis desipere homines, imo hunc esse prodigiosum stuporem, ubi tribuunt aliquam deitatem, vel ligno, vel lapidi, vel metallo. Quare? Sunt enim ipsorum figmenta, inquit." (Commentary on the Twelve Minor Prophets, "Habakkuk" 2:18; CO 43:558.) Cf. also Commentary on Psalms 79:7; CO 31:750.

[61] "Nam unde idolis principium, nisi ex hominum arbitrio?" (Commentary on Psalms 115:4-7; CO 32:186.) Cf. also Commentary on Daniel 11:38-39; CO 41:274.

[62] See footnote 3, this chapter.

[63] See footnote 61, this chapter.

Although the obvious connecting link is human decision, human decision indicates that there is a specific human nature involved in decision making. In a description of human nature Calvin offers information concerning both the labyrinth and idolatry:

> Here arises that immense and vile medley of errors with which the whole earth has been stuffed and overwhelmed. For the nature of each human being is like a labyrinth, such that it is no wonder that individual nations have been scattered amidst various fabrications. Not only is this true for individual nations, but almost every man has his own gods. For when rashness and petulance are added to ignorance and darkness, scarcely a single person has ever been found who did not fashion for himself an idol or spectre in place of God.[64]

This description of human nature as a labyrinth has a definite interconnection with the human being's capacity for idolatry. This is so because Calvin also describes human nature as a "perpetual workshop of idols."[65] This interconnection of human nature being both a labyrinth and a workshop of idols will become apparent through an analysis of Calvin's concept of idolatry.

Thus Calvin's concept of idolatry should disclose at least two things with respect to human decision making: (1) how the imagination functions in relation to idolatry and (2)

---

[64] "Hinc immensa illa errorum colluvies, qua totus orbis refertus ac coopertus fuit; suum enim cuique ingenium instar labyrinthi est, ut mirum non sit singulas Gentes in varia commenta diductas esse; neque id modo, sed singulis prope hominibus proprios fuisse deos; nam ut ad inscitiam et tenebras accedit temeritas et lascivia, vix unus unquam repertus est qui non sibi idolum vel spectrum Dei loco fabricaret." (Institutes I, 5, 12; OS III, p. 56.)

[65] "...hominis ingenium perpetuam, ut ita loquar, esse idolorum fabricam." (Institutes I, 11, 8; OS III, p. 96.)

how the image of the labyrinth is interconnected with the phenomenon of idolatry. In attempting such disclosures it should be stated that although human nature is a perpetual workshop of idols, Calvin would not say that because of the capacity for idolatry the image of God has become completely obliterated in the human person. On the contrary, for Calvin:

> ... from the beginning of the world there has been no region, no city, in fact no home which was able to exist without religion. In this there is a certain tacit confession that the sense of Divinity is inscribed within the hearts of all. Indeed, idolatry is ample proof of this conception. We surely know that man does not willingly cast himself down in order to esteem other created things in comparison with himself. Accordingly, since he prefers to worship wood and stone rather than to be thought of having no God, it is indisputable that there is this most powerful impression of the Divine which cannot be obliterated from the mind of man. In fact, it would be easier to break into pieces man's entire natural disposition than to obliterate such an impression from his mind. Certainly man's entire natural disposition is broken into pieces when, by his own natural pomposity, he willingly allows himself to fall to the basest depths so that he may honor God.[66]

[66] "Nulla ergo quum ab initio mundi regio, nulla urbs, nulla denique domus fuerit quae religione carere posset: in eo tacita quaedam confessio est, inscriptum omnium cordibus divinitatis sensum. Quin et idololatria, huius conceptionis amplum est documentum. Quam enim non libenter se deiiciat homo, ut alias prae se creaturas suspiciat, scimus. Proinde quum lignum potius et lapidem colere malit, quam ut nullum putetur habere Deum: constat vehementissimam istam esse de numine impressionem, quae adeo ex hominis mente obliterari nequeat, ut facilius sit naturae affectum frangi: quemadmodum certe frangitur, dum homo ex illa naturali inflatione ad infima quaeque sponte se demittit, quo Deum revereatur." (Institutes I, 3, 1; OS III, p. 38.)

The phenomenon of having a god or gods of some sort is for Calvin an indelible characteristic of human nature. It springs from the remnant traces of the image of God in the human soul. Calvin will even allow that some sense (sensu) of the true God is naturally within the human person:

> For since men are imbued by nature with some sense of God, from that source they derive true principles. But as soon as the knowledge of God creeps up into men's minds the true principles vanish amidst distorted fragments of the imagination, and thus the pure seed generates into corruption. Still, the first general knowledge of God remains in men for a time.[67]

In the previous discussion of reason and will, reason was described as still possessing remnant traces of the image of God. Reason seeking to know its source, its "whence," its own origin, examines varied forms of ultimacy. Reason finding many of its supposed idols or forms of ultimacy reason-created and not creating reason turns against itself. Reason desires to know. Reason knows that it should know. But to actually know the nature of the true Deity – that reason does not know. Yet a general knowledge of God does remain for a time. This general knowledge spurs reason on to continually investigate and be at war with itself.

Manifestations of this phenomenon of reason struggling for the truth about the true Deity have taken the form of philosophical formulations. Calvin would assert that some such formulations are "true principles" which partake of

[67] "Nam quia naturaliter aliquo Dei sensu imbuti sunt homines, ex illo fonte vera principia hauriunt. Tametsi autem simul ac eorum figmentis evanescunt: atque ita purum semen degenerat in corruptelas: prima tamen generalis Dei notitia interim in ipsis manet." (Commentary on the Acts of the Apostles 17:28; CO 48:417.)

"the first general knowledge of God." This first general knowledge of God lasts for "a time." For how long? For the extent of time consumed by a lightening flash.[68] Just as the nighttime wayfarer sees the darkness fade for a second beneath the lightening flash, so the human person sees only for a second the general knowledge of God. If that second of light produces aids in forming "true principles" these true principles are limited in scope. These principles do not carry that enduring brightness which would enable the wayfarer to guide his steps safely. Such true principles would only add to his confusion.

"Behold, there is a field you must traverse. The field is the time you have yet to live. Sickness, death, despair, and self-destruction are waiting amidst the chasms and quicksand. You must cross over. Even to destroy yourself is to cross over. You intuit a possible Way to cross over, but you do not completely know that Way." Is not this a terrible inward recognition? To know that there is some deity, but not to understand who or what this deity is – certainly this only adds to the confusion which follows the lightening flash.

Calvin's statements concerning such confusion are as follows: "Those who know there is some deity, but who do not know what it is, perpetually hesitate and entangle themselves in strange labyrinths."[69] How does this entangling begin? It

---

[68] See footnote 42, this chapter.

[69] "Qui norunt aliquod esse numen, nec quid sit intelligunt, perpetuo vacillant, mirisque involucris sese implicant." Commentary in Isaiah 43:10; CO 37:89.) The general lexicographical meanings of "involucrum" are: that in which something is wrapped, a wrapper, covering, case, envelope. (Lewis and Short, A Latin Dictionary. Oxford: Clarendon Press, 1969, p. 997.) It is my contention that, given the context of use, the term should be interpreted with that meaning of the verb "implico" which connotes bondage or entanglement. A good single English word for the human phenomenon of being wrapped, cased, covered, or enveloped would certainly be found in the term "labyrinth."

should be observed that darkness immediately engulfs the human soul after the lightening flash of transitory truth. Reason sees that something can be known concerning the true Deity. However, to actually pursue the source of such knowledge is impossible for reason. What is reason to do? Constantly hesitating amidst the possible deities which reason examines and finds to be false, reason exhausts itself. In attempting to know the origin of itself, reason proves to itself its own impotence.

However for reason to know itself as impotent before itself does not mean that the rest of the faculties of human soul automatically shut themselves off. Indeed, the entire human soul continues with its remnant traces of the image of God. If reason is dissatisfied and impotent, it does not mean that the imagination will roll over and die. On the contrary, imagination will attempt to comfort the human person.[70] That is, imagination speaks to the wanderer after the lightening flash and the collapse of reason: "You have seen some light. Although you do not know the Way, you can make your own way. Use your projective capacities. I will aid you."

Then, amidst the possible earthly goods of wealth, love, success, power and prestige, the imagination weaves the idol ridden labyrinth. Phantasms upon phantasms build each winding corridor. And the human person, agitated by the threatening darkness and the building storm, enters into the most absurd and destructive darkness. Human capacities become extolled by the self and other human beings as "heavenly things." Humans become the absolute judges of all things. Human works become absolutes in themselves needing only more human beings to bow down and worship

---

[70] Commentary on Jeremiah 30;12; CO 38:625.

them. "Earthly things" take on the significance of "heavenly things."[71] In Calvin's words:

> Yet, whenever we might happen to conceive some sort of Divinity, without delay we sink into the delirious or distorted fabrications of our flesh and corrupt by our vanity the pure truth of God. In this we are indeed dissimilar – each one privately summons up something from his own particular labyrinth. However we are, one and all, similar in this respect – we desert the one true God for prodigious trash.[72]

Although the imagination attempts to comfort the human person, the imagination's comfort does not last for long. All too soon false fabrications of the Deity actually mislead the human person.[73] The Way of deliverance out of the labyrinth is lost to the sudden allurements and enticements of each newly projected "god."[74] Each new god forms a new channel or tunnel in which to wander. The fertility of desperate imagination is able to form a multitude of gods simultaneously. Money, sex, beauty, power, deified human love – all have their immediate objects and immediate paths of pursuit. And the human person, desiring to find comfort in the darkness, is actually "broken into pieces"[75] as he attempts to pursue his gods. He is prone to be carried away

---

[71] See footnote 36, this chapter.

[72] "...tamen ubi temere divinitatis alicuius sensum concepimus, extemplo ad carnis nostrae deliria vel prava commenta delabimur, ac puram Dei veritatem nostra corrumpimus vanitate. In eo quidem dissimiles, quod quisque sibi privatim aliquid peculiaris erroris accersit: in hoc tamen simillimi, quod ad unum omnes, ab uno vero Deo ad prodigiosa nugamenta deficimus." (Institutes I, 5, 11; OS III, p. 55.) With respect to the translation of "erroris" as "labyrinth" see Lewis and Short, A Latin Dictionary, Oxford: Clarendon Press, 1969, p. 657.

[73] "Car permierement les hommes s'esgarent du droit chemin de salut quand ils suyvent leurs imaginations propres..." (Sermons on Job 4:20-5:2; CO 33:219.)

[74] Ibid.

[75] See footnote 66, this chapter.

here or there as he chases each new projection.[76] Multiple gods mean multiple pursuits of those gods. The soul is torn now this way, now that way. Inward stability vanishes. Inward peace vanishes. There remain only the flirtatious new possibilities of another new god. New paths are traversed, and new dead-ends are discovered.

Amidst the instability, inward warfare, and final disappointment of god-chasing in the labyrinth; the human person faces spiritual exhaustion. The lightening flash of a true yet transitory knowledge of God has faded. Imagination has brought the seeker into the depths of the labyrinth. Energy to attempt to pursue the real Way of deliverance is difficult if not impossible to find within the human soul. Energy is difficult to procure because the soul's resources have been divided amidst so many marvelous "earthly things" which have taken on "heavenly" proportions.

The individual wandering in the labyrinth may encounter others like himself. Just as there are many deceptive paths in a labyrinth, so there are in the world varied communities of idolaters. For the sake of brevity I will suggest a more than academic division of such idolaters. There are non-religious idolaters, and there are religious idolaters. By non-religious idolaters I mean those who simply accept the goods of this world as the highest good and, with a total lack of any further spiritual striving, pull the cover of unmitigated opulence over their heads in order to enjoy themselves. In further describing the non-religious idolater, I will cite a few of Calvin's words:

> many are so delighted with marble, statues, gold, and paintings that they become marble statues, they turn, as it were, into metals, and

---

[76] "Car nous sommes subiets à estre transportez de nostre phantasie et çà et là." (Sermons on Job 12:14-16; CO 33:590.)

> are like painted figures. The smell of the kitchen or the sweetness of its odors so stupefies others that they cannot smell anything spiritual.[77]

Another statement of Calvin's aids in describing non-religious idolaters:

> Thus when men pile up much wealth and accumulate a great heap from the property of others, they become more and more blind. Hence we see that prosperous fortune ought to be distrusted by us lest our fatness so increase that we see nothing – for the eyes are dimmed by excessive fatness.[78]

But to guard against the snares of those with the fat-dimmed eyes is not any easy task. It is not any easy task because in the labyrinth of this world

> scarcely one person in a hundred is found who does not venture to promise any power to himself according to his own industry and virtue. Thus it is that those who give credit to themselves for the prosperous occurrences of things do not hesitate to neglect God when they begin any undertaking.[79]

---

[77] "...multi marmore, auro, picturis ita delectantur ut marmoreit fiant, vertantur quasi in metalla, similes sint pictis figuris. Nidor culinae vel odorum suavitas alios obstupefacit, ne quid spirituale olfaciant." (Institutes III, 10,3; OS IV, p. 179.)

[78] "Ubi ergo homines sibi opes multas accumulant, et ex aliena substantia contrahunt acervum, tunc magis ac magis excaecantur. Hinc videmus merito debere nobis suspectam esse prosperam fortunam, ne pinguedo ita crescat, ut nihil cernamus: quemadmodum obstupescunt oculi nimia pinguedine." (Commentary on the Twelve Minor Prophets, "Habakkuk" 1:16; CO 43:515-516.)

[79] "Atqui vix centesimus quisque reperitur, qui non quidvis sibi de propria industria aut virtute promittere audeat: hinc fit ut posthabito Deo quidvis etiam machinari non dubitent, qui sibi arrogant prosperos rerum eventus." Commentary on a Harmony of the Gospel, Matthew 6:27; CO 45:210-211.)

To say that God is neglected is not the same as saying there is no "god" projected. On the contrary, "gods" are projected. The "gods" of the non-religious idolater are two: (1) prosperity and (2) fortune or chance or fate. Both gods are interrelated. Both gods feed the hunger for security found in each person making his way through the labyrinth. Both gods give a type of false security which lasts for a time. Both gods finally leave the human person in a state of dull-grey lethargy.

In commenting on the "god of prosperity" Calvin states the following:

> And let it be noted that when the ungodly estimate their prosperity in the light of preconceived considerations, they imagine that God is in a certain manner bound to themselves.[80]

What stands behind such "preconceived considerations"? It is not to be denied that within the labyrinth of the world countless anxieties attack each human person. Such questions as: "Where shall I live?" "How shall I make a living?" "How shall I provide for myself?" "How shall I provide for others?" abound at one time or another in every human soul. Even those privileged from birth still need to manage and maintain their privileged positions. Necessity is no idle force. Doubts as to future economic security, the constant witness of those overcome by poverty, and the incessant fear of privation all threateningly combine to force anyone to "take care of number one." Number one, one's self, will strive to establish some form of security. But striving

---

[80] "Notandum autem quod impii ex praesenti intuitu sic aestimant suam fortunam, ut Deum quodammodo sibi obstrictum imaginentur." Commentary on Psalms 10;11; CO 31:115.) Cf. also Commentary on the Twelve Minor Prophets, "Hosea" 9:15; CO 42:405.)

means that there must be an object for which one strives. Projections must be made as to who or what will aid each person in obtaining "economic security." However, in the labyrinth of this world, the seeker need not be forced to rely solely on himself. Amidst the growing corporate trusts, amidst the empire builders and slick hucksters, amidst the well-manicured drummers, the "god of prosperity" arises. Surely it can be recognized. Its origin derives from the world's concupiscence for gain. It is fed by each individual's fear of poverty. In the confusion caused by that anxious question: "What is to become of me?" the idol of prosperity is voraciously pursued. It is not to be denied that "the ethics of good business" are also pursued along with this idol. And thus it is not to be denied that one can be described as "good" along with one's fellow idolaters. But, this criterion of "good" is man-made and subject to the opening of new markets, the most for the least, and all the other deities which combine to form the god of prosperity's pantheon.

It can of course be argued that business sense would, in Calvin's thought, be specified as an "earthly thing."[81] This is true provided that business sense would remain(!) an "earthly thing." But the human being's capacity for idolatry,[82] and the human being's ignorance as to the real nature of the true Deity,[83] deny the possibility of business sense remaining an "earthly thing." On the contrary, material prosperity has appeared as a "heavenly thing." All the capacities of the soul are then employed to pursue this idol.

As "the god of prosperity" with its benefit of human security looms large before the soul, decisions upon decisions are made to possess such prosperity completely. Actions follow these decisions. Corridors composed of hours, days, and

[81] See footnote 36, this chapter.
[82] See footnotes 64, 65, 66; this chapter.

years of prosperous well-being are perceived in the labyrinth. Ambition–no minor messenger in the pantheon of prosperity's attendant gods – is ready with supposed infinite energy. However, in Calvin's words:

> ... in fact, those whom ambition seduces will inevitably find themselves in a labyrinth of wanderings. And thus we see how God frustrates those grand endeavors into which the children of this world proudly hurl themselves. They run to and fro for a long time. They violently twist the whole world to their will and let nothing go untouched. They are satisfied with themselves because of their own shrewdness and industry. But suddenly, when they have carried out a great multitude of their plans, everything is overthrown because there is no solidity in them.[84]

There is no solidity either in the ambitious or in their plans because, with death as a constant menace, there is nothing certain or solid.[85] This does not mean that the worshippers or prosperity will stop their initial calculations. However:

> even one who is best at arithmetic, one who can clearly and accurately examine and master millions upon millions, still cannot count up eighty years in his own life. Likewise

---

[83] See footnote 69, this chapter.

[84] "...quoscunque vero ambitio sollicitat, necesse est in labyrintho vagari. Et sane videmus ut magnificos istos conatus, in quibus fastuose se iactant filii saeculi, frustretur Deus. Per longos suos discursus obequitant, versant totum mundum suo arbitrio, et nihil intactum praetereunt: placent etiam sibi in suo acumine et industria, verum ubi in magnum acervum extulerunt sua consilia, repente everitur: quia nihil inest solidum." (Commentary on Psalms 131:1; CO 32:340.)

[85] "...car nous sommes advertis quelle est la fragilité de nostre vie, ce sont autant de messages que Dieu nous envoye pour dire, Apprestez vous: car vous n'avez rien de certain ne ferme au monde." (Sermons on Job 21;13-15; CO 34:229.)

> it is certainly a strange phenomenon that men can measure all the distances beyond themselves, can know how many feet separate the moon from the center of the earth, what space there is between the different planets; in short, can know all the dimensions of heaven and earth, while they cannot number seventy years in themselves.[86]

It could be argued that in the modern day medicine may or will eternalize one's time before the "god of prosperity." In this way the earthly good of medicine would also take on divine proportions in the pantheon of prosperity's attendant gods. That is, modern medical science could project the fantasy of endless life on earth. Realistically this has yet to be seen. Realistically "the sepulcher devours the great and the small."[87] Realistically

> the bodies of princes, like those of the common people, must finally be spoiled and gnawed by worms regardless of the expensive and magnificent tombs which may have been erected for them.[88]

Thus the psuedo-security offered by prosperity is, before the reality of death, no security at all. However, this realization does not strike home with prosperity's worshippers

---

[86] "Nam qui optimus erit arithmeticus, et myriades myriadum distincte ac subtiliter tenebit ac excutiet, non tamen poterit octoginata annos supputare in propria vita. Hoc certe prodigio simile est, homines extra se ipsos metiri omnia intervalla, cognoscere quot pedibus distet luna a centro terrae, quam longis inter se spatiis planetae dividantur, denique omnes coeli et terrae dimensiones tenere, quum in se ipsis septuaginta annos non numerent." (Commentary on Psalms 90:12; CO 31:839.)

[87] "...le sepulchre engloutist et grands et petis..." (Sermons on Job 4:20-5:2; CO 33:214.)

[88] "Principum enim corpora, ut plebeiorum, corrumpi et corrodi a vermibus tandem necesse est, quamvis etiam iis sumptuosa et magnifica sepulcra exstruantur." (Commentary on Isaiah 14:10; CO 36:277.)

"for we know that men are blinded by prosperity."[89] This blindness arises not only from the tunnel-vision necessary to procure wealth. It also arises from the cares of this world attendant upon seeking and maintaining such wealth. These cares are overloaded with energy-depleting anxieties.

> Therefore it is no wonder if the cares of the world overwhelm us and make us drowsy and if the appearance of present things dulls our eyes, for almost all of us promise ourselves an eternity in the world; an end, at least, never enters our minds.[90]

Thus amidst the false securities and blindness promulgated by "divine prosperity" a dull-grey lethargy or dullness overtakes the non-religious idolater. His supposed "heaven on earth" has led him to a constant subservience beneath earthly things. Deified earthly problems now possess him entirely. Whatever energy he can summon up in himself is spent on a god which must fail him in a contest with death.

If objections are raised at this point that in fact prosperity breeds prosperity, that industry breeds industry, and that the prosperous man is of course (of course) the proverbial "go-getter" and anything but lethargic; such objections would fail to face the facts of lives wasted in earthly worries, lives destroyed for false security, and the victorious worms. The visible world of the empire-builder is in most cases blind to any form of spiritual progression. In Calvin's words:

---

[89] "Scimus enim homines excaecari prospera fortuna." (Commentary on the Twelve Minor Prophets "Hosea" 4:7; CO 42:276.) Cf. also footnote 78, this chapter.

[90] "Non mirum igitur si nos obruant mundi curae, sopitosque teneant: si oculos perstringat praesentium rerum adspectus: quia omnes fere nobis aeternitatem in mundo promittimus: saltem nunquam finis venit in mentem." (Commentary on the First Epistle of Peter 4:7; CO 55:274.)

> We know how much a moderate quantity of riches hinders many so that they do not raise their heads to heaven. Those who truly overflow with great wealth are not only sluggish in their inactivity but are utterly submerged in the earth.[91]

Herein lies the dull-grey lethargy: whatever remaining traces of the image of the true God in man are absorbed in the worship and service of prosperity. Whatever may have been the sparse indications of a higher life of union with the true God are forgotten. Instead, one's time is used before the fabricated idol of perfect, eternal, and "prosperous" life in this world. All energies are drained in the impossible and desperate hope of achieving such a life. What can now be seen and heard from the human soul in the labyrinth? All that can be seen is an exhausted and indifferent shrug. All that can be heard is the listless subterranean question: "Who ultimately cares?"

Precisely at this point "the god of prosperity" is reinforced by the extremely deceptive "god of fortune." Indeed, there is already a linguistic affinity between the two gods. In Calvin's Latin the god of prosperity is often termed "prosperous fortune" (prosperam fortunam).[92] The god of prosperity is also termed "the prosperous occurrences of things" (prosperos rerum eventus)[93] or simply "fortune" (fortunam).[94] The Latin term for the deity of fortune is "fortuna."[95]

---

[91] "Scimus quantopere multos impediant modicae facultates, ne in coelum caput attollant, qui vero abundant maiore copia, non modo pigri torpent, sed prorsus in terra demersi sunt." (Commentary on Genesis 13:1; CO 23:188.)

[92] See footnote 78, this chapter. Cf. also footnote 89, this chapter.

[93] See footnote 79, this chapter.

[94] See footnote 80, this chapter.

[95] Lewis and Short, A Latin Dictionary. Oxford: The Clarendon Press, 1969, p. 773.

However, there is more than a linguistic interrelationship between the "god of prosperity" and "the god of fortune." To investigate this interrelationship it is necessary to return to the non-religious idolater as he comes to the realization of his own spiritual lethargy. Somewhere between the shrug and the murmur, deep-seated metaphysical questions occur to him. Quietly addressing himself he asks: "What else could be done?" "Was it not fated that I come to my own spiritual inactivity?" "What other chance did I have?" "If the world's maligned indifference only offers me probable success on the wheel of fortune, how can I be at fault?" Thus the non-religious idolater becomes a speculative metaphysician. Inwardly traversing the projected deities variously called "fate," "chance," "probability," and "fortune"; he all too readily excuses himself from any culpability. Further, the "god of fortune" or any of its synonymous idols (i.e., fate, chance, or probability) reinforces his excusing of himself.

In the labyrinth of this world the non-religious idolater will find many bar-stool metaphysicians like himself. There will be any number of like-minded idolaters with "fortuna" bottled and bonded for immediate use. "Oh FORTUNA! – There is no cognac like thee! Drunken with thee, all is answered! There is no end to speculation once thou art in the blood. Oh FORTUNA! – The world is thine!" And thus amidst the innumerable odes to fortune, the non-religious idolater is lured deeper into the labyrinth.

Calvin was not totally unaware of fortune's possible inebriation. He would admit that events can occur in the world so that it appears as if "everything were ravished by fortune (fortuito) and blind impulse."[96] He would also admit

---

[96] "Ubi ergo videntur omnia fortuito et caeco impetu rapi..." (Commentary on Daniel 7:27; CO 41:81.)

that things can become so confused in the world as to imply the indifference of God and the connotation that fortune rules and governs all.[97] Calvin would even go so far as to ask the reader:

> In fact, with respect to those things which happen daily outside the ordinary course of nature, how many of us do not think that men are whirled about and twisted by the blindness and accident of fortune (fortunae) rather than governed by the providence of God?[98]

However, Calvin rigorously asserts that blind fortune is a fabrication originating from "profane men":

> For nothing is stable in the world; but continuous revolutions, as they are commonly called, occur. Thus amidst things that are constantly being changed, where indeed all things are violently whirled about at random, profane men are unable to decide on how the world is governed by the fixed counsel of God. Rather profane men fabricate for themselves blind fortune (fortunam).[99]

Thus for Calvin the "god of fortune" is an imaginative human construct promulgated by the world's confusion. The decision that fortune exists is made by profane men. What is

---

[97] "...quand les choses sont confuses au monde, et qu'il semble que Dieu ne s'en mesle plus: mais que fortune gouverne et domine." (Sermons on Job 24:1-9; CO 34:371.)

[98] "Quantum vero attinet ad ea quae preater naturalis decursus ordinem quotidie eveniunt, quotusquisque non magis reputat, caeca potius fortunae temeritate rotari et volutari homines quam Dei providentia gubernari." (Institutes I, 5, 11; OS III, p. 55.)

[99] "Nam nihil stabile est in mundo: sed accidunt continuae revolutiones ut vulgo loquuntur. Quum ita subinde res mutentur, imo quum tumultuarie omnia versentur, non possunt statuere profani homines mundum regi certo Dei consilio: sed fabricant sibi caecam fortunam." (Commentary on the Prophet Ezekiel 10:9; CO 40:214.)

the consequence of depending on such a "god"? Just as with depending on "the god of prosperity" dependence upon "the god of fortune" ends in blindness.

> Because perverse error possesses their minds, profane men determine that everything has occurred by fortune (fortuito). Thus they become blind to the conspicuous works of God and think that the human race is violently whirled about accidentally by chance (casu temere).[100]

This same blindness outlines the interrelationship between "the god of prosperity" and "the god of fortune" as found in the non-religious idolater:

> First, being drunken with prosperity (rebus prosperis), they imagine that God is their friend as though God had no regard for good people who are oppressed by many hardships. Then they imagine that the world is turned by fortune (fortuito), thus they willingly become blind in the clear light.[101]

The "conspicuous works of God"[102] as well as "the clear light"[103] have thus far been seen to be the remnant traces of the image of God in the human person. It should be remembered that the human soul with its capacities of reason, will, and imagination were all asserted to be such traces of the image of God. It should also be remembered that

---

[100] "Fortuito accidisse omnia dicerent profani, quia perversus error mentes eorum occupat, ut ad conspicua Dei opera caecutiant, dum putant casu temere versari genus humanum." (Commentary on the Four Last Books of Moses in the Form of a Harmony 2:4-9; CO 24:24.)
[101] "Ac primo quidem rebus prosperis ebrii, Deus sibi amicum esse fingunt: bonos vero qui multis aerumnis oppressi sunt, ab eo non curari: denique fortuito rotari mundum: ita sponte caecutiunt in clara luce." (Commentary on Psalms 28:5; CO 31:283.)
[102] See footnote 100, this chapter.

these remnant traces were all but annihilated by the worshipper of the "god of prosperity" who drained himself in pursuing an impossible eternal life in this life. Prosperity was pursued on a very immediate level. Prosperity had seemed to follow the simple law of cause and effect or the simple law of so much received for so much given. Self-aggrandizement was to be a simple thing. But somewhere in the labyrinth the non-religious idolater began to speculate about the nature of the world. He needed a god to satisfy the reflective capacities of reason. Fortune was ready to satisfy him ... temporarily. Thus the immediate pursuit of prosperity gave birth to the more reflective "god of fortune."

But now in the deeper descent into the labyrinth the blindness caused by both gods has become manifest. The striving for prosperity has blinded the eyes from seeing any real and vital eternality. Such striving has only discovered the false eternality of a man-made heaven which is subject to death. The remnant traces of the image of God have been exploited in pursuit of a false god. The capacities of the soul have been disciplined by that false god. Striving for the True God has now become a pastime for fools who have "time to spare." Now even the reflective capacities have begun to do service before the "god of fortune." Whatever of the "conspicuous works of God" that remained in the human soul are swallowed up by dependence upon "fortune." Whatever of "clear light" which may have been indicated by the imminent remnant traces of reason, will, and imagination has been darkened by the capacity for idolatry. The capacity for idolatry has fabricated fortune to reinforce the prior idol of prosperity. The capacity for idolatry has attempted to extinguish any sparks of the image of the True God in man. The capacity for idolatry has been employed in fabricating

---

[103] See footnote 101, this chapter.

idols and has thus blinded the human person from seeing any possible indications of union with the True God.

This is not to say that reason, will and imagination have become satisfied with fortune as a metaphysical construct. How could they be? Reason must sooner or later question fortune. Then reason asks the human person: "Did you not at least once plan something that subsequently occurred? Did you not have some freedom to use your mind in some small way? Why must I be sacrificed on the altar of fortune so as to establish the doctrine that fortune rules all?" The will asks the human person: "Did you not once act out a plan? Did you never have some freedom to act independently? Why must I become incense for an idol of fortune which contends that I have no real power to act or effect change?" Imagination asks the human person: "Have I not shown you the aesthetic productions of poets, writers, musicians and artists who asserted their freedom? Indeed many of them wrote, composed and painted precisely to express their individual freedom in opposition to the wheel of fortune, chance accident, and/or fate. Am I now to kneel in impotence before the idol of fortune?"

Although the human capacities of reason, will, and imagination are not sufficient to produce a true and complete knowledge of the True God, they are not to become entirely quieted before the "god of fortune." Whatever remnant traces of the image of God can be found in the soul still continue to be active in indicating the freedom of the individual. But the indications of freedom are not the full actualization of freedom. Still, fortune argues against even the indications of freedom. Fortune points to the hurricanes which destroy populations, the visible power of those who are both rich and evil, and the impotence of the good and the innocent. Thus the wanderer in the labyrinth, staggering to the dead-end to which the gods of prosperity and fortune have brought him, sits down exhausted and contemplates his "fate."

The security he thought he might have through the metaphysical construct of fortune has only left him in a state of anxiety. Fortune seemed to explain many things but it could not answer the questions of his reason, will, and imagination. Looking up at the dull-grey wall of the blind alley in which he finds himself, he can barely note his own listless exhaustion. At this point the non-religious idolater has one of two choices. He can attempt to retrace his steps in the labyrinth at the risk of only finding more dead-ends. Or, he can in despair answer the question "Who ultimately cares?" with the tired and dreary words: "No one."

If the non-religious idolater retraces his steps in the desperate hope of extricating himself from the labyrinth, he may yet look for a way of escape. Although Calvin has remarked that, "When human life is spoken of, it is compared to a way"[104] he would not concede that the right way for human life could be discovered solely through human effort. In explaining this it would be advantageous to follow the non-religious idolater who has decided to retrace his steps in the hope of finding an escape from the labyrinth.

Anxious to discover some way of leading his life aright, the non-religious idolater could very easily, in the labyrinth of this world, make the "noble" decision to become religious. If this is his decision, he will find numerous "religious" organizations and "religious" comrades. Calvin's comment that "from the beginning of the world there has been no region, no city, in fact no home which was able to exist without religion"[105] will certainly be verified by the non-religious idolater in his search. A maudlin sigh can now be

[104] "Ubi agitur de humana vita scimus conferri viae." (Commentary on Jeremiah's Lamentations 3:9; CO 39:566.)

heard in those religious establishments which have taken in the once non-religious wanderer. From the church, the mosque, the synagogue, and the temple rises up the bellowing refrain: "Now he is converted! Now he will be 'happy'! Now he has (sigh) RELIGION!"

Calvin would agree that the non-religious idolater was indeed "taken in." The unsuspecting wayfarer was "taken in" deeper into the labyrinth. Calvin's remarks concerning religious idolaters far outnumber his remarks concerning non-religious idolaters. The worshippers of prosperity and fortune are only street hawkers and alley peddlers compared with their "religious" relatives. It is the religious idolaters who own and operate the massive emporiums of the gods. It is the religious idolaters who add blindness to blindness. It is the religious idolaters with innumerable sanctions and rituals who attempt to lead one and all into the most recessed depths of the labyrinth.

Commenting on fictitious religions and the human person's search for God, Calvin states:

> ... there is a horrible licentiousness in fictitious religions, and those who are submerged by their own inclination are carried away into the labyrinth. Thus men do nothing but weary and torment themselves in vain when they seek God, but do not know the way.[106]

The origin of fictitious religions derives from an overestimation of the powers of the human soul or human spirit. Reason and intelligence leave the human being without

---

[105] See footnote 66, this chapter.

[106] "...in fictitiis religionibus esse horribilem licentiam, et quicunque proprio sensu feruntur demergi in labyrinthum, ita ut nihil quam se frustra fatigent ac macerent homines, ubi Deum quaerunt, nec viam tenent." (Commentary on the Twelve Minor Prophets, "Jonah" 1:6; CO 43:215.)

excuse before God; they do not give the human being the ability to form correct religions. Still, the capacity for idolatry inclines the human person to fabricate false worship of false gods according to the fancy of one's own disposition.

> Briefly, there is so much reason and intelligence prevailing in men as to render them inexcusable in the presence of God. But in reality as long as men are allowed to live according to their own inclination, they can do nothing but wander from the truth, hesitating and then dashing against all their purposes and actions. Thus it appears how many and how costly are fictitious adorations when they are estimated in the sight of God, for these same fictitious adorations come forth from an abyss of vanity and a labyrinth of ignorance.[107]

It is not to be doubted that the founders and devotees of such fictitious religions deem themselves wise. However, for Calvin, such founders and devotees have been deluded by their imaginations, and their imaginations have given them a false view of wisdom.[108] The source of this false view of wisdom lies in the "flesh" or the human person subjugated to original sin:

> Daily experience teaches that the flesh is always restless until it stumbles upon a resembling figment in which the flesh has vainly accustomed itself to find the likeness of God. In almost every age from the creation of

---

[107] "Tantum denique ratione et intelligentia pollent homines, ut reddantur coram Deo inexcusabiles. Verum quamdiu sinuntur ingenio suo vivere, nihil quam errare, labi et impingere in omnibus tam consiliis quam factis possunt. Hinc etiam apparet quanti aestimentur, et quo in pretio sint fictitii cultus apud Deum, quum ex abysso vanitatis et labyrintho ignorantiae prodeant." (Commentary on the Epistle to the Ephesians 4:17; CO 51:205.)

[108] "Omnia figmenta quae sibi homines fabricant, habere speciem aliquam sapientiae. Scimus enim quo feratur nostrum ingenium: ideo sapimus nobis ipsis..." (Commentary on Jeremiah 19:7; CO 38:327.)

> the world, men, in order that they might obey these blind longings, have erected images in which they believed God was observable to them before their bodily eyes.[109]

These "blind longings" apply not only to the products of the human imagination as manifested in tangible objects such as statues, paintings, tokens, amulets, and totems. They also apply to whatever reflective dogmas, ideologies, doctrines, philosophies and theologies may be forthcoming from such statues, paintings, tokens, amulets and totems. The mind easily becomes addicted to the products of the imagination. "The human mind conceives nothing about God except what is gross and earthly, thus it transfers all signs of the Divine Presence into the same grossness."[110] Again, the proclivity of the human person to change "earthly things" into "divine things" is seen. Products of the imagination could have been considered traces of the image of God in man. Instead, due to the influence of original sin, the traces have become gods.[111]

The mind cannot cease reflecting upon and formulating doctrines concerning these gods. Thus Calvin's remark that: "The mind therefore begets the idol; the hand gives it birth"[112] applies not only to ancient cultures and the musty corridors of museums displaying primitive artifacts. It also applies to the universities, the libraries, and the

---

[109] "Id quotidiana experientia docet, inquietam semper esse carnem, donce sibi simile figmentum nacta est in quo se pro Dei imagine inaniter soletur. Omnibus fere a conditio mundo seculis, huic caecae cupiditati ut obsequerentur homines, erexerunt signa in quibus Deum sibi prae oculis carnalibus obversari credebant." (Institutes I, 11, 8; OS III, p. 97.) Cf. also Commentary on Genesis 31:19; CO 23:426.

[110] "...mens humana, ut nihil nisi crassum et terrenum de Deo concipit, ita ad eandem crassitiem transfert omnia divinae praesentiae symbola." (Commentary on the Acts of the Apostles 7;40; CO 48:153.)

[111] Sermons on Job 22:12-17; CO 24:295-298, passim.

[112] "Mens igitur idolum gignit: manus parit." (Institutes I, 11, 8; OS III, p. 97.)

seminaries of today. Any doctrine, philosophy, world-view or theology could have its gross idol. The worship of idols is not reserved solely for the uncultivated and the vulgar.[113] Rather, the most prudent and those most endowed and gifted with the capacity for learning are entangled by idolatry.[114]

Since the human mind with its ability to reason is always for Calvin in a dialectical relationship with the human will,[115] there is also necessity that the human will must be infected with idolatry.

> The knowledge of God which now remains in men is nothing other than a horrible gushing spring of idolatry and all superstitions. Judgment for choosing and distinguishing things is partly blind and absurd, partly mutilated and confused. Whatever industry we have disappears into vanity and trifles. And the will itself, premature in its furious vehemence, is totally carried away into evil.[116]

The human will, unable to derive the proper divine object from reason alone, still continues in its energy. However, the energy of the will is "premature" because the proper divine object or the True God is still unknown. All that is known are the idols which the mind and imagination have

---

[113] "Negare certe non audebunt ubicunque ad cultum prostant in templis simulacra, maximam et prope universam hominum multitudinem divinis ipsa honoribus prosequi: ac in eo in secundum legis praeceptum, quod est de non colendis idolis, impingere. Non stolidum hominum vulgus, sed prudentissimos quosque, et summis ingenii doctrinaeque dotibus praeditos, hoc errore captos involutosque esse dico..." (De Fugiendis Impiorum Illicitis Sacris, et Puritate Chritianae Religionis Observanda; CO 5:253-254.)

[114] Ibid.

[115] See footnotes 21 and 22, this chapter.

[116] "Notitia enim Dei, quails nunc hominibus restat, nihiil aliud est quam horrenda idololatriae et superstitionum omnium scaturigo: iudicium in rerum delectu ac discrimine, partim caecum ac praeposterum, partim mutilum et confusum: quidquid industriae habemus in vanitatem et nugas defluit: voluntas autem ipsa furioso impetu praecox tota ad malum rapitur." (Commentary on the Gospel of John 3:6; CO 47:57.)

devised. The will, however, has a "furious vehemence" to pursue and serve some "god." This pursuit and service of the will result in self-imposed acts of worship or superstitions. "Under the term 'self-imposed acts of worship' (ἐθελοθρησκίας). is included all false adorations which men fabricate apart from the command of God."[117]

> Accordingly men undertake voluntary adorations – which the Greeks call superstitions (ἐθελοθρησκίας) – but which are nothing other than the self-imposed acts of worship. Thus when men begin this or that in order to give honor to God, there appears to flash a type of wisdom; but this supposed pure devotion is an abomination in the sight of God.[118]

The manifestations of self-imposed acts of worship or superstitions are as varied as the individual religious idolaters. Who has not heard of "holy men?" Certainly there are records of innumerable founders of religions who prescribed their own rituals and disciplines. But what stands behind the kneeling, bowing, and fasting? Simply the superstitious belief that another human being's self-imposed worship was the truth. That self-imposed act of worship has become deified through the passing of time and has continued to be worshipped as the final wisdom for forthcoming generations.

---

[117] "Ideoque Paulus (Col. 2, 23) sub nomine ἐθελοθρησκίας complecititur perversos omnes cultus, quos sibi absque Dei mandato fabricant homines." (Commentary on Isaiah 1:29; CO 36:56.) Cf. also Institutes IIII, 10, 24; OS V, p. 187.)

[118] "Quum ergo homines suscipiunt cultus voluntarios, ἐθελοθρησκίας vocant Graeci superstitiones: sed nihil aliud sunt quam voluntarii cultus. Quum ergo homines hoc vel illud in honorem Dei agendum suscipiunt, species sapientiae illic refulget: sed coram Deo mera est abominatio." (Commentary on the Twelve Minor Prophets, "Hosea" 4:13-14; CO 42:285.) Cf. also Commentary on the Twelve Minor Prophets, "Amos" 5:25-26; CO 43:100.

The task of listing the innumerable founders, devotees, and cults (not to mention their modern counterparts) is being done and will continue to be done indefinitely. The forthcoming volumes when added to the existent tomes may fill every tunnel in the labyrinth. However, for the present, a single sentence of Calvin should give some perspective upon the possible manifestations of self-imposed worship or superstition: "One person sets up a statue, another constructs a chapel, another appoints the annual sacred festival and the boundless number of similar things."[119]

Although the manifestations of self-imposed acts of worship or superstitions are boundless, the consequences of self-imposed acts of worship or superstitions can be specified. The consequences are ceaseless wanderings, blindness, vanity, and destruction. In analyzing these consequences it is beneficial to keep in mind the universality and complexity of religious idolatry. For Calvin, "no mortal ever contrived anything that did not basely lead to the corruption of religion."[120] The remnant traces of the image of God in the human soul or spirit which are vitiated by original sin may strive to approach and worship God. This striving will then take on the appearance of "true" religion in the eyes of the founder or his devotees. However,

> religion immediately becomes corrupt and degenerates into superstition as soon as men wish to become legislators for themselves. They say, "In doing we shall do every word that comes forth from our mouth."[121]

[119] "Eriget hic simulacrum, alius sacellum exstruet, alius anniversaria sacra constituet, et infinita eius modi." (Commentary on Isaiah 1:14; CO 36:41.)
[120] "...nihil unquam excogitavit ullus mortalium, quo non turpiter courrupta fuerit religio." (Institutes I, 5, 12; OS III, p. 56.)
[121] "...religio prorsus vitiosa est, et in superstitionem degenerat simul atque homines volunt sibi ipsis esse legislatores. Dicunt, Faciendo faciemus omnem

Added to the "god" attempted to be worshipped through superstitions or self-imposed acts of worship are the numerous "gods" forged by superstitions or self-imposed acts of worship.

> Therefore as soon as we allow ourselves this license to worship God in this way or that, or imagine God to be such and such, just so many gods are created.[122]

Whatever may have been the good intentions of the religious idolater in worshipping his "god(s)," he has decided upon an indirect way of confronting the Deity[123] -- a way which in fact has dire consequences. One of these consequences is ceaseless wandering.

> Let us observe this distorted inclination which is always found in the superstitious. This distorted inclination is that they are led here and there after their own fabrications and have nothing stable in themselves.[124]

For Calvin "superstitious men never consider that their devotion is observed by God unless there is some sign of His Presence before their bodily eyes."[125] This being the case, there is little wonder that the religious idolater scurries from

---

sermonem, qui egressus fuerit ex ore nostro." (Commentary on Jeremiah 44:17; CO 39:262.)

[122] "Simul ergo atque permittimus nobis hanc licentiam, ut Deum hoc vel illo modo colamus, vel ut imaginemur Deum esse talem, vel talem, totidem sunt deorum creationes." (Commentary on Jeremiah 16;21; CO 38:259.)

[123] Sermons on Job 11:13-20; CO 33:550 passim.

[124] "...notemus hoc praeposterum studium semper dominari in superstitiosis, quod scilicet post sua commenta huc et illuc ferunture, et nihil havent in se stabile." (Commentary on the Twelve Minor Prophets, "Hosea" 3:1; CO 42:258.) Cf. also Sermons on Job 5:8-10; CO 33:238.

[125] "...superstitiosi homines nunquam putant suum studium curae esse Deo, nisi habeant prae oculis aliquod signum carnalis praesentiae..." (Commentary on the Twelve Minor Prophets, "Sophonias" 1:5; CO 44:9.)

one inward or external place of devotion to the next. Monday – the mosque; Tuesday – the quiet temple; Wednesday – lectures from "holy" men; Thursday – the shrines; Friday – adorations to any known or unknown god; Saturday – the synagogue; and Sunday (alas) the "Christian" church! What a schedule! No vacation itinerary of a one-week tour devised to traverse Europe and Asia could match the religious idolater's inward and external wanderings in the labyrinth. And in each "place of worship" what ceremonies! What bowing! What pomposity! What pretense! All the kings and queens of the earth have been virtually ignored by their courts if devotions designed to please them were to be compared with the devotions offered to idols.

With the "infinite possibilities" of gods, religions, and rituals there is also every possibility that the religious idolater will lose himself in the labyrinth. Unlike the non-religious idolater who may simply come to spiritual exhaustion, spiritual blindness, and despair, the religious idolater has a multitude of fabrications gushing forth. If one tunnel dead ends, he is quick to project another god, religion, or ritual. Quickly he can retrace his steps as his spirit moves him, and again he can pursue his idol. Farther and farther he goes into the labyrinth. He honestly believes that he is seeing the lighted exit from the maze. In fact, he is becoming more blind and is enveloping himself in the blackest darkness, vanity and destruction.

To explain the interrelationship between the ceaseless wanderings in the labyrinth and the blindness of the religious idolater, the following words of Calvin should be cited:

> Accordingly if you represent to yourself either God or a creature in an image (in simulachro), as soon as you prostrate yourself before it in

> veneration, you are bewitched by some superstition.[126]

It should be noted and noted well that the Latin term "simulacrum" can be translated as "a likeness, image, form," or "semblance."[127] These are the most general equivalents. More specifically "simulacrum" may be translated as "an image, figure, portrait, effigy," or "statue."[128] These latter equivalents would apply to the material and/or physical manifestations of "simulacrum." The more elusive and/or ethereal translations of "simulacrum" would be "an image, form, shade," or "phantom."[129] Philosophically "simulacrum" connotes "the form or image of an object of sense or thought represented to the mind" i.e., "a representation, idea" or "conception."[130] Philosophically "simulacrum" would therefore imply the speculative components of philosophies, theologies, ideologies, doctrines and dogmas in so far as they assume the forms of representations, ideas or conceptions. Therefore, when Calvin says that men are blinded by superstitions,[131] this blindness applies not only to the false worship of physically manifested statues or paintings. It also applies to any flitting phantom, speculative idea, or projected conception.

Calvin will also state that: "We know from abundant experience that our minds are sublimely carried away by vain

---

[126] "Itaque sive Deum sive creaturam tibi in simulachro repraesentes, ubi ad venerationem prosterneris, iam superstitione aliqua fascinatus es." (Institutes I, 11, 9, OS III, p. 97.)
[127] Lewis and Short, A Latin Dictionary (Oxford: The Clarendon Press, 1969) p. 1704.
[128] Ibid.
[129] Ibid.
[130] Ibid.
[131] Commentary on Jeremiah 9:13-25; CO 38:42, passim.

speculations."[132] Who has not been "carried away" by the numerous legends of the gods? Who has not been "elevated" by the sublime thoughts of noble thinkers? Who has not restlessly pursued such legends and such thoughts to their mythological conclusions? And in the act of pursuing how many new legends and thoughts have presented themselves? Tunnel upon tunnel and chamber upon chamber has opened in the labyrinth.

Since for the superstitious religious idolater "nothing is determined or constant, he is whirled around by varied speculations, now trying this, now trying that";[133] endless hours, days and years are spent in the corridors of phantom hopes, specter beliefs, projected myths and speculative thoughts. The source, the "whence" of all this restlessness may have been partly derived from the remnant traces or sparks of the image of God in one's self or in others. But the products of these remnant sparks have now become deified. These products are now objects of faith. Man now worships man and the things of man. His blindness has become very complex. He maintains that he is pursuing some "god" but is in fact blind to the realization that he is pursuing a concoction of his or some other human's making. Like a dog chasing his own tail he perpetually spins through libraries, religious organizations, and projected images. The incessant favor of "the gods" echoes in his spirit. He maintains that he is serving a deity when in reality he is burning up hour after hour wandering in the labyrinth. He becomes blind to the fact that life on earth is not infinite. He also becomes blind to the fact that the remnant sparks of the image of God which are

---

[132] "Vanis speculationibus in sublime ferri nostra ingenia plus satis experimur." (Commentary on the Four Last Books of Moses in the Form of a Harmony, "Deuteronomy" 18:16; CO 24:273.)

infected by original sin are not leading him to God but are rather leading him into greater and greater darkness.

Commenting on human beings "religiously" relying on human beings, Calvin states:

> At length, they entangle themselves in such a huge accumulation of wanderings that the darkness of malice suffocates and finally extinguishes those sparks which once flashed to show them God's glory. Yet that seed remains which can in no way be uprooted: that there is some sense of divinity; but this seed is so corrupted that it only brings forth from itself the worst fruits.[134]

The "worst fruits" are the fabrications of idols which are unreal and cannot be depended upon.[135] The "worst fruits" are the devotions contrived to serve the idols in the minds of men – devotions which are of themselves false and vain.[136]

Even if the knowledge of the blindness of idol worship did become apparent to the religious idolater, the vanity of continued idol worship despite such knowledge would remain as a complex phenomenon in the religious idolater. That is, in the labyrinth the human person could become aware that he is wandering in darkness when he serves idols[137] and that he is entangled in his idolatry.[138] But why is there the

---

[133] "Nam quia nihil illis certum est vel firmum, per varias speculationes circumaguntur, nunc hoc, nunc illud tentant." (Commentary on the Four Last Books of Moses in the Form of a Harmony, "Numbers" 23:13; CO 25:282.)

[134] "Tandem se tanta errorum congerie implicant, ut scintillas illas quae micabant ad cernendam Dei gloriam suffocet, ac demum extinguat malitiae caligo. Manet tamen semen illud quod revelli a radice nullo modo potest, aliquam esse divinitatem: sed ipsum adeo corruptum, ut non nisi pessimos ex se fructus producat." (Institutes I, 4, 4; OS III, p. 44.)

[135] "...quoniam in eorum idolis nihil sit firmum, nihil sit denique probabile." (Commentary on Jeremiah 10:9; CO 38:71.)

[136] Commentary on Isaiah 37:18-19; CO 36:629, passim.

[137] Commentary on Galatians 4:8; CO 50:229, passim.

[138] Commentary on the Four Last book of Moses in the Form of a Harmony, "Deuteronomy" 29:16-18; CO 25:48-49.

persistence of the religious idolater's going astray after false gods in his superstitious devotions?[139] The answer to this lies in Calvin's contention that superstition or self-imposed worship is pure vanity.[140] For Calvin, this vanity is formed and augmented in that:

> We indeed know that religion possesses the souls of everyone and that no one dares to withdraw himself openly and totally from this compliance. Yet the greater part of mankind turns aside into tortuous winding paths.[141]

This same vanity is also formed and augmented due to the fact that: "man's folly cannot restrain itself from constantly falling into superstitious rites."[142]

The capacity and desire for religion contain enormous energy which constantly propels the religious idolater to worship. He may say to himself, "I know that I am ignorant as to how my adorations will free me from the labyrinth. Still, I must continue to worship something. It is too horrible a thought that I am alone with nothing higher than my life which is doomed to extinction. Perhaps through some god I will be liberated. Let me search indefinitely amidst the multitude of indefinite deities. Let me speculate awhile. After all, it is better to have a false god or even myself as god than to have no god at all."

---

[139] Commentary on the Twelve Minor Prophets, "Hosea" 3:2-5; CO 42:258-265. Commentary on the Twelve Minor Prophets, Amos" 5:25-26; CO 43:97-101, passim.

[140] "....θM9=θρ5=κ0α meram esse vanitatem." (De Necessitate Reformandae Ecclesiae, CO 6:461.)

[141] "Scimus autem quum omnium animos occupet religio, ut nemo se palam et in totum ab eius obsequio subducere audeat: magnam tamen partem flexuosis ambagibus divertere." (Commentary on Psalms 40:7; CO 31:410.)

[142] "...quia sibi temperare non potest hominum stultitia, quin protinus ad superstitiosos cultus delabatur." (Institutes I, 11, 13; OS III, p. 102.)

As soon as this soliloquy is inwardly delivered, there is every temptation to defend mercilessly "the god of the hour." By "the god of the hour" I mean whatever deity may arbitrarily present itself as worthy of worship. If it is "the sacred land" of one's own country, the rifle is loaded. If it is "the holy family" of which one is a member, the knife is sharpened for the ritual of vendetta. If it is "the local religion," the pen is filled with venomous black ink designed to castigate any non-local religion. If it is another human being, the dark fires of passion begin to blaze.

The decision to defend mercilessly "the god of the hour" thus brings forth the less noble products of the human spirit: war, murder, "religious" persecution, suicide, adultery, and every other form of misery. Are not these products noticeable as one wanders down the "tortuous winding paths" of human history? Are not these products also the consequences of human folly which "cannot restrain itself from constantly falling into superstitious rites?" Is this not the real vanity of the human spirit – to defend to the death gods which are in reality not gods at all?

There is little wonder then that Calvin sees religious idolatry ending in the destruction of human persons. His words are as follow:

> In turn some sink into oblivion in their own superstitions, while others with malicious intent revolt from God, yet all fall away from a true knowledge of Him. As a result, no proper piety remains in the world. But as to what I have said concerning those who by error slip into superstition, I do not accept the contention that their own innocence frees them from blame. For the blindness under which they labor is almost always mixed with proud vanity and obstinacy. Indeed, vanity joined with pride can be apprehended in the

> fact that when miserable men seek God they do not rise above themselves as they should. Rather, they measure him by the standard of their own dullness and neglect solid investigation. Thus out of curiosity, they fly off into vain speculations. They do not therefore apprehend God as He offers Himself, but imagine Him according to the fabrications of their own unfounded opinions. When this raging abyss opens, in whichever way they move their feet they cannot but plunge violently headlong into destruction. Indeed, however henceforth they exert themselves in the worship or service of God, they are unable to bring tribute to Him because they are not worshipping Him. Rather, they are worshipping a figment and dream of their own heart in place of Him.[143]

The destruction of human persons does not therefore apply only to the destruction of one's own time and the remnant sparks of the image of God in the human person. Nor does the destruction apply only to war, murder, "religious" persecution, suicide, and adultery. The destruction also applies to the possibility of worshipping the True God. Amidst so many confused gods, phantasms, speculations, and myths there is no real possibility of the human person coming to the

[143] "Porro sive alii evanescant in suis superstitionibus, sive alii data opera malitiose a Deo desciscant, omnes tamen degenerant a vera eius notitia. Ita fit ut nulla in mundo recta maneat pietas. Quod autem errore aliquos in superstitionem labi dixi, non ita accipio quasi sua eos simplicitas a crimine liberet: quia caecitas qua laborant, semper fere et superba vanitate, et contumacia implicita est. Vanitas et quidem superbiae coniuncta, in eo deprehenditur quod neque miseri homines in Deo quaerendo supra se ipsos, ut par erat, conscendunt, sed pro carnalis sui stuporis modo ipsum metiuntur: et neglecta solida investigatione ad vanas speculationes curiose transvolant. Itaque non apprehendunt qualem se offert, sed qualem pro sua temeritate fabricati sunt, imaginantur. Quo gurgite aperto, quaquaversum pedem moveant, in exitium praecipites semper ruere necesse est. Quidquid enim postea in cultum aut obsequium Dei moliantur, impensum illi ferre nequeunt: quia non ipsum, sed cordis sui figmentum potius et somnium, pro ipso colunt." (Institutes I, 4, 1; OS III, p. 41.)

True God. He can only increase and continue his wanderings – wanderings which sooner or later in the depths of the labyrinth force him to confront the roaring abyss of his own vanity and ruin.

In illustrating how the possibility of worshipping the True God is destroyed, a quotation from Calvin should again be cited. This quotation initially applied to imaginative productions:

> But because sculpture and painting are gifts of God, I seek a pure and legitimate use of each, lest those things which the Lord has conferred upon us for His glory and for our good are not only contaminated by absurd waste but are also turned to our destruction.[144]

It was seen that the imagination combined with the human capacity for idolatry led both the non-religious idolater and the religious idolater to a false worship of God. However, where the non-religious idolater either came to despair or attempted to retrace his steps in the labyrinth, the religious idolater continued amidst myriad speculations deceiving himself as to the nature of the True God. Despite the varied forms of destruction with which both the non-religious and the religious idolater are plagued, the distinctiveness of religious idolatry lies in the threat of the destruction of the possibility of proper worship. This is most easily seen in the manner in which the religious idolater uses the products of the imagination. Let it be remembered that the religious idolater desires to worship. During the process of his devotions he actively projects himself and all his thoughts. Any "earthly thing" can not only become an object of devotion

[144] See footnote 59, this chapter.

but also a stimulus for further projections. Two most manifest "earthly things" which are susceptible to devotion and stimuli for projection are paintings and sculpture. Calvin, citing Augustine, describes the religious idolater making eye-contact with a painted or sculptured image of "god" or a "saint" in a place of worship:

> "When they (i.e., images) are placed in these temples," he (i.e., Augustine) says, "so that in esteemed sublimity they are given heed to by those praying and sacrificing, by the very likeness of living bodily members and sense – although they are devoid of life and sense – they influence infirm souls so as to seem to live and breathe, etc."[145]
>
> For the shape of bodily members makes and in a certain sense compels the spirit living in a body to make the decision that the idol's body also has feeling, because it (i.e., the idol's physical appearance) appears to be like its own body (i.e., the body which actually does have a living spirit within it).[146]
>
> "Images (simulchra) have more power to bend the unhappy soul because they have a mouth, eyes, ears and feet; than to straighten it because they do not speak, see, hear, or walk."[147]

---

[145] "...Quum his sedibus locantur, inquit, honorabili sublimitate, ut a precantibus atque immolantibus attendantur, ipsa similitudine animatorum membrorum atque sensuum, quanvis sensu et anima careant, afficiunt infirmos animos, ut vivere ac spirare videantur, etc." (Institutes I, 11, 13; OS III, p. 101-102.) This is quoted from Augustine's letter, no. 102 (Migne, Patrologia cursus completus, series Latina, vol. 33, p. 377, section 18.)

[146] "...Hoc enim facit et quodammodo extorquet illa figura membrorum, ut animus in corpore vivens magis arbitretur sentire corpus, quod suo simillimum videt, etc." (Institutes I, 11, 13: OS III, p. 102.) Although in this case Calvin is quoting Augustine, the exact location of the citation in Augustine's works is not given.

[147] "...Plus valent simulachra ad curvandam infoelicem animam, quod os, oculos, aures, pedes habent: quam corrigendam quod non loquuntur, neque

These three prior quotations can best be summarized by one quotation which fully describes the spiritual disease of religious idolatry in its most malignant stage:

> "no one prays or worships looking at an image (simulcrum) without becoming impressed that the image is listening to him."[148]

This "idolomania". (idolomaniam)[149] has no limits in bringing forth "absurd waste."[150] This "idolomania" is also inevitably "turned to our destruction."[151]

Some of the more hilarious examples of absurd waste and the destruction of the possibility of worshipping the True God come from Calvin's own time. In the sixteenth century it was the practice of many Roman Catholics to buy and worship the supposed relics of the prophets, Jesus Christ and the saints. These relics were generally thought to make things better between "god" and the "believer." Some relics supposedly possessed the powers for healing physical infirmities. Other relics were thought to relieve part of the time of bondage in purgatory after the relic-worshipper died. Some relics were thought to do both of these things. Calvin wrote a small satirical work entitled Very Useful Information Concerning the Great Profit Which Would Occur in Christianity if an Inventory of All the Bodies of the Saints

---

vident, neque audiunt, neque ambulant." (Institutes I, 11, 13, OS III, p. 102.) Calvin is quoting from Augustine's Enarratio in Psalmum, "Psalm 113:5-7" (Migne, Patrologiae cursus completus, Series Latina, vol. 37, pp. 1484-5). Cf. also De Necessitate Reformandae Ecclesiae CO 6:476-477.)

[148] "...neminem orare vel adorare, simulacrum intuentem, qui non sic afficitur, ut ab eo exaudiri se putet." (De Necessitate Reformandae Ecclesiae, CO 6:476.) Calvin is again quoting from Augustine's letter no. 102; see footnote 145, this chapter.

[149] De Necessitate Reformandae Ecclesia, CO 6:476.

[150] See footnotes 59 and 144, this chapter.

[151] See footnotes 59 and 144, this chapter.

Were Made as They Are Found in Italy, France, Germany, Spain and Other Realms and Countries in 1543.[152] In this work which will henceforth be abbreviated as An Inventory of Relics, Calvin caustically shows the destructive lunacy of religious idolatry.

Outlining the interconnection between relics and superstition, he writes:

> But it is a very rare thing for the crowd to be at all devoted to relics, without the same crowd also being contaminated and polluted with respect to some superstition. I admit that they do not at the outset break into open idolatry; but little by little, from one abuse to the next, they move along until they err in the most outrageous way. The fact remains that a crowd calling itself "Christian" has come to a condition which exhibits an idolatry unimaginable even in paganism. For they have prostrated themselves and knelt before relics as though before God; as a sign of homage they have lighted torches and candles before the relics; they have put their trust in relics; they appeal to relics as if the power and grace of God were contained in them.[153]

[152] Advertissement Tresutile du Grand Proffit Qui Reviendroit a la Chrestienté S'il Se Faisoit Inventoire de Tous les Corps Sainctz et Reliques Qui Sont Tant en Italie Qu'en France, Allemaigne, Hespaigne, et Autres Royaumes et Pays (1543), CO 6:405.

[153] "Mais c'est une chose bien rare, d'avoir le cueur adonné a quelques reliques que ce soit, qu'on ne se contamine et pollue quant a quant de quelque superstition. le confesse qu'on ne vient pas du premier coup à idolatrie manifeste: mais petit à petit on vient d'un abus à l'autre, iusque à ce qu'on tresbuche en l'extremité. Tant y a que le people qui se dict Chrestien en est venu iusques là, qu'il a pleinement idolatré en cest endroit, autant que feirent iamais payens. Car on s'est prosterné et agenouillé devant les reliques, tout ainsi que devant Dieu: on leur a allumé torches et chandelles en signe d'hommage: on y a mis sa fiance: on a là eu son recours, comme si la vertu et la grace de Dieu y eust esté enclose." (Inventory of Relics, CO 6:411.)

Examples of this outrageous idolatry are then listed throughout An Inventory of Relics. A few citations would be appropriate. In one city it was rumored that the arm of Saint Anthony could be venerated.[154] "While it was encased, everyone kissed and adored it. But when the relic was brought into plain view, it was discovered to be the limb of a stag."[155]

> The brain of St. Peter was supposed to be contained within a great altar. As long as it was encased, no one doubted for it was considered blasphemy if anyone failed to trust in it. But when the nest was disturbed and someone could accurately inspect the thing, it was discovered to be a pumice stone.[156]
>
> They have not even allowed the body of Jesus Christ to escape entirely. For besides the teeth and the hair, the Monastery of Charroux, in the diocese of Poitiers, boasts of having the Foreskin, that is to say the skin which was cut off at the Circumcision. And from whence, I entreat you, did this skin come to them? The Evangelist Saint Luke does indeed recount that our Lord Jesus had been circumcised; but it is nowhere mentioned that the skin had been put away in order to be preserved as a relic. All the ancient histories say not a word about it, and for the period of five hundred years it was never mentioned in the Christina Church. Where had it been hidden in order to return so suddenly? Moreover, how did it fly to Charroux? But, in order to authenticate their

[154] Ibid., p. 413.

[155] "...quand il estoit enchassé, on le baisoit et adoroit: quand on le mist en avant, on trouva que c'estoit le member d'un cerf." (Ibid.)

[156] "Il y avoit au grand autel de la cervelle de sainct Pierre. Pendant qu'elle estoit enchassée, on n'en faisoit nulle doubte; car ce eust esté un blaspeheme de ne s'en fier au billet Mais quand on esplucha le nid, et on y regarda de plus pres, on trouva que c'estoit une pierre d'esponge." (Ibid.).

> claim, they say that some drops of blood have fallen from it. They indeed say this, but they should prove it. One clearly sees that this is nothing but mockery.[157]

Calvin discovered that not only was Christ's manger on display,[158] but that the table, utensils, and dishes from the last supper could be seen by all.[159] If all the pieces of the true cross were gathered together, they would fill a good-sized ship.[160] It was even contended that someone had a piece of the broiled fish which Peter offered to Jesus Christ after the resurrection.[161] Calvin said of such a fish: "It must have been especially well-spiced, or it must have been wonderfully salted to have lasted for such a long time!"[162] Relics of the Virgin Mary, including her milk, could be venerated in numerous places.[163] The gullibility of the populace had become so astounding that:

> if someone had shown them the dung-droppings of goats and they had been told, "These are the rosary beads of our Lady," they would have adored them without debate, or, they would have transported them in ships to

---

[157] "Combien encore qu'on n'a point laissé eschapper le corps de Iesus Christ sans en retenir quelque loppin. Car outre les dens et les cheveux, l'Abbaye de Charroux, au diocese de Poytiers, se vante d'avoir le Prepuce, c'est à dire la peau qui luy fut couppée à la Circoncision. Ie vous prie, dont est ce que leur est venue ceste peau? L'Evangeliste sainct Luc recite bien que nostre Seigneur Iesus a esté circonciz; mais que la peau ayt esté serrée, pour la reserver en relique, il n'en faict point de mention. Toutes les histories anciennes n'en a iamais esté parlé en l'Eglise Chrestienne. Où estce donc qu'elle estoit cachée, pour la retouver si soudainement? D'avantage, comment eust-elle vollé iusque à Charroux? Mais, pour l'approuver, ilz disent qu'il en est tombé quelques gouttes de sang. Cela est leur dire, qui auroit mestier de probation. Parquoy on veoit bien que ce n'est qu'une moquerie." (Ibid, p. 415.)

[158] Ibid, p. 416.

[159] Ibid., p. 418.

[160] Ibid., p. 420.

[161] Ibid., p. 429.

[162] "Il faut dire qu'il ayt esté bien espicé, ou qu'on y ait fait un merveilleux saupiquet, qu'il s'est peu garder si longtemps." (Ibid.)

[163] Ibid., p. 432.

> any place where they could be respectably enshrined.[164]

All in all, Calvin saw the adoration of relics as a labyrinth[165] in which people who had succumbed to the blindness[166] of religious idolatry and brutish stupidity[167] must lose themselves. However, the loss of one's self in the labyrinth of relic-filled idolatry does not excuse the human person from culpability. The responsibility for the loss of one's self is briefly outlined in An Inventory of Relics:

> I add the case of Saint Michael and his attendance upon the Virgin Mary. Someone may think that I am simply having fun when I mention the relics of an Angel, for that is the sort of thing with which the buffoons of the farces have such great sport. Regardless, sanctimonious hypocrites have continued to deceive the common people. For at Carcassone they boast of having relics belonging to him as do the parishioners of the church of Saint Julian at Tours. At the great church of Saint Michael, which is frequented by pilgrims, his short-sword is on display. This short-sword looks like a dagger a small boy would play with. Michael's shield has a like appearance. It resembles the little round metal circles found on a horse's bridle. There is no man or woman so simple-minded as not to see that this is ridiculous. But because such lies are hidden under the shadow of devotion, the evil

[164] "...si on leur eust monstré des crottes de chievres, et qu'on leur eust dit: voyla des patenostres de nostre Dame, ilz les eussent adorées sans contredit, ou les eussent apportées en leurs navires par deçà, pour les colloquer honnorablement en quelque lieu." (Ibid., p. 429.)
[165] "...car en tel abisme qui n'y seroit confuz?" (Ibid., p. 441.)
[166] Ibid., pp. 411-413.
[167] Ibid., p. 431.

> of mocking God and His Angles is not perceived.[168]

The lies hidden under the shadow of devotion deceive not only the human person worshipping before the reliquaries. They also deceived the human person as he worships before every image and every doctrine about such an image. Natural reason itself (i.e., reason under the dominion of original sin) may still be able to bear iconoclastic witness to the truth that in reality idols are dependent on men. However, natural reason itself is not powerful enough to completely overcome human superstition.

> Even superstitious persons know that idols need the help and assistance of men, instead of men needing the help and assistance of idols which are not able to stand without the agency of men .... What, therefore, is more insipid than to direct vows and prayers to wood or stone? Yet the infidels run hither and thither seeking deliverance through dead statues.[169]

> For what is more alien to reason than for a man to prostrate himself before the trunk of a tree or before stone in order to expect

---

[168] "Ie mettray icy sainct Michel, afin qu'il face compagnie à la vierge Marie. On pensera que ie me gaudisse en recitant des reliques d'un Ange, car les ioueurs de farces mesmes s'en son moquez. Mais les Caffars n'ont pas laissé pourtant d'abuser tout à bon escient le povre people. Car à Carcassonne, ilz se vantent d'en avoir des reliques, et pareillement à sainct Iulien de Tours. Au grand sainct Michel, qui est si bien frequenté de pelerins, on monstre son braquemart, qui est comme un poignart à usage de petit enfant; et son bouclier de mesme, qui est comme la bossete d'un mors de cheval: il n'y a homme ny femme si simple, qui ne puisse iuger quelle moquerie c'est. Mais pource que telz mensonges sont couvers soubz ombre de devotion, il semble advis que ce n'est point mal faict de se moquer de Dieu et de ses Anges." (Ibid., p. 435.)

[169] "Sciunt enim superstitiosi, idola hominum ope et auxilio potius indigere, quam homines idolis: quae sine hominum opera consistere non possunt.... Quid enim insulsius quam vota et preces dirigere ad lignum vel lapidem? et tamen salutis petendae causa ad mortuas statuas cursitant increduli." (Commentary on Isaiah 45:20; CO 37:146-147.)

deliverance through it? Indeed, infidels put on their disguises and say that they seek God in heaven; and since idols and images are forms of God, it is obvious what they are doing. Consequently their excuses completely vanish because their stupidity is openly observed when they bend their knees before stone or wood.[170]

For those who seek life from dead things, do they not entirely extinguish in themselves all the light of reason? In a word, if they had a speck of mental sanity, they would not attribute divinity to the works of their hands, to which they could impart no vital sensation. And certainly this consideration alone suffices to destroy any excuse of ignorance, for they are fabricating for themselves false gods in opposition to natural reason. Thus it follows that they freely blind their eyes, envelop themselves in darkness, and stupefy themselves. This voluntary blindness renders them absolutely inexcusable in order that they not be allowed to pretend that their error was a result of pious zeal.[171]

Besides, the eyes of men are dulled by indolence because they neither question, nor reflect, nor scrutinize. Thus they are stupefied by idols because they are willingly deceived.

---

[170] "Nam quid magis alienum ratione est, quam hominem se prostituere coram ligneo trunco, vel coram lapide, ut inde salutem expetat? Increduli quidem fucos suos inducunt, nempe se quaerere Deum in coelo: quoniam autem idola et imagines, Dei sunt figurae, ideo illuc accedere: sed interim apparet quid ipsi faciant. Colores igitur illi sunt prorsus evanidi, quia stupor ipsorum palam deprehenditur, quum ita genua flectunt coram lapide vel lingo." (Commentary on the Twelve Minor Prophets, "Hosea" 8:6; CO 42:6.)

[171] "Nam qui a rebus mortuis vitam petunt, nonne quantum in se est exstinguunt omne rationis lumen? Summa est, si qua esset gutta sanae mentis, no tribuerent operibus manuum suarum deitatem, quibus sensum dare nequeunt. Et certe hoc unum praeter naturae rationem falsos deos sibi fabricant. Unde sequitur, sponte claudere oculos, obducere sibi tenebras, seque obstupefacere: quae voluntaria caecitas eos prorus inexcusabiles reddit: ne obtendere liceat, errorem in pio zelo profectum esse." (Commentary on Psalms 115:8; CO 32:187.)

> For they would immediately discover the deception of idols, if they diligently applied their minds in examining them. Thus it is obvious that the worshippers of idols cannot excuse themselves under the pretext of ignorance, for they choose to be blind and wander in darkness rather than to see the light and embrace the truth.[172]

Although for Calvin natural reason does not permit the pleas of ignorance for idolatry, natural reason does not itself afford the human person the possibility of conducting his life properly. This latter statement is true not only because natural reason is vitiated by original sin, but also because natural reason is dialectically interrelated to the natural emotions or passions. This dialectical interrelationship between reason and the emotions as well as the dialectical interrelationship between the emotions and the other faculties of the human soul will be investigated in the forthcoming section.

(d) Emotion

In initially examining Calvin's thoughts concerning human emotions a few quotations should be cited again and supplemented. It should be remembered that during the pre-fall condition, Adam

> was happy in every way. Consequently in his life he esteemed equally his body and his soul. While he lived with correct judgment in his

[172] "Caeterum hebetantur hominum oculi socordia, quod neque interrogent, neque considerent, neque observent. Obstupescunt ergo in idolis: quia sponte hallucinantur. Nam protinus vanitatem deprehenderent, si diligentiam in considerando adhiberent. Unde apparet idolorum cultores ignorantiae praetextu excusari non posse: quia caeci esse atque in tenebris errare quam lucem intueri et veritatem amplecti malunt." (Commentary on Isaiah, 41:28; CO 37:55.)

> soul and the proper moderation of his affections, life also reigned.[173]

Correct judgment was possible through the pre-fall condition of intellect and will. Without the influence of original sin correct judgments would have, through intellect and will, manifested in the soul "the living image of the divine wisdom and justice."[174] That is, intellect and will would have operated in accord with the Will of the True God.

It was also seen that the interrelationship between reason and will was as follows:

> the intellect is as it were the leader and ruler of the soul. The will always considers the command of the intellect, and in its own desires awaits the decision of the intellect.[175]
>
> Moreover, the function of the intellect is to distinguish between objects according to the value or worthlessness of each object. However, the will chooses and conforms to that which the intellect has declared good, and rejects and flees that which the intellect disapproves.[176]

Calvin then remarked that no faculty can be found in the soul which did not refer to either intellect or will.[177] Further, he subsumed sense perception (sensum) under intellect,[178] and desire (appetitus) under will.[179]

Prior to the fall, the intellect would have had no difficulty in distinguishing the True God as the Highest Good.

---

[173] See footnote 5, this chapter.
[174] See footnote 6, this chapter.
[175] See footnote 21, this chapter.
[176] See footnote 22, this chapter.
[177] See footnote 23, this chapter.
[178] See footnote 24, this chapter.
[179] See footnote 25, this chapter.

Therefore the will would have obediently served the True God as the Highest Good. Further, all the other faculties of the human soul would have been in accord with the intellect and therefore in accord with the Highest Good or the True God. This would also mean that the faculty of human emotion would, prior to the fall, also be obedient to intellect (i.e., the rational capacity) and in accord with the True God. This is substantiated by Calvin's assertion that: "When God created man, He placed emotions (affectus) in him. But these emotions were compliant with reason and obedient to reason."[180]

However, with the fall and the vitiation of the human spirit by original sin, different characteristics of human nature became evident.

> For those who are not totally blind perceive that no part of us is sound. The mind is stricken with blindness and infected with innumerable wanderings. All the affections of the heart are full of obstinacy and perverseness, and either horrible longings or other equally fatal diseases reign there so that all the senses gush forth with many vices.[181]

In further describing the emotions infected with original sin, Calvin states that "blind affections predominate in ruling the lives of men."[182] "All are so carried away by wandering passions that nothing sound and blameless remains in their lives. This is a universal defect which

---

[180] "Deus quum hominem crearet, affectus illi indidit, sed morigeros et rationi obsequentes..." (Commentary on the Gospel of John 11:33-35; CO 47:266.)

[181] "Quicunque enim non prorsus caecutiunt, vident nullam nostri partem esse integram: mentem esse percussam caecitate, innumerisque erroribus infectam: omnes cordis affectus contumacia et pravitate plenos: et illic regnare vel foedas libidines, vel alios non leviores morbos: multis vitiis sensus omnes scatere." (Commentary on Genesis 3:6; CO 23:62.)

[182] "...ut regendae hominum vitae praesideant caeci affectus." (Commentary on Psalms 119:24; CO 32:224.)

extinguishes all true worship."[183] "In fact, we are held entangled in our passions. Then we long for that which is pleasing to our flesh. And thus, for the most part, men wish to subjugate God to themselves."[184] "The desires that agitate a carnal man are like antagonistic waves which beat against each other, whirling the man around violently this way and that way so that he hesitates and changes at almost every moment."[185]

The last description of the emotions vitiated by original sin (i.e., that the desires are like antagonistic waves which beat against each other) is comparable to Calvin's description of vitiated human reason (i.e., that the disharmonies within reason itself are like armies at war).[186] Further, the descriptions of wandering passions (i.e., as (a) inclining men to wish to subjugate God to themselves, and (b) extinguishing all true worship) are also comparable to the description of the non-religious idolaters' imaginations convincing them that God is "in a certain manner bound to them,"[187] and the description of the religious idolaters' imaginations obeying "blind longings" in erecting images.[188] Residing somewhere amidst conflicting reason, deceptive imagination, and violent passions, the human will can only be drawn in opposite directions simultaneously. With this many erupting volcanic elements in the human spirit, the human

---

[183] "...sic omnes vagis cupiditatibus fuisse abreptos, ut nihil in eorum vita sincerum vel integrum maneat. Haec est universalis defectio, quae omnem pietatem exstinguit." (Commentary on Psalms 14:2-3; CO 31:138.)
[184] "Tenemur enim impliciti nostris cupiditatibus: deinde appetimus quod nobis arridet secundum carnem: et hoc modo, ut plurimum, vellent Deum sibi sibiicere homines." (Commentary on Jeremiah's Lamentations 2:19; CO 39:559.)
[185] "...libidines, quibus homo carnalis circumagitur, veluti contrarii sunt fluctus: qui dum inter se confligunt, hominem ipsum versant huc et illuc, ut variet atque alternet fere in singula momenta." (Commentary on the Epistle of Paul to Titus 3:3; CO 52:428.)
[186] See footnotes 28 and 29, this chapter.
[187] See footnote 80, this chapter.
[188] See footnote 109, this chapter.

will can only err in serving any pseudo-divine object and must, amidst so many conflicting faculties, face exhaustion.

This conflict and vitiation of reason, imagination, will, and emotion will give some indication of the all-encompassing effect of original sin on the total human person. In Calvin's words we would indeed have to be totally blind to perceive that no part of us is sound.[189] However, to perceive that no part of us is sound is not the same thing as making us healthy. This is only to diagnose the disease. The cure is still needed. In a very real sense reason's leaving us without excuse with respect to the actual existence of a Deity[190] and (!) reason's convicting us of our own false worship of the Deity[191] have performed this diagnostic function. But reason's diagnosis cannot directly or immediately lead us to the cure. This is so not only because reason is at war with itself, but also because of reason's dialectical interrelationship with the emotions. Commenting on the interrelationship between reason and the emotions, Calvin states:

> We see how each person loosens the bridle on his passions. When we make decisions, do we decide with regard to reason in order to be directed by it? Not at all. But our passions rule in such a way that we do not perceive a single thing without becoming preoccupied with some fantasy.[192]

This dialectic of vitiated reason and vitiated emotion is further described by Calvin's statement: "It is perceived

---

[189] See footnote 181, this chapter.

[190] See footnotes 44 and 45, this chapter.

[191] See footnotes 169, 170, 171 and 172, this chapter.

[192] "Nous voyons comme chacun lasche la bride à ses passions. Quand nous iugeons, est'ce regardans à la raison, pour nous conduire par icelle? Nenni: mais nos passions dominent en telle sorte que nous n'y voyons goutte, d'autant que nous sommes preoccupez de quelque phantasie." (Sermons on Job 21:22-34; CO 34:262.)

that within the human mind there is an intemperate madness for perverse worship, a madness which no confining bridles are able to restrain."[193] A predominate factor in forming and actualizing this madness is the faculty of emotion. Reason may for a time abhor and even attempt to "bridle" the madness of idolatry. However, inevitably, reason itself is swallowed up by the power of the passions. This is illustrated by another statement of Calvin's concerning the madness of idolatry:

> Everyone will testify that he earnestly detests such madness. And yet men are led by indiscriminate and insane passion to fabricate gods so that no warning can recall them.[194]

Here lies the truth of the statement that "blind affections predominate in ruling the lives of men."[195] Reason's diagnostic warning against idolatry is no match for the fury of the emotions in pursuit of their gods. Reason cannot predominate in a contest with such passions. Rather, reason is itself overcome and placed under the dominion of the emotions. Who has not heard the political orator manipulate the emotions of the masses for his purpose and for his god of power? Who has not read the persuasive lines of a gifted poet which extol to "divine heights" human and earthly love. Who has not remarked to himself or others after listening to a "religious" leader, "Surely this is a man of 'god'!"? And reason, reason which is critical of deifying "earthly things," where is that reason in the face of thousand-year empires, "perfect" human love, and a feeling of the "holy"? Such critical reason is

---

[193] "...perspicitur humani ingenii intemperies ad perversos cultus, quae nullis fraenis cohiberi satis potest." (Commentary on Joshua 23:12-16; CO 25:561.)
[194] "Nemo profecto erit qui tantam dementiam non magnopere detestetur. Et tamen homines promiscue insana libidine feruntur ad deos fabricandos, nec ulla monitione revocantur." (Commentary on Isaiah 44:10; CO 37:112-113.)
[195] See footnote 182, this chapter.

hard to find. Even if it can be found, what are its chances of combating the political herd, swooning lovers, and the "people of 'god'"? Such critical reason is simply swallowed up. It's once active potency of showing the human person his or her culpability for idolatry becomes ineffective. The human person is rushing through the labyrinth. The "gods" and delights of the countless and fascinating tunnels want nothing to do with the sober self-examination of iconoclastic reason. Iconoclastic reason cannot even be heard much less recall the mad wanderers.

Regardless of this passionate fury of pursuing gods or goddesses there is still the possibility that the idolatrous wanderer in the labyrinth may again come to himself and analyze his predicament. The possibility arises from the nature of the vitiated emotions themselves. These emotions have great energy for a time. They do not have infinite energy. Further, in attempting to worship the "deity of the hour" the emotions have been frustrated many times. The desired god or goddess was not always available. Even when the god or goddess was available somehow it was not always a continuously "divine" affair. The emotions, examining themselves, begin to discover an earth-bound lethargy. Calvin describes this lethargy in the following manner:

> The consequences of our disordered passions and our anxieties which are, as it were, bound to the earth are that our souls either eroneously wander or our souls sink down into listlessness so that they are not free to rise up to God. And, as the essence of God is hidden from us, this makes us all the more sluggish in seeking Him.[196]

---

[196] "Nam ut sunt inordinati nostri affectus, et sollicitudines nos quasi terrae affixos tenent, animi nostri aut perperam vagantur, aut per ignaviam subsidunt, quominus ad Deum libere assurgant. Quum autem essentia Dei nobis

Concomitant with this earth-bound lethargy is the realization that our souls "are not free to rise up to God." Latently contained within the is statement is it apprehension that our souls should indeed freely rise up to God. What faculty or human capacity makes this apprehension possible? It has been shown that he capacity cannot be reason because reason has been swallowed up in the emotions. Likewise it cannot be will or imagination because reason predominates dialectically over both will and imagination. Thus this apprehension that one should or ought to freely rise up to God must come from another faculty. The analysis of conscience in the forthcoming section will offer some information concerning he origin of the apprehension that one should or ought to freely rise up to God.

(e) Conscience and Natural Law

Calvin's concept of conscience has already been briefly outlined at the beginning of this chapter. In establishing the assertion that the human soul was immortal and an essence, the following quotation was cited:

> Surely conscience, which, distinguishing between good and evil, responds to the judgment of God, is a certain sign of the immortal spirit. For how could a motion without essence penetrate into the tribunal of God and inflict itself with terror at its own guilt. Certainly the body is not affected by the fear of spiritual punishment, but it falls heavily on the soul alone. From this it follows that the soul is endowed with essence.[197]

abscondita sit, eo fit ut tardiores simus ad ipsum quaerendum." (Commentary on Isaiah 26:8; CO 36:431.)

[197] See footnote 13, this chapter.

In clarifying this initial statement concerning conscience, a new quotation should be recorded. In defining conscience Calvin states that

> the definition should be sought from the origin of the term. For just as when through the mind and intelligence men grasp the knowledge of things, about which they are said to know, there is then derived the term "science": so when men have a sense of the divine judgment, as a witness joined to them, which does not allow them to hide their sins but rather drags the sins before the judge's tribunal, this sense is called "conscience." For it is a certain mean between God and man because it does not allow a man to suppress in himself what he has come to know, but pursues and persuades him until he stands accused.[198]

To clarify the meaning of conscience (<u>conscientia</u>) derived from the last quotation, examine the English word "conscience" made up of "con" and "science." "Con" in Latin means "with." The English word "science" or "structured knowledge of things" derives from the Latin word "scientia." Thus "conscience" means "with knowledge." Calvin is simply saying that by experience we are "with the knowledge" of good and evil; i.e., we know that there is a moral law within us and we cannot escape this sense of morality.

---

[198] "...ac definitio quidem ex etymo vocis petenda est. Nam sicuti quum mente intelligentiaque homines apprehendunt rerum notitiam, ex eo dicuntur scire, unde et scientiae nomen ducitur: ita quum sensum habent divini iudicii, quasi sibi addiunctum testem, qui sua peccata eos occultare non sinit quin ad iudicis tribunal rei pertrahantur, sensus ille vocatur conscientia. Est enim quiddam inter Deum et hominem medium: quia hominem non patitur in seipso supprimere quod novit, sed eousque persequitur donec ad reatum adducat." (<u>Institutes</u> III, 19, <u>OS</u> IV, p. 295.) Cf. also <u>Institutes</u> IIII, 10, 3; <u>OS</u> V, p. 166.

For Calvin the conscience lies within the heart or "the innermost part of the soul."[199] Conscience is thus for Calvin an extremely significant faculty of the human soul and/or human spirit. It should be remembered that the proper seat of God's image is in the human spirit or soul.[200] It should also be remembered that the capacities for reason and will distinguished the human soul from the soul of beasts.[201] Although vitiated reason was supposed to dialectically predominate over the other faculties of the soul[202] and manifest the absurdity of idolatry,[203] vitiated reason was not powerful enough to overcome the passionate idolomania of the emotions.[204] However, although blind affections predominate in ruling the lives of men,[205] Calvin would not consent to the idea that man has become excusable or without fault because blind affections predominate. If iconoclastic reason finally succumbs to blind affections, there is still a sense of guilt despite the power and force of the passions.

> But yet there is no diminution of guilt before God when men, blinded by their passions, no longer make distinctions but follow their passions without any discrimination and shame.[206]

---

[199] "Corda hic pro conscientia posuit, vel intima animae parte..." (Commentary on First Thessalonians 3:13; CO 52:159.)
[200] See footnote 16, this chapter.
[201] See footnote 15, this chapter.
[202] See footnotes 21-25, this chapter.
[203] See footnotes 169-172, this chapter.
[204] See footnotes 192-194, this chapter.
[205] See footnotes 182 and 195, this chapter.
[206] "Sed tamen hoc non minuit culpam coram Deo, ubi homines excaecati sua libidine nullum amplius dicrimen tenent, sed absque ullo delectu et pudore sequuntur suam libidinem." (Commentary on the Twelve Minor Prophets "Amos" 2:7; CO 43:26.) Cf. also Sermons on Job 32:1-3; CO 35:10.

The conscience, despite the fall of man into original sin, still maintains enough potency to point out good and evil. Yet, even the conscience has its limitations.

> Here another inquiry arises. It is certain that in this degenerate and vitiated nature some residue of God's gifts remain; thus it follows that we are not perverted in every part. The explanation is easy: the gifts which the Lord left for us after the fall are certainly worthy of praise if judged in themselves. But since the infection of evil has proceeded with violence through every part, nothing unspoilt and free from all corruption will be found in us. That some knowledge of God is innate in us, that some distinction between good and evil is engraved on our consciences, that we are able to maintain our present life naturally, that, in short, we surpass brute cattle in so many ways, is excellent in itself inasmuch as it originates from God. But all these things are contaminated in us, just as when wine which has been completely spoiled and tainted by its rank-smelling cask loses the agreeableness of good flavor so that the taste is bitter and offensive.[207]

That conscience in fallen man is a significant gift of God cannot be doubted. This is especially true within the context of the labyrinth. Despite the myriad tunnels,

---

[207] "Suboritur etiam alia quaestio. Certum enim est, in hac degenere vitiataque natura manere tamen aliquid donorum Dei residuum: unde sequitur, non omni ex parte nos esse perversos. Solutio facilis est: Dona quae nobis reliqua fecit Dominus post lapsum, si per se aestimentur, laude quidem esse digna, sed quum per omnes partes grassetur mali contagio, nihil in nobis sincerum reperietur et omni inquinamento vacuum. Quod aliqua Dei notitia nobis annascitur, quod in conscientia insculptum est aliquod boni et mali discrimen, quod ingenio pollemus ad tuendam praesentem vitam, quod denique tot modis antecellimus brutas pecudes, id per se ut a Deo proficiscitur praeclarum est, sed in nobis perinde inquinata sunt haec omnia, atque vinum vasis sui foetore

fantasies, and inticements of the maze, the capacity "to distinguish between good and evil recalls us from our wanderings."[208] Despite the fall, "God has registered such a certitude in our consciences that we are not able to obliterate the knowledge which we have of good and evil."[209]

Coupled with the activity of conscience is the phenomenon of natural law. For Calvin:

> natural law is that apprehension of the conscience which sufficiently distinguishes between what is just and unjust in order to annul in men the excuse of ignorance, for they are convicted by their own testimony.[210]

In explaining the interrelationship between conscience and natural law it is important to realize that both are gifts excellent in themselves in that they originated from God.[211] However, conscience and natural law are also things which are contaminated in us due to the vitiation or original sin.[212] Conscience with its concomitant of natural law may be able to recall us from our wanderings,[213] but presently where do we now find ourselves in the labyrinth? Surely we have not yet freely risen to God. On the contrary, according to Calvin, we stand convicted by our own testimony.[214] To stand

---

prorsus infectum ac imbutum boni saporis gratiam perdit, imo gustu et amarum et noxium est." (Commentary on the Gospel of John 3:6; CO 47:57.)

[208] "...ut boni et mali discrimen ab errore nos revocet..." (Commentary on Psalms 36:4; CO 31:360.)

[209] "...Dieu a enregistré en nso consciences une certitude telle, que nous ne pouvons point effacer la congnoissance que nous avons du bien et du mal." (Sermons on Job 32:1-3; CO 35:6.)

[210] "Quod sit conscientiae agnitio, inter iustum et iniustum sufficienter discernentis: ad tollendum hominibus ignorantiae praetextum, dum suo ipsorum testimonio redarguuntur." (Institutes II, 2, 22; OS III, p. 265.)

[211] See footnote 207, this chapter.

[212] See footnote 207, this chapter.

[213] See footnotes 208 and 210, this chapter.

[214] See footnote 210, this chapter.

convicted is to stand with a burden upon ourselves, a burden which does not allow us to freely rise up to God.

For Calvin a misinformed or partially informed conscience restrains a person from fleeing to God.[215] Again, this is not to say that conscience itself is evil. It is a gift of God still active in the human person. Yet this gift has been contaminated. The consequences of this contamination are twofold. First, the conscience may accuse a person of transgressing the laws of idols and not the law of nature. This is a conscience which none the less accuses and convicts the human person. Second, the conscience may accuse the person of transgressing the natural law. In this second case the person has a consciousness of the natural law but feels that he has not fulfilled the natural law. Thus the human person feels accused and convicted. Both phenomena of conscience are interrelated and active in the human person and can best be described under the single category of "the bad conscience."

Calvin describes the bad conscience as "the forecourt of hell."[216] The approach to this forecourt is through the inner windings and recesses o the labyrinth. The worship of human traditions has its horribly destructive consequences and quickens the approach to the same forecourt.

> Human traditions are a labyrinth in which consciences are more and more entangled. Further, human traditions are snares which initially bind in such a way that they finally strangle.[217]

---

215 "...non possunt ad Deum confugere, quia conscientia tenet ipsos constrictos." (Commentary on the Twelve Minor Prophets "Obadiah" 1:7-8; CO 43:186.)
216 "...atrio inferorum..." (Commentary on Ephesians 4:19; CO 51:206.)
217 "...humanas traditiones labyrinthum esse, quo magis ac magis implicantur conscientiae: imo esse laqueos, qui sic initio stringunt, ut successu tandem temporis strangulent." (Commentary on Colossians 2:21; CO 52:114.)

The bondage and strangulation of human traditions doing homage to man-made gods have already been partially discussed in the analyses of no-religious and religious idolatry. There is no "earthly" thing which cannot take on "heavenly" proportions. Once the man-made absolute has been accepted, traditions concerning how such an absolute is to be worshipped are promulgated. The conscience, under the influence of such traditions, attacks the human person for not having fulfilled the devotions prescribed by the latest finite deity.

This is not to say that conscience under the influence of human traditions will not struggle with itself. One impetus which attempts to free the conscience from the bondage of human traditions is natural law. Natural law as has been previously stated is an apprehension of the conscience which annuls in man the excuse of ignorance.[218] For Calvin, this excuse of ignorance is destroyed because natural law is also sufficient "to instruct (institui) the human person in a right standard of conduct."[219] Further, natural law as an apprehension of conscience points to a very valuable knowledge of the truth. Calvin describes this knowledge in the following manner:

> ...although avarice and perverse passions take away judgment and soundness of mind, a knowledge of the truth still remains engraved in the souls of men which, being stirred up, sends forth sparks to prevent the universal triumph of malice.[220]

---

[218] See footnote 210, this chapter.

[219] "Et nihil est vulgatius, quam lege naturali (de qua istic Apostolus loquitur) hominem sufficienter ad rectam vitae normam institui." (Institutes II, 2, 22; OS III, p. 264.)

[220] "...licet avaritia perversique alii affectus iudicium et sanam mentem eripiant, manere tamen in animis hominum insculptam veri notitiam, quae scintillas

Both conscience and natural law are factors which stir up sparks of the truth. These sparks in turn show the need for human justice.[221]

However, to be instructed in a right standard of conduct is not the same thing as having mastered and actualized that same standard of conduct. In the same manner, sparks of the knowledge of the truth are not the same as continuous light from the knowledge of the truth. Conscience and natural law leave the human person inexcusable and point to the need for justice. They do not ease the guilt of being inexcusable nor do they totally satisfy the need for justice.

An illustration of both the power and limitations of conscience and natural law are found in the following words of Calvin:

> This example is certainly worthy of notice: men seldom err in general principles, thus they unanimously confess that each person should receive what is due to him. However, as soon as they descend into their own affairs, perverse self-love blinds them or at least envelops them in such foggy mists that they are driven away in the opposite direction.[222]

The context to which this quotation pertains is in conjunction with the general principle that "justice ought to be mutually

excitata emittit, nisi in totum malitia dominetur." (Commentary on Genesis 31:43; CO 31:431.)

[221] Ibid, ff.

[222] "Notabile certe exemplum: nam raro in generalibus principiis errant homines, ideo fatentur uno ore ius suum cuique reddendum. Simul autem atque ad propria negotia descendunt, excaecat eos perversus sui amor vel saltem tales nebulas obducit ut in contrariam partem ferantur." (Commentary on Genesis 29:14; CO 23:401-402.)

cultivated."[223] This general principle is "engraved in the nature of men"[224] as a "law of equity"[225] and comprises the true substance of the natural law as the right standard of conduct.[226] Men may be unanimously aware of this general principle and preach this general principle, but their individual actions do not actualize this principle. On the contrary, their individual actions take a quite different course.

For Calvin, the cause of this non-actualization lies in the reality of self-love. Now self-love is not only a love of one's self but also a love of the idols that the self has projected and/or accepted. Here the conflict within the bad conscience can again be seen.

It will be remembered that the bad conscience was prone to be bound by the labyrinth of human traditions.[227] Conscience may struggle with such traditions with the aid of natural law. However, to struggle is not the same as to conquer. Natural law, although a possible aid to the conscience, can itself become contaminated by human traditions. Who is not aware of the deification of certain "earthly goods" such as the family or the nation? And once these goods have been deified, who has not heard that it is "the natural thing" to control or destroy any other alien family or nation? Certainly this is the cause of a labyrinth of evils which has always plagued this world. Certainly both conscience and natural law can become strangled once the rhetoric of warfare announces the "natural" process of tribal and political history.

---

[223] "Iustitiam mutuo colendam esse..." (Ibid., p. 401.)
[224] "...insculpsit hominum naturae..." (Ibid.)
[225] "...aequitatis iudicium..." (Ibid.)
[226] See footnote 219, this chapter.
[227] See footnote 217, this chapter.

I use the murderous history of warfare among families and nations as only one example of how human traditions can bind and strangle conscience and conscience's apprehension of natural law. The tales of sexual warfare, war within the individual, and every sort of destruction point to conscience's failure to actualize and solidify natural law's authentic precept that "justice ought to be mutually cultivated."

However, even if conscience is bound and strangled for a time by human traditions and/or self-love, conscience will still struggle to make itself known. "The worm of conscience, hotter than any cauterizing iron, gnaws away within."[228] Like the other faculties of the human soul, conscience is a remnant trace of the image of God in the person – a remnant trace which cannot be wholly obliterated.[229] Conscience still functions "like a warden assigned to man, which observes and searches out all man's secrets so that nothing is buried in darkness. Hence the ancient proverb: 'Conscience is a thousand witnesses'."[230]

In the myriad inward tunnels of the labyrinthine self the wanderer is aware of those thousand witnesses. Like the unrelenting accusations of a prosecutor, the recriminating voices of conscience can be heard: "Why did you not do this?" "You did something well, but perhaps you could have done better." "What did you forget to do?" "Did you correctly and fully employ your reason, will, imagination and emotions?" "Are you at all times doing all the good that is in your power?" "Why do you eat and drink while others have nothing?" "Why

---

[228] "..intus eos mordet conscientiae vermis cauteriis omnibus acrior." (Institutes I, 3, 3; OS III, p. 40.)
[229] Ibid. Cf. also Calvin's Commentary on Seneca's De Clementia, book I, chapter 13, section 94 (Battles and Hugo eds., Leiden: E.J. Brill, 1969, p. 228.)
[230] "...est quasi appositus homini custos, qui omnia eius arcane observet ac speculetur, ne quid in tenebris sepultum maneat. Unde et vetus illud proverbium, Conscientia mille testes." (Institutes IIII, 10, 3; OS V, p. 166.) Cf. also Calvin's

do you attempt to sleep while others suffer privations?" Whether the voices originate from human traditions or natural law or an amalgam of both, the result is the same:

> We are tossed about here and there by our anxieties and cannot find any refuge in which to stay.[231]

It is true that the individual may temporarily find relief from the accusations of his conscience by rushing to some secular and/or religious society. In such a society he may attempt to silence the constant murmurs of the thousand inward witnesses. However, a bad conscience is a persistent worm which even gnaws away at the good-natured acceptance of the individual by the group. Questions still resound in the individual's soul as he finds himself alone: "What is human society? Is it possible for such a society to be anything else than a mass of chattering voices trying collectively to hide its own guilt?" "What authority do other humans have? How could they possibly have any more authority than one's self?" "Have other human beings overcome the thousand witnesses of a bad conscience or have they simply tried to quiet those witnesses with incessant verbosity?" "Who cares what other have or haven't done once you apprehend your own failings?"

Given the possible idols, deceptions, and wanderings in the maze; given the mists of the mind, the nebulous vision of the wanderer and the insecurity of each step; given the constant darkness, exhaustion, and retracing found in each labyrinthine path; who can be assured that he is really seeking the way of deliverance? Conscience, even conscience struggling with itself, has only uncovered the confusion and

---

Commentary on Seneca's De Clementia, book I, chapter 13, section 94 (Battles and Hugo eds., Leiden: E.J. Brill, 1969, p. 228.)

blindness within the human soul. It has not actualized the light and clarity necessary for escape. In Calvin's words: "when consciences wrestle with themselves for a long time and exert themselves in lengthy battles, they still do not find a refuge in which to rest."[232]

Thus a bad conscience, as a remnant trace of the image of God, indicates that one should or ought to seek the way of deliverance from the labyrinth. The bad conscience in and of itself cannot clearly indicate or actualize that way of deliverance. Conscience in its contaminated condition sends forth those sparks which point to an anxiety-filled culpability of the human being. However, for Calvin, even this bad or contaminated conscience is better than no conscience at all.

> Let each person serve his nearest neighbor as far as charity will allow and as the occasion demands. Meanwhile no one ought to allow himself to be turned in opposite directions contrary to a bad conscience, for once this free agency is lost, he will be known to permit the most abusive actions and obey the most hideous commands.[233]

That a bad conscience is better than no conscience at all is emphasized by Calvin in that although a bad conscience is the forecourt of hell, the false security and drowsiness of the human being is "a deadly whirlpool."[234] A bad conscience

[231] "...ut anxii huc atque illuc volvamur, nec protum conspiciamus ubi tuto pedem figere liceat." (Commentary on Isaiah 7:2; CO 36:146.)
[232] "Ubi ergo diu secum luctatae, et longis certaminibus exercitae conscientiae, portum tandem in quo resideant non inveniunt..." (Institutes III, 4, 2; OS IV, p. 88.)
[233] "Serviat quisque proximis suis, quantum fert caritas: diende ut postulat etiam usus. Interea nemo mala conscientia flecti se sinat in hanc vel illam partem: quia ubi desinit esset liber, cogetur perferre quascunque contumelias, et obsequi foedissimis imperiis..." (Commentary on Daniel 6:17; CO 41:20.)
[234] "Tormentum malae conscientiae, quo eam cruciat horror divini iudicii, atrio inferorum conferri potest. Sed talis securitas et veternus exitialis est gurges."

at least actually struggles to discover the exit from the labyrinth. As a remnant trace of the image of God in the soul, it can aid the human person to actualize a limited degree of justice and charity in relation to one's nearest neighbors. This is conscience actualizing itself within the context of "earthly things."[235] This does not mean that conscience has led the person out of the labyrinth. It only means that while in the labyrinth a limited form of justice and charity is possible among human beings. Further, the bad conscience recognizes the limitations of this justice and charity and still proclaims that greater, unlimited justice and charity is required.

Although "the bad conscience" has not become "a good conscience" "the bad conscience" still bears witness to the contaminated yet Divine gift of conscience in the human person. It should be remembered that the gift of conscience as well as the other faculties or capacities of the human soul distinguish the human race from "brute cattle."[236] As long as even the infected or contaminated conscience struggles with itself, struggles to search out the exit from the labyrinth, struggles for light and clarity; the human person continues to be something other than a brute. It is true that he or she is still an exhausted wanderer in the labyrinth. It is true that he or she has been deceived by idols. It is true that a thousand voices have torn apart his or her soul. Regardless, the struggle has been carried on and that very struggle has indicated that some spark of the image of God remains in the human person – a spark which prevents the universal triumph of malice.[237]

(Commentary on Ephesians 4:19; CO 51:206.) Cf. also footnote 216, this chapter.

[235] Cf. footnote 36, this chapter.

[236] Cf. footnote 207, this chapter.

[237] See footnote 220, this chapter.

However, the proddings of the bad conscience also indicate something else. The very fact that the universal triumph of malice is halted means that malice does in fact exist as a threatening and destructive force. Conscience in its weakened and contaminated condition may not always have the power to do battle with such a force. For how long can conscience struggle? What aid will conscience find in the labyrinth? Let us remember that in the labyrinth of the ancient world there were not only sacrificial victims (i.e., the youth of Athens). There was also the hybrid monster-child, part human and part beast (i.e., the Minotaur). The wanderer must be aware that the beast can at any moment toss its horns into the air for an attack. That is, the wanderer must recollect that if the agency of conscience is abandoned, he will himself become capable of "the most abusive actions."[238] He himself will be prone to obey "the most hideous commands."[239] In short, if the struggle with conscience is abandoned, the wayfarer will find himself so overcome by the malicious beast within the labyrinth of himself and the labyrinth of the world that his condition will be that of a person caught in a "deadly whirlpool."[240] How and why this can occur is the subject of the next chapter.

C. Conclusion

This chapter was concerned with how a person enters the labyrinth. It was discovered that a person enters the labyrinth by making decisions "above God." The components of human decision-making were then analyzed within the context of Calvin's conception of self-knowledge. Calvin's

[238] See footnote 233, this chapter.
[239] See footnote 233, this chapter.
[240] See footnote 234, this chapter.

conception of self-knowledge as being the knowledge of human nature before and after the fall of Adam afforded the possibility of dialectically examining the human soul and its faculties of reason, will, imagination, emotion, and conscience. It was established that the human soul and its faculties were so vitiated by original sin that only remnant traces of the image of God were detectable. These remnant traces were so contaminated that they led the human person into idolatry or deciding "above God" and consequently into the labyrinth.

It was also shown that a particular faculty of the soul was not only in conflict with itself (e.g., reason in conflict with reason), but that a particular faculty was also in conflict with another faculty (e.g., reason in conflict with imagination) or with other faculties (e.g., reason in conflict with imagination and emotion). The conflicts within the soul displayed the labyrinthine nature of human life seeking liberty from its predicament. In this very search the responsibility of the human person to arise to the True God presented itself. It was established that the soul and its faculties attempted such an ascension but were so limited and confused by the effects of original sin that the human person actually became more and more ensnared in the labyrinth.

CHAPTER THREE
THE MONSTER-BEAST

In Chapter Two there was a partial examination of the remnant traces of the image of God in the human person. It was initially stated in that chapter that these remnant traces were unable in and of themselves to again attain primal perfection.[1] Further, it was contended that the remnant traces, because they were contaminated by original sin, may tend to obliterate totally the image of God.[2] Chapter Two explained how the human person entered and entangled himself in the labyrinth. Towards the conclusion of that chapter it was also remarked that the labyrinthine wanderer had not only to contend with the deceptions of the myriad tunnels, but he also had to contend with the possible attacks of a lurking monster or beast.[3] From whence comes the origin of this monster-beast? What is the nature of its powers? What is the extent of its powers? Seeking answers to these questions, we must again find ourselves apprehensively wandering in the labyrinth.

A. The Monster-Beast is Man as "god."

[1] See Chapter II, discussion of footnotes 16-18.
[2] Ibid.
[3] See Chapter II, discussion of footnotes 237-239.

In Chapter Two it was shown that forms of blindness darkened the vision of both the non-religious[4] and the religious idolater.[5] For Calvin there are two general types of blindness:

> ... among unbelievers there are some blind in such a way that they are ignorant due to a false mental image of what is right. Others, however, are blind in such a way that malice is the dominant factor.[6]

These two general types of blindness are directly correlated to Calvin's assertion that the knowledge of God which has been implanted in men's minds is, because of the effects of original sin, either smothered or corrupted – partly by ignorance, partly by malice.[7]

In Chapter Two false mental images of God were examined as they developed themselves in both the non-religious and the religious idolater. It was seen that idolatry did in fact smother or corrupt the light of the knowledge of God implanted in the human soul. To smother and corrupt such light is of course to darken the soul, and increasing darkness is simply another name for blindness. But this blindness for the most part was not maliciously intended. Rather, because of false conceptions of God, the human person became entangled in the labyrinth. That is, ignorance of the True God's full nature opened the corridors of idolatry. There is still a responsibility for such ignorance in that the human person still struggles to find the exit from the labyrinth. This

---

[4] See Chapter II, discussion of footnotes 87-95.

[5] See Chapter II, discussion of footnotes 119-140, and 165-167.

[6] "...ex infidelibus alios ita esse caecos, ut falsa recti imaginatione fallantur: alios autem sic excaecatos, ut malitia tamen praevaleat." (Commentary on the First Epistle to Timothy 1:13; CO 52:258.)

[7] "Eandem notitiam partim inscitia, partim malitia vel suffocari vel corrumpi. " (Institutes, Title to Chapter IV of Book I; OS III, p. 40.)

search for the exit manifests the fact that there is not complete satisfaction with a subterranean life of wandering, that there is still the hope of extrication, and that the human person feels some responsibility to struggle for the light.

But there remains another form of blindness – a form of blindness that connotes ill-will or malice. The origin and effects of this malicious blindness describe and explain how the human person as an ignorant wanderer in the labyrinth is transformed into something inhuman, something bestial, something monstrous.

It should be remembered from Chapter Two that Calvin described fallen human nature as follows:

> Nothing is more inconstant than man. Contrary motions stir up and variously perplex his soul. Continually he wanders because of ignorance. He yields, overcome by the slightest temptations. We know his soul to be a chasm and a lurking place for every sort of filth.[8]

This description initially sets forth the interrelationship between the blindness of ignorance and the blindness of malice. The remnant traces of the image of God (i.e., reason, will, imagination, emotion, and conscience) are incapable in and of themselves of knowing the complete and full nature of the True God. Thus the human person wanders amidst the phantasms, speculations, and images of false gods. Any temptation of any new deity will call him into another labyrinthine corridor. This is the blindness of ignorance.

However, the human soul is also a "chasm and a lurking place for every sort of filth." Within this chasm there are ferociously destructive possibilities. Hidden in the most

---

[8] See footnote 18, Chapter II.

darkened lurking places there is a hybrid monster-child capable of producing relentless misery. This touches upon the blindness of malice.

I say this touches upon the blindness of malice because the origin of this monster-beast is still unknown. How does the ignorant wanderer become the bestial agent of human destruction? How does the seeker of labyrinth's exit become a menacing threat to himself and to others? Commenting on the origin of violence in general, Calvin states: "Pride, therefore, is the mother of all violence."[9] Like the Cretan Minotaur, pride in the human soul has two horns.

> Pride, we know, has two horns, so to speak. Certainly one of them is when men forget about their own condition and claim for themselves not only more than is right, but what God claims for Himself alone. This, therefore, is one horn of pride: when men trusting in their own greatness, superiority, wealth, and works are so inebriated by false imaginings that they think themselves equal to God. The other horn of pride is when men do not acknowledge their own vices, despise others in comparison with themselves, and please themselves with dissolute acts as though they were free from rendering an account.[10]

---

[9] "Ergo superbia omnis violentiae mater." (Commentary on Psalms 73:6; CO 31:677.)

[10] "Scimus autem duo esse cornua superbiae, ut ita loquar, nempe dum homines suae conditionis obliti sibi arrogant non modo plus quam fas est, sed quod Deus sibi uni vendicat. Hoc igitur unum superbiae cornu, ubi homines sua dignitate, praestantia, copiis, et opibus confisi inebriantur falsis imaginationibus, ut putent se esse quasi pares Deo. Iam alterum cornu superbiae est, ubi non agnoscunt sua vitia, et alios prae se despiciunt, imo perinde ac si immunes forent a reddenda ratione, sibi placent in flagitiis." (Commentary on Ezekiel 16:50; CO 40:380-381.)

In explaining the origins of pride it would be systematically suitable to analyze the human monster-beast horn by horn. With respect to the first horn of pride Calvin states that its initial origin arises "when men forget about their own condition." For Calvin human life is anything but secure.

> Innumerable are the evils which besiege human life; innumerable also are the deaths which threaten it. We need not go beyond ourselves: since the body is a receptacle for a thousand diseases – in fact the body holds confined within itself and fosters the causes of disease – a man is not able to move about without carrying in himself many forms of his own destruction and without in a certain manner dragging out a life entwined with death. Indeed, what else could you say when he neither has chills nor perspires without danger? Assuredly, whichever way you turn, all the things around you not only are untrustworthy but almost openly menace, and seem to threaten immediate death. Embark upon a ship, a single foot separates you from death. Mount a horse, if a single foot slips, your life is endangered. Walk through the streets of a city, you are subject to as many dangers as there are tiles on the roofs. If there is a weapon in your hand or a friend's, harm awaits. All the fierce animals you see are armed for your destruction. Even if you attempt to enclose yourself in a walled garden where everything appears to be lovely, occasionally there lies hidden a serpent. Your house, continually in danger of fire, threatens in the daytime to impoverish you, and during the night threatens to collapse upon you. Your field, since it is exposed to hail, frost, drought, and other calamities, threatens you first with barrenness and then with famine. I pass over

> poisonings, ambushes, robberies, and open violence which partially besiege us at home and partially pursue us abroad. Amid these tribulations must not man be most miserable, since, but half alive in life, he weakly draws his anxious and languid breath, as though he perpetually had a sword hanging over his neck?[11]

> The human condition is one of tenuous fragility.[12]

> It is advisable to recognize that we are not made of iron, that we are not like rocks, but that we are mortal men full of fragility.[13]

Although the human soul contains remnant traces of the image of God, those traces have become so weakened and infected with original sin that no immortal essence can be

---

[11] "Innumera sunt quae vitam humanam obsident mala, quae totidem ostentant mortes. Ut extra non exeamus: quum mille morborum receptaculum sit corpus, imo intus inclusas teneat ac foveat morborum causas, seipsum homo ferre non potest quin multas exitiorum suorum formas secum ferat, ac vitam quodammodo cum morte implicitam trahat. Quid enim aliud dicas, ubi nec frigetur, nec sudatur sine periculo? Iam, quo cunque te vertas, quae circa te sunt omnia, non modo ambiguae sunt fidei, sed aperte fere minantur, ac praesentem mortem videntur intentare. Conscende navem, pede uno a morte distas. Equo inside, in lapsu pedis unius vita tua periclitatur. Incede per vias urbis, quot sunt in tectis tegulae, tot discriminibus es obnoxius. Si ferramentum in tua aut amici manu sit, exerta est noxa. Quotquot animalia ferocia vides, in tuam perniciem armata sunt. Quod si vel horto munito includere te studeas, ubi nihil quam amoenitas appareat, illic serpens interdum delitescet. Domus assidue incendio subiecta, interdiu tibi paupertatem, noctu etiam oppressionem minatur. Ager grandini pruinae, siccitati, aliisque tempestatibus expositus quum sit, sterilitatem, atque ex ea famem tibi denuntiat. Omitto veneficia, insidias, latrocinia, vim apertam, quorum pars nos domi obsident, pars peregre consequuntur. Inter has augustias annon oportet miserrimum esse hominem, utpote qui in vita semivivus anxium et languidum spiritum aegre trahat, non secus acsi imminentem perpetuo cervicibus gladium haberet?" (Institutes I, 17, 10; OS III, p. 214.)

[12] Sermons on Job 7:7-15; CO 33:347. Sermons on Job 31:33-34; CO 34:703. Semrons on Job 35:1-7; CO 35:223. Sermons on Job 36:20-24; CO 35:293. Sermons on Job 37:14-24; CO 35:339. Sermons on Job 39:36-40:6; CO 35:441. Sermons on Job 40:7-19; CO 35:457.

apprehended. Rather, human life appears to be like smoke or a shadow[14] which disappears into nothingness. It appears that every person flows away like water in a river, or that human life is simply a non-substantial image in a mirror.[15]

However, although the human person is like a snail who is born to be menaced by death,[16] although his life is held by a small thread and death is always between his teeth,[17] the human person usually remains unmindful of his mortality.

> If some corpse is being buried, or we are walking among the graves, then I confess that we philosophize brilliantly about the vanity of this life because then the image of death is observable to our eyes. However, we do not do this consistently, for the most part all these things do not affect us at all. In truth when it happens, our philosophy is for the moment; it vanishes as soon as we turn our backs and leaves not a trace of remembrance behind it. Finally, like the applause in the theatre for some pleasing spectacle, it vanishes. Forgetful not only of death but also of mortality itself, as if no inkling of it had ever reached us, we return to the indolent security of an earthly immortality.[18]

---

[13] "Il est expedient de cognoistre que nous ne sommes point de fer, que nous ne sommes point comme des rochers, mais que nous sommes homes mortels pleins de fragilité." (Sermons on Job 6:1-9; CO 33:285.)

[14] Institutes III, 9, 2; OS IV, p. 172. Cf. also Sermons on Job 14:5-12; CO 33:676. Sermons on Job 23:1-7; CO 34:342.

[15] "Certe in imagine transit homo, quod tantundem valet ac fluere instar aquae, cui nulla inest soliditas: vel potius instar figurae, quae in speculo refulgens substantia tamen caret." (Commentary on Psalms 73:20; CO 31:684.) Cf. also Sermons on Job 22:18-22; CO 34:310.

[16] "Voici les hommes qui sont comme les escargots, si tost qu'ils sont nez la mort les menace." (Sermons on Job 38:12-17; CO 35:378.)

[17] "...car nostre vie est pendante d'un filet, la mort est tousiours entre nos dents." (Sermons on Job 14:1-4; CO 33:663.)

[18] "Si effertur funus aliquod, vel inter sepulchra ambulamas, quia tunc oculis obversatur mortis simulachrum, egregie, fateor, de vitae huius vanitate philosophamur. Quanquam ne id quidem facimus perpetuo: plerunque enim nihil nos afficiunt ista omnia. Verum ubi accidit, momentanea est philosophia, quae,

The apparent fact that the human being does not live for ever but dies like a beast[19] is in no way acceptable to the human being. How could it be acceptable to a creature who does in fact have an undying though perverted spirit? Such a constant admission of mortality would imply that there is nothing so excellent in man that it cannot quickly fade and perish.[20] Such an admission of finitude would also verify that icy cold truth that human beings, in and of themselves, are poor and miserable creatures,[21] and that the human condition, in strictly human terms, is vile and abject.[22] No, quite simply, the human person will not accept such a merciless, demeaning sentence concerning his destiny. He will both consciously and unconsciously find someone or something to justify his existence, and in the pursuit of this justifying entity he will hope to escape the threatening menace of death.

But it is precisely here in the pursuit of justification that real and blinding pride is born. When one seeks an entity of justification, he attempts to escape the meaninglessness doomed to extinction. That is, he attempts to forget the temporality of the human condition. For Calvin this is the initial stage of pride's first horn.[23] To actually forget his finitude the human being must discover an entity with at

---

simul atque terga vertimus, evanescit, ac ne minimum quidem post se recordationis vestigium relinquit; denique non aliter effluit atque theatralis plausus in iucundo aliquo spectaculo. Neque enim mortis tantum, sed mortalitatis quoque ipsius obliti, acsi nullus unquam de ea rumor ad nos pervenisset, in supinam terrenae immortalitatis securitatem revolvimur." (Institutes III, 9, 2; OS IV, p. 172.)

[19] Commentary on Psalms 49:13; CO 31:487. Cf. also Institutes II, 10, 17; OS III, pp. 417-418.

[20] Commentary on Isaiah 40:6; CO 37:11.

[21] Sermons on Job 7:1-6; CO 33:338.

[22] Sermons on Job 7:7-15; CO 33:351.

[23] See footnote 10, this chapter.

least the appearance of immortality. That is, he must have a "god" to justify himself.

As was seen in Chapter Two, there are any number of enticing idols within the labyrinth. These idols may have been originally produced through weakness or ignorance. But now, with the human person in dread of nothingness, any criticism of idolatry is forgotten. Something divine in proportions must be had. It makes little difference to the human person if he is really the producer of these gods or not. He desires to be secure, to have all things under his control, to conquer death on his own terms. It is in this attempt to form his own immortality that the human person claims for himself "not only more than is right, but what God claims for Himself alone."[24]

The immediate manifestations of this man-made immortality are the proud declarations of men concerning their idols and their idol worship. Since these idols are in reality man-made projections, the human person has no difficulty in identifying himself with these projections. Soon he sees himself to be like his idols. As soon as he can make himself "god," the dread of nothingness subsides. Proudly and arrogantly he defends his will as the "absolute" truth. It is precisely at this point that he is in reality not God, not a human being, but a brutal monster.[25]

Calvin describes these types of idolatrous human beings as "butting bulls" running directly against God.[26]This form of idolatry can no longer be attributed to ignorance. Rather, the ignorance of false worship has grown to full proportions – proportions which are best summarized in the first horn of pride. Not only has this form of idolatry shunned

---

[24] See footnote 10, this chapter.
[25] Sermons on Job 4:20-5:2; CO 33:214. Institutes I, 11, 9; OS III, p. 97.

and forgotten the finitude of the human condition, it has also placed absolute faith in human "greatness, superiority, wealth, and works."[27]

Let us analyze the labyrinthine sojourner as he transforms himself into a monster-beast. It may be true that he was once a wanderer in the maze. Perhaps from exhaustion, perhaps from despair, he began to rage in the midst of his confusion. His "gods" had deceived him and had not indicated to him the way of deliverance. With maniacal fury he reflects upon his wanderings. Seizing upon some form of earthly justification, he begins to integrate into himself the imaginings of his past. Let us say at first he accepts prosperity as his justification for life. Although riches are only temporal goods and will, just as himself, vanish like smoke,[28] he begins to idolize himself as a man of wealth. He may know that he does not have solid truth, his reason and his conscience will at first tell him this, but now he refuses to listen to his reason and his conscience. Instead, he becomes obstinate in his fantasies.[29] Now his idol, prosperity, has become one with himself. That is, his idol has become himself.

I use wealth or prosperity as only one example. Although Calvin specifically states that "it is out of prosperity that men rear the horns of pride,"[30] prosperity is only one example of that human longing to justify and deify one's self. All ultimate faith in human "greatness, superiority, and

---

[26] "...tauri cornupetae..." (Commentary on the Four Last Books of Moses in the Form of a Harmony "Deuteronomy" 4:12-18; CO 24:385.)
[27] See footnote 10, this chapter.
[28] Commentary on First Timothy 6:17; CO 52:334. See footnote 14, this chapter.
[29] Sermons on Job 6:24-30; CO 33:321.
[30] "Nam ex secundo rerum suarum statu cornua superbiae induunt homines." (Commentary on the Acts of the Apostles 2:19-20; CO 48:35.) (Cf. also Sermons on Job 12:17-25; CO 33:594-5. Sermons on Job 1:6-8; CO 33:68. Commentary on Isaiah 17:4; CO 36:313.)

works"[31] is also the fodder which fattens and strengthens the human monster-beast.

If the first horn of pride can be summarized by the phrase that men "think themselves equal to God,"[32] the second horn of pride can be summarized by the phrase "when men... despise others in comparison with themselves...."[33] The content of both phrases outlines the interrelationship between both horns of pride. Once the human person has made himself "god," he does not want to be reminded of the weakness, sickness, poverty and death of other humans. This would, after all, disturb his divine image of himself. Consequently, in order to feel secure within himself and safeguard his image of himself, he begins to despise others.

It is in this despising of others that the socially destructive power of pride is seen. Little by little self-deification leads to a monstrous inhumanity. Where else could it lead? To turn away from one's own weakness and finitude inevitably makes one intolerant of another's weakness and finitude. Intolerance of others leads to a lack of compassion. The twisted judgments of a divine self-image then condescendingly sneer at what is in reality basically human and humane. The consequences are a lack of compassion and an inhumanity which are characteristic of a savage beast.[34]

Examples of this bestial and monstrous inhumanity fill the dark caverns of human history. Observe that tyrannical pride which has formed and destroyed nations. Visit the historical monuments of dungeons and torture chambers which testify to something other than "the ascent of

---

[31] See footnote 10, this chapter.
[32] See footnote 10, this chapter.
[33] See footnote 10, this chapter.
[34] Sermons on Job 31:16-23; CO 34:663.
Sermons on Job 6:15-23; CO 33:309-310.
Sermons on Job 22:9-11; CO 34:289.
Sermons on Job 19:17-25; CO 34:115.

man." Do I deceive you? Is it not verifiable that the body-stretching rack, the cat-o'-nine-tails, the scimitar, the group gas oven and every other sort of sophisticated torture machine have been designed and used by humans against humans? Listen to the collected screams of the ages, screams which originated through the hands of humans. Will not all this tell us that there is certainly something vile and malicious in the spirit of man?

Calvin, commenting on the nature of tyranny, describes those who are strong and powerful as fierce and terrible bulls.[35] In numerous works he refers to unjust rulers as monstrous beasts[36] who, once they have become accustomed to plundering, ceaselessly work destruction.

> A kind of fury (rabies) is kindled in their hearts such that they seek nothing else but to devour and to tear into pieces, to mangle and to torture.[37]

---

[35] "...hic figurate tauros nominat eos qui praevalent viribus et potentia." (Commentary on Isaiah 34:7; CO 36:583.) Cf. also Commentary on Psalms 22:13-14; CO 31:227.

[36] Commentary on Genesis 31:22; CO 23:427. Commentary on the Four Last books of Moses in the Form of a Harmony "Exodus" 10;23-24; CO 24:128.
Commentary on Psalms 101:2; CO 32:56-57.
Commentary on Isaiah 36:21; CO 36:613-614.
Commentary on Isaiah 37:9; CO 36:622-623.
Commentary on Isaiah 51:9-10; CO 37;232-233.
Commentary on Jeremiah 23:5-6; CO 38:408-409.
Commentary on Jeremiah 49:19; CO 39:368.
Commentary on Daniel 2:5; CO 40:563-564.
Commentary on Daniel 2:32-35; CO 40:590.
Commentary on Daniel 2:39; CO 40:597.
Commentary on Daniel 2:44-45; CO 40:606.
Commentary on Daniel 3:29; CO 40:645-646.
Commentary on Daniel 7:5; CO 41:42-43.
Commentary on the Twelve Minor Prophets "Hosea" 1:3-4; CO 42-208.
Commentary on the Twelve Minor Prophets "Nahum" 2:13; CO 43:472.
Commentary on the Twelve Minor Prophets "Habakkuk" 2:17; CO 43:555-6.
Commentary on the Twelve Minor Prophets "Zephaniah" 3:2-3; CO 44:48-50.

[37] "...imo quaedam rabies accenditur in eorum cordibus, ut iam nihil aliud appetant quam vorare, et discerpere, et laniare, et strangulare." (Commentary on the Twelve Minor Prophets "Nahum" 2:11-12; CO 43:471.)

The savage exploits of tyrants are only one historical and verifiable example which testifies to the destruction caused by pride. In fact, once the two horns of pride become fully grown, the overall malicious blindness of the human monster-beast becomes clearly apparent. It is most clearly apparent when human beings who have been blinded by pride[38] boldly despise God[39] and say, "There is no God[40] except for ourselves and our own powers."[41]

At this point the remnant traces of the image of God in the human person (i.e., reason, will, imagination, emotion, and conscience) become totally blind in relation to their past origin and their future direction. Reason, originally a distinguishing factor between the human being and the brute beast,[42] is now energized by the proud arrogance of human self-deification. Reason should have been seen as a Divine spark in the human person.[43] Reason should have, with the help of the True God, eventually aided in leading the human person to the True God.[44] Instead, because of the blindness of pride, reason is transformed into a malicious power.

---

[38] Commentary on Ezekiel 11:14-16; CO 40:236-240. Commentary on Ezekiel 16:55; CO 40:388-389. Commentary on Daniel 3:3-7; CO 40:619-625. Commentary on the Twelve Minor Prophets "Hosea" 10:13; CO 42:426-429.
[39] Commentary on Psalms 20:7; CO 31:210.
[40] Commentary on Psalms 10:4; CO 31:110-111.
[41] Commentary on Psalms 75:5-6; CO 31:702-703. Commentary on Joshua 24:8; CO 25:564-565.
[42] See footnote 34, Chapter II.
[43] See footnote 33, Chapter II.
[44] "Nam sicuti Deus ad imaginem suam initio nos finxit, ut mentes nostras tum ad virtutis studium, tum ad aeternae vitae meditationem erigeret: ita, ne socordia nostra obruatur tanta generis nostri nobilitas quae nos a brutis animalibus discernit, cognoscere operaepretium est, ideo nos ratione et intelligentia praeditos esse, ut sanctam et honestam vitam colendo ad propositum beatae immortalitatis scopum tendamus." (Institutes II, 1, 1; OS III, pp. 228-229.)

> Reason has another form which is vicious. It is observable in a corrupted nature, and it is manifested when mortal man wishes to subject "heavenly things" to his own judgment instead of receiving them with reverence.[45]

This is no longer a form of reason which is ignorant yet seeking truth. Rather, it is a depraved form of reason which is unique to the human species. Once the human person considers himself to be a "god," reason's cunning is ready to do homage to the most destructive idol – man's divine image of himself. I have only briefly mentioned the torture devices of tyrants. From whence did such devices originate? Surely depraved reason played its part in designing and implementing the scream machines of the past.

But perhaps such torture devices seem antiquated and crude. Indeed the are. As the human being's reasoning powers have become more sophisticated, they have also become more destructive. Now entire cities and civilizations can be destroyed through the ingenuity of human reason. Now the whole earth fears the "rational" monster-beast who is able to devour the entire world with a gulp and a belch.

Of course depraved reason is not alone in its endeavor. Depraved reason is dialectically interrelated to the other faculties of the human soul.

With respect to the dialectical interrelationship between reason and will, it must be deduced that the depraved machinations of reason will be carried out and actualized by a depraved will.[46] For Calvin, "the depravity of

[45] "Altera ratio vitiosa est, praesertim in natura corrupta: dum mortalis homo res divinas, quas suspicere debuerat, suo iudicio vult sibiicere." (Dilucida Explicatio Sanae Doctrinae de Vera Participatione Carnis et Sanquinis Christi in Sacra Coena, ad Discutiendas Heshusii Nebulas 1561; CO 9:474.) For the distinction between "earthly" and "heavenly" things, see footnote 36, Chapter II.

[46] See footnotes 21 and 22, Chapter II.

the will is all too well known."[47] Go to a library and select any volume which deals with the savage history of the human race. Notice the statistics dealing with maimings, mutilations, destruction, and death. A ferocious energy within human nature becomes apparent. Go to the newsstand; buy a newspaper or periodical and read about the incessant conquests of invading armies, mercantile exploitations and all else that makes for "exciting" headlines. Certainly there are activities in process which touch upon the antiquated but descriptive word "depravity."

Thus Calvin's' statement that "the will of man is completely inclined towards evil and is even carried headlong into the commission of evil"[48] is verifiable. What is also verifiable is that this "will to and for evil" is a definite characteristic of the proud human monster-beast.

In addition to the bestial depravity of human reason and human will, there are also the monstrous projections of the human imagination. In Calvin's words:

> ... we see how vain imaginations perniciously intoxicate a large part of the world ... the more shrewd people are in their own estimation, the more do they deceive themselves.[49]

This pernicious intoxication becomes evident when the human person becomes vain and obstinate about his own

[47] "...pravitas voluntatis plus satis nota est." (Institutes II, 2, 12; OS III, p. 255.)
[48] "...ut tota hominis voluntas ad malum inclinet, atque etiam feratur." (Commentary on Psalms 95:8; CO 32:33.) Cf. also Acta Synodi Tridentinae cum Antidoto (1547); CO 7:446.
[49] "...videmus quam exitialiter bonam mundi partem inebrient vanae suae cogitationes ... quo sibi videntur magis perspicaces, magis sibi imponere." (Commentary on Psalms 119:118-119; CO 32:267.)

projections of what is "divine."[50] Calvin would in every way contend that:

> However obstinate they may be, they follow doubtful and uncertain opinions instead of the truth, they grope in the dark and worship their own imagination instead of God.[51]

In relation to the human monster-beast it is to be noted that in fact what is being obstinately worshipped is the human imagination itself. Since the imagination is a faculty of the human person, the human person is in reality simply worshipping himself. Consequently, imagination ultimately leads the human person to both self-deification and self-worship.

What are the consequences of self-deification and self-worship? The consequences can be summed up in two words: bestial license. The destruction involved in this bestial license is at once seen when individuals, because of deceitful imaginings, keep themselves from the common condition of men[52] and imagine that there is no God.[53] Thus depraved imagination not only causes the two horns of pride to grow, but also strengthens and sharpens them. Infatuating doctrines and ideologies are now proposed which give deified human beings the supposed right to act without regard to natural reason or natural law.[54] The result is "The Ode to Viciousness" which is the unique description of human history.

---

[50] Commentary on Psalms 110:1-3; CO 32:54-55.

[51] "Utcunque sint pervicaces, vagas opiniones et incertas sequuntur pro veritate: palpant in tenbebris, et imaginationem suam colunt loco Dei." (Commentary on Isaiah 25:9; CO 36:420.)

[52] Commentary on Psalms 10:5-6; CO 31:113. Cf. also Institutes II, 8, 50; OS III, p. 389. Sermons on Job 39:36-40:6; CO 35:441-442.

[53] Commentary on Isaiah 37:18-19; CO 36:628.

[54] Commentary on Psalms 82:1; CO 31:768.

Combined with pride, depraved reason, depraved will, and depraved imagination are the depraved emotions. For Calvin, when pride unifies itself with blind impulse, humans hurry headlong into a bestial and unrestrained madness.[55] Commenting on The First Epistle of John 2:16, Calvin states:

> The desire of the eyes, in my judgment, comprises wanton glances as well as that vanity which diffuses itself in ostentation and inane splendor. Finally follows arrogance or pride, with it is joined ambition, vainglory, contempt of others, blind love of one's self and rash self-confidence. The sum of it is that, as soon as the world offers itself, our desires are carried away by it like unbridled beasts, because our hearts are perverse. And so various longings, all against God, rule over us.[56]

These various longings can be described under the single term "concupiscentia" or concupiscence. In its broadest context concupiscence simply means an insatiable desire to devour the world.[57] It is massive greed for the things of the

---

[55] Sermons on Job 7:1-6; CO 33:352.
Sermons on Job 8:7-13; CO 33:392.
Sermons on Job 9:7-12; CO 33:532.
Sermons on Job 13:1-10; CO 33:615.
Sermons on Job 31:29-32; CO 34:694.
Sermons on Job 39:36-40:6; CO 35:450.
Commentary on Jeremiah 35:12-15; CO 39:109.
Commentary on Ezekiel 11:19-20; CO 40:246.
Commentary on Ezekiel 18:25; CO 40:451.

[56] "Cupiditas oculorum (meo iudicio) tam libidinosos adspectus comprehendit, quam vanitatem quae in pompis et inani splendore vagatur. Sequitur postremo loco fastus aut superbia, cui coniuncta est ambitio, iactantia, aliorum contemptus, caecus amor sui, praeceps confidentia. Summa est, simul ac mundus se offert, appetitus mostros, ut cor nostrum peversum est, quasi effraenes beluas, illuc rapi: ita sominari varias concupiscentias, quae omnes Deo sunt adversae." (Commentary on the First Epistle of the Apostle John 2:16; CO 55:319.)

[57] Commentary on Psalms 37:19; CO 31:375. Commentary on Genesis 31:1; CO 23:421-422.

world, a greed which hurls the human monster-beast into every form of iniquity.[58] The best description of the truly concupiscent individual would be that of a person who would willingly try to take the sun from the poor.[59]

It should be remembered that human (!) longing, or human (!!) concupiscence is being described. This means that human reason, will, and imagination are also vitally active in attempting to procure the longed for object of gratification. These capacities within the human spirit so distinguish the human monster-beast that there is "no lion or any other savage beast on earth which has the destructive force of man's malicious greed."[60]

The meaning of this last quotation will become obvious if we examine human nature in ourselves. Once an object or person is desired, reason immediately begins conniving to acquire and possess that object or person. Reason, in its depraved form, is constantly ready to rationalize away and argue down any possible objections the conscience or natural law might raise. The depraved will with its impulsive torrents of energy constantly seeks action and the happiness of pursuit. The will's ferocity demands that the human monster-beast "make up its mind" at once. Wild and destructive fantasies pour forth from the imagination. The depraved imagination even projects alternative plans and methods of acquiring the desired object or person. Now the impatient human monster-beast lifts and hurls his head, a head crowned with the two horns of pride, with menacing

---

[58] Second Epistle of Peter 2;10; CO 55:464-465.

[59] Commentary on Isaiah 5:8; CO 36:108. Calvin maintains that this description derives from Chrysostom.

[60] ":...ne lion, ne autre beste sauvage en terre qui ait une telle violence comme ont les meschantes cupiditez de l'homme." (Sermons on Job 7:7-15; CO 33:354.)

gestures.[61] The capacities which were once gifts of God in the human person are now used against God and the natural law.[62]The human monster-beast is now full grown. He wanders in the labyrinth of this world seeking unlimited gratification and causing constant misery.[63]

In this vicious pursuit of unlimited gratification, the conscience may be temporarily silenced. That is, an analysis of the human monster-beast inflamed with desire would indicate that he could no longer distinguish between good and evil.[64] His passions have overcome him; he has lost contact with his conscience or has tried to annihilate his conscience.[65] In fact, the beast has in reality come to revel in evil. He has attempted to justify himself as a "god" above all laws and codes of good and evil. The agency of even the bad or contaminated conscience has been lost.[66] The human monster-beast is now notoriously known "to permit the most abusive actions and obey the most hideous commands."[67]

After a time, after the most abusive actions have been permitted and the most hideous commands have been obeyed,

---

[61] "Quand donc nous serons solicitez de nous fascher et d'estre impatiens, que ce passage nous vienne en memoire, Que fais-tu povre creature, en quell labyrinthe est-ce que tu entres? Il n'est point question ici d'une simple tentation, mais tu leves les cornes contre Dieu." (Sermons on Job 34:33-37; CO 35:209-210.) "Unde enim fit ut suis cupiditatibus ita serviant homines, ut volitent per medium aërem, ut omnia miscendo mundum conturbent, ut denique sua audacia ferantur praecipites, nisi quia superbia turgent?" (Commentary on Psalms 131:1; CO 32:339.) Cf. also Commentary on Psalms 73:8; CO 31:678 and Sermons on Job 35:1-8; CO 35:223.

[62] Ibid.

[63] Ibid.

[64] "...perinde est ac si quis inflammatus sua libidine rueret: quemadmodum videmus brutos homines ferri interdum caeco et pudendo impetu, quia iam ablatum est discrimen omne ex oculis, nullus est delectus, nullus pudor." (Commentary on the Twelve Minor Prophets "Hosea" 4;12; CO 42:283.)

[65] Sermons on Job 23:8-12; CO 34:249-250.

[66] See footnotes 233 and 234, Chapter II.

[67] See footnote 233, Chapter II.

the worm of conscience may again be felt.[68] However, in this context with the human monster-beast thinking himself to be "god," there is no shame and no remorse.[69] Instead there is a hardened murmuring against the True God. Calvin describes this phenomenon in the following manner:

> ... the ungodly, although convicted of evil by their own consciences, murmur against God like fierce and wild beasts who gnaw at their constricting chains.[70]

This murmuring against God is accompanied with desperate anxieties and a total lack of inward peace. To remedy the situation, the human monster-beast may seek any and all forms of escape.

> ... the ungodly, since they are terrified by even the sound of a rustling leaf and whirl about in constant restlessness, envelope themselves in the bestial thick skin of dull insensitivity. Consequently they bring themselves to such a state of mad frenzy that being, as it were, carried out of themselves, they may not feel their calamities.[71]

In order to escape the stings of conscience, the human monster-beast will seek out secure hiding places in the labyrinth of this world and in the labyrinth of his individual

---

[68] "En cela donc les meschans monstrent qu'il y a mesmes une loy en nature qui ne se peut abolir, qu'il y a une discretion entre le bien et le mal." (Sermons on Job 24:10-18; CO 34:386.)

[69] See footnote 64, this chapter.

[70] "...impii quantumvis male sibi conscii sint, Deo tamen obmurmurent, non secus ac ferae indomitae catenas quibus constringuntur, dentibus mordent." (Commentary on Psalms 38:4-5; CO 31:388.)

[71] "...impii vero quamvis expavescant ad strepitum folii cadentis, et in continua inquietudine versentur, callum tamen stuporis sibi obducunt, vel accersunt sibi insanam vertiginem, ut extra se positi mala sua non sentiant." (Commentary on Psalms 10:5-6; CO 31:113.)

soul. He attempts to hide, but in his hiding he is always prepared with bestial force for the frenzies of destruction. Calvin compares these hiding places to the "lurking places" (latebras) of ferocious beasts.

> It is indeed true that even the worst of men are often tormented by the stings of conscience; but, by closing their eyes, they plunge themselves into numbness as though it were a lurking place, and thus they harden all their senses.[72]

> Thus it often happens when a person seeks lurking places, he brings upon himself an almost brutal stupor – he thinks of nothing, he cars for nothing, he is anxious for nothing.[73]

It may at first appear contradictory that a numb, rational, conscience-stricken beast would pose any threat. After all, the humane thing to do may be simply to let the horned monster go his own listless and grunting way into the darkened caverns of the labyrinth. This would be acceptable if the beast would only grunt, ruminate, sit back on his haunches and leave everyone else alone. In fact, in reality, the human monster-beast will not be ignored nor will he ignore others. On the contrary, this depraved spiritual creature still seeks his own justification and self-deification in defiance of the accusations of conscience. Now he will ferociously justify himself on his own terms. Every "god" of the fellow beasts in the labyrinth will be cunningly and mercilessly used in the

---

[72] "Verum quidem est, pessimos quosque conscientiae aculeis interdum pungi: sed oculos claudendo in torporem non secus atque in latebras se demergunt, sensus denique suos omnes obdurant..." (Commentary on Isaiah 47:10; CO 37:169.)

[73] "Sed ita saepe contingit ubi quis captavit latebras, ut tandem fere brutum stuporem sibi inducat, nihil cogitet, nihil curet, nulla de re sit anxius." (Commentary on the Twelve Minor Prophets "Jonah" 1:5; CO 43:214.)

self-deification process. If wealth is esteemed, then the wealthy beast has a "divine" right to devour any victim in the labyrinth. If beauty is honored, then the beautiful have the "sacred" right to sharpen their teeth in sexual and psychological warfare. If social position is valued, then every beast is a king ready to maul the peasants beneath him. Once the dictum that "justice ought to be mutually cultivated"[74] is numbed, the human monster will feed on any human fodder he can find.

Thus the danger of the lurking places becomes clear. The lurking places are the hidden and secret caves within the soul's and the world's labyrinth where the adult beast fattens and strengthens himself on the lives of others. Indeed, gnawing through the lives of others adds to the beast's stupor and gives him an elated feeling of security, artificial peace, and man-made divinity.

B. Conclusion and The Relation of the Labyrinth and the Human Monster-Beast to the Knowledge of Our Deliverance.

It would seem at this stage of analyzing both the nature of the labyrinth and the nature of the human monster-beast that darkness and terror would be the only descriptions of human life. Any labyrinthine wanderer could either be attacked by monsters or become a monster. The germs of pride in the lurking places of the human soul are all too quick to generate the horns of destruction. The lurking or hiding places of already full-grown beasts are infamously established in history and in the present.

What shall we do then? Shall we become more proud and bestial? Shall we turn back to the dying "god" called "fate" and howl in despair about the nature of things? Shall we say

[74] See footnote 223, Chapter II.

there is no hope? Shall we connive and murder until it is irrevocably proven that all is blindness, darkened caverns, and mayhem?

Although such responses are tempting, although such actions are the order of the day, although depravity seems to have won out, Calvin would still maintain that a recognition of the labyrinth and the human monster-beast is necessary and beneficial for the knowledge of our deliverance. That is, the knowledge of whom we are and what we can become will prod us into seeking the lighted way out of the labyrinth. Further this knowledge of ourselves is extremely valuable because it inwardly teaches us to look to another source other than ourselves for our liberty. Calvin has stated this in the following ways:

> ...whoever is totally dejected and overwhelmed by the knowledge of his own destructiveness, weakness, exposure to harm, and despicable conduct has thus advanced farthest in the knowledge of himself.[75]

> Accordingly, the knowledge of ourselves not only arouses us to seek God, but also, as it were, leads us by the hand to find Him.[76]

> ... for liberty is not promised to any but those who acknowledge that they are captives, and light and deliverance are not promised to any but those who acknowledge that they are plunged in darkness.[77]

---

[75] "...Ut quisque maxime suae calamitatis, inopiae, nuditatis, ignominiae conscientia deiectus est et consternatus, ita optime in sui cognitione profecisse." (Institutes II, 2, 10; OS III, p. 252.)

[76] "Proinde unusquisque sui agnitione non tantum instigatur ad quaerendum Deum, sed etiam ad reperiendum quasi manu ducitur."

Who it is that can promise, liberty, light and deliverance to both the labyrinthine wanderer and the monster-beast will be the subject of the second part of this work.

[77] "Libertas enim non aliis promittitur, nisi qui se captivos esse agnoscunt: lux et salus, qui se in tenebris demersos esse confitentur." (Commentary on Isaiah 49:9; CO 37:201.)

PART II

THOMAS THE SKEPTIC

CHARACTERS

THE BEAST-MAN
THOMAS

[The time is the evening on which Jesus Christ reportedly first appeared to ten of the remaining apostles after His resurrection. According to The Gospel of John (20:19-29), Thomas was absent from this occurrence. When the other apostles told him of Jesus' appearing to them, Thomas doubted their words.

The place is a tavern owned by a man once called "The Beast-Man of the Caves." Regardless of the overall shabbiness of the setting, the owner has made every effort to improve the place. Torn but bright colored tapestries hang on the walls. Bottles of varied colors, shapes, and sizes can be seen on the shelves in the background. Each of the two tables has a candle burning on it. As the conversation begins, Thomas is seen sitting at the center table staring at a glass of wine.]

The Beast-Man: The wine is not very good. Especially for someone who has climbed the hill to this lonely place. I paid too much for the whole cask. It will be vinegar in another week. Maybe you would like to try something else.

Thomas [in a monotone voice, like a man talking to himself in a dream]: No...I mean yes. Yes it will turn to vinegar soon, like everything else. [He gulps down the whole glass.]

The Beast-Man: Actually some good stuff came in from the north country. Here, try this. [He refills Thomas's glass.]

Thomas [draining the second glass in a single gulp]: Not bad. I'll buy the whole bottle. [As soon as the bottle is set on the table Thomas pours another glass and drinks it immediately. He then covers his mouth and runs off stage. Sounds of retching can be heard. After a few seconds, Thomas returns.] I made a mess of things out there. Let me pay you something for your trouble.

The Beast-Man: That's all right. There's some water in the back. I'll...

Thomas: I'll take care of it. [He exits immediately. A few seconds pass and he returns.] It's been taken care of. I'm really sorry.

The Beast-Man [laughing]: That's all right. At least you left the room in the first place. The Roman soldiers just vomit right on the table. When they get drunk and arrogant they wouldn't move to please Caesar himself.

Thomas: Well, I don't want to have anything in common with Roman soldiers.

The Beast-Man [smiling]: I wouldn't give a glass of vinegar for a whole legion myself.

Thomas [wild-eyed]: Do you know what those bastards did last week?

The Beast-Man: You mean the crucifixion of Jesus of Nazareth.

Thomas: Yes, that's what I mean.

The Beast-Man [somberly]: That was not the first crucifixion that I have witnessed. They did the same thing long ago to my father. I do not see how anyone bears the torture.

Thomas: What had your father done?

The Beast-Man: My father was a madman, at least that's how I remember him. He used to import wood from the north country for wine casks. One day he made a deal with the Romans. They told him they wanted to export Judean wine to Rome for Caesar's throat. They paid him well. I think at first my father was just a simple man who had to make money like anyone else. He sold them the wood. The next day he watched the Romans crucify five men on the same wood. Something happened to him after that day. He began drinking all the time and wouldn't work. He sat at home and used to stare into his wine glass the way you were doing a little while ago. He vomited a lot too.

Thomas: How old were you then?

The Beast-Man: I must have been five or six. I can't really remember. I only remember my mother crying a lot and fearing for our lives. You see, my father would get so drunk that he would wander out into the streets at night and scream about Caesar's throat. Then he would mumble something about red wine and Caesar's blood and the blood on the wood of those five crucified men. It was always confusing and horrible. At first the townspeople tried to quiet him down. Finally, they grew afraid to be seen with him. Then the soldiers came and took him away. He was in prison for a while. They said he turned into an animal in prison. He would sit in the corner and hiss at the guards and throw his food at them. In the end, they crucified him.

Thomas [intently]: And your mother, what happened to your mother?

The Beast-Man: She went to see him on his cross. Two days after his death, she hanged herself. I became a slave of the Romans trained to serve my father's executioners and those who indirectly caused my mother's suicide. At the Roman military school designed for the patrician sons of the elite, I was forced to bring meat and drink to the young aristocrats. Whenever I had time, I watched the young boys use the sword and the shield in their training for death. Death--that was the thing--whether on the cross, at the end of a rope, or on the battlefield--that was the thing.

Thomas [returning to his own thoughts]: Yes, that <u>is</u> THE THING.

The Beast-Man: Times change but THE THING was always there. When I was about twelve years old, the Romans transferred me to view THE THING anew. I became a gravedigger for those who had been crucified. Mangled body after mangled body was laid to rest with these hands. I worked with an old man who saw his task as just one more insult in the darkness. He too raged at the Romans, but he raged quietly and inwardly. He also raged about THE THING ITSELF saying that he and I knew something which all turn from yet something finally true--that there is only darkness and nothing else.

Thomas: I once believed there was something else, but He was crucified and buried also.

The Beast-Man: You mean Jesus of Nazareth.

Thomas [pouring another glass of wine]: Yes, that is who I mean.

The Beast-Man: He is someone death will not conquer.

Thomas: I once believed that, but He is dead. You've been a gravedigger for the crucified ones. You know what the Romans can do to a human body. They did it to Him.

The Beast-Man [staring at Thomas]: I know I've seen you before.

Thomas [staring at his untouched glass of wine]: I probably remind you of your father.

The Beast-Man: No, you are one of the twelve, are you not?

Thomas: I was one of the twelve. I think there are ten left. Judas who betrayed Him, hanged himself. I left. [staring at the glass of wine.] Yes, without me there are ten left.

The Beast-Man: What are the other ten doing now?

Thomas [nervously]: They are either going mad or are already mad. The last time, this evening in fact, I met with them. They say Jesus has appeared to them. They are like hysterical, superstitious women who see a ghost in every darkened corner. [He takes a gulp of wine.]

The Beast-Man [watching him intently]: Perhaps you had best eat something. Here, I'll get...

Thomas: Don't bother, please. My stomach couldn't take it. I am not used to drinking, and food on top of everything else would only make me more sick.

The Beast-Man: All right, but let me tell you where I first saw you. There is great risk in my telling you, yet you should know, you must know.

Thomas [half-interested]: Why is that?

The Beast-Man: Because it concerns Jesus of Nazareth.

Thomas: Then please go on.

The Beast-Man: I was telling you that I was a gravedigger.

Thomas: Yes.

The Beast-Man: One day a Roman soldier came to the cemetery looking for an assistant.

Thomas: An assistant?

The Beast-Man: Yes...someone to assist at the crucifixions. Someone to "help" in the torture rooms, nailing the hands to the crosses, and placing the crosses in the ground. He promised me more money and all sorts of things.

Thomas: And what did you say?

The Beast-Man: Nothing.

Thomas: Nothing?

The Beast-Man: Yes, I said nothing. But I grabbed a pick and drove the sharp end through the left side of his forehead. At first the pick stayed stuck in his head and blood began to spray in every direction. He gave a horrible cry and fell to the ground. As he fell, the pick was dislodged. Blood poured out like a river all over his face and body. I saw what I had done, let out with a cry more horrible than his, and then I began to run. I ran it seemed for days though it was probably a few hours, and then I collapsed.

Thomas [staring intently at him]: You killed a Roman soldier, and yet you're alive...that's impossible.

The Beast-Man: Let us say that I wished I was dead when I awakened. Fear drove me to the high country near the region of the Gerasenes.*

Thomas [surprised]: The Gerasenes...no, it couldn't be. You couldn't have been there. Did you know "The Beast-Man"...Yes, that's what they called him--"The Beast-Man of the Caves"?

The Beast-Man: I was he.

Thomas [staring intently at his face]: No...it is not possible. I was with Jesus the day the Beast-Man was brought back to his right mind. He didn't look like you.

The Beast-Man [quietly]: I was the Beast-Man of the caves. Neither my hair nor my beard had been cut since the pick was driven into that Roman soldier's forehead. It was ten years' time between my killing that torturer and my meeting Jesus of Nazareth. Ten years in which I lived with the real torturer: myself

---

* The Gospel According to Mark 5:1-20. The Gospel According to Luke 8:26-39.

Thomas: But you don't look that old.

The Beast-Man: Remember, I killed the killer when I was fifteen. I am now twenty-seven. Two years have passed since my meeting your Master and mine.

Thomas: I am afraid that He is our dead Master.

The Beast-Man [vehemently]: It cannot be!

Thomas [sadly]: It is.

The Beast-Man: It is not. I believe He lives. I will tell you why. For ten years I hid and wandered alone in the caves of the Gerasenes. After a short time, no one would or could come near me. At the beginning, the swineherders thought I was just another holy man seeking solitude. [laughing mildly] Me! Holy! What a misunderstanding! In truth, I was at first so afraid of the Romans and their crucifying me that I was fearful of seeing anyone [looking at Thomas] Have you ever faced your own possible tortured death alone?

Thomas: Only once, when Jesus said He was going to Jerusalem to be crucified and die. I knew what the religious authorities would do if He went to Jerusalem. Oh, I was brave then. The other apostles were confused and afraid, but I said to them, "Let us also go, that we may die with him."* I said this before I saw the mob's torches, swords, and spears in the garden at Gethsemane.** Then I ran away with all the others. [He drinks in a single gulp his glass of wine.]

The Beast-Man: Well, then perhaps you understand. I also ran, but where or to whom or to what was I to run?

Thomas [pouring another glass of wine]: I feel the same at this very moment.

The Beast-Man: I will tell you what I did. I ran from myself, and yet I ran up against myself. A ten year running to and from myself, that's what it was! I ran from my fear of death, but death was in me. Wherever men were, there was also certain death. The caves--that is the place for

* The Gospel of John 11:5-16.
** The Gospel ofJohn 18:1-11. The Gospel of Matthew 26:36-56.

hiding. The caves of the Gerasenes are winding and inviting much like the inward imaginings of all of us. A person can hide there just as a person in the world can hide from the fact of his own certain death.

Thomas [vengefully]: The world--that is something worth hiding from! The world, the religious authorities, the Romans, the indignant and hostile mob which screams: "GIVE US BARABBAS!* That's what the mob yelled at the trial of Jesus! The world which honors the bandit and strives to destroy the good. Why, the world will always say "GIVE US BARABBAS THE BANDIT!" And the world will devour those who strive for The Light which is true, bright, and humane. The world did it last week; it did it to the prophets and wise men, and it will do it again. ** If the world could only be buried we could write on its tombstone: "GIVE US BARABBAS THE BANDIT!" That alone would say enough for the earth's wretched lands, skies, seas, and hordes of murderers!

The Beast-Man [smiling]: You sound like a man who knows the caves of the Gerasenes.

Thomas [drinking another glass of wine]: All that I know is that this world is not worth tolerating much longer.

The Beast-Man: Then you are a man of the caves. You've come to understand the absurdity of being born simply to feed and to breed and then, like some over-bloated slug, to die.

Thomas [irritated]: I understood that long ago. Why do you think I wandered like a vagabond all over the countryside with Jesus of Nazareth? That man was The Truth; He was from God; He was...

The Beast-Man [also becoming irritated]: He was, according to you, just another man who died.

Thomas [still irritated]: I didn't say He was just another man who died. I said He was dead and that's that.

---

* The Gospel of Matthew 27:15-23.
** The Gospel of Matthew 23:29-36.

The Beast-Man [becoming irate]: Well, if he died and that's that, then He's just another man as far as I'm concerned.

Thomas [also becoming irate]: Look, He was not just another man. [Thomas reaches for the wine bottle, holds it up to the light and sees that it is empty.] The wine's gone. Bring me another bottle.

The Beast-Man [smiling sarcastically]: Are you sure you're up to it?

Thomas [sullenly]: Just bring me another bottle. [The Beast-Man brings a bottle with another glass. He sits down. The angle should be such that he can see Thomas, and the audience can see both of them.]

The Beast-Man [filling Thomas's glass]: Here, this is a gift from "The Beast-Man of the Caves."

Thomas [very irritated]: Look, I'll pay for it.

The Beast-Man [sternly]: I said it's on me. [smiling] Besides, I intended to drink some myself.

Thomas [indifferently]: Whatever you want. [The Beast-Man fills his own glass to the brim. Thomas drinks half of the glass previously poured for him and then sets it down. Thomas speaks matter of factly] Now, where were we?

The Beast-Man [indifferently]: I don't know, and I don't care. [after a few sips of wine] I was telling you about the caves.

Thomas [indifferently]: Yes, go on.

The Beast-Man: In a sense I really liked the caves of the Gerasenes.

Thomas: You what?

The Beast-Man: Well, think about what you just said about the world and the world's viciousness. The world tears down, maims, and crucifies whomever and whatever it can. The brighter the light, the more the darkness of the world tries to overcome it.

Thomas [sadly]: True, very true.

The Beast-Man: And the caves, well the caves were a type of freedom from the world. No demands, no worries, no authorities to obey, no annoying humans with their paltry problems...just one's self screaming wild words and the silence after the caves stopped echoing the screams. Although I screamed and howled alone for ten years, it was not always unpleasant.

Thomas [drinking]: I'm starting to howl and scream inwardly myself and, for me, it is anything but pleasant.

The Beast-Man: You are new to your inward caves. Wait a while. At first I was so frightened and terrified that I was sure I would destroy myself simply to get some type of relief from my fear and terror. But gradually, after months of my mind racing backward and forward from thought to thought and from alternative to alternative, a new image of myself came to me. Was I at fault for my father's going mad, being crucified and my mother hanging herself? NO! Did I do wrong when I was solicited by a professional Roman torturer and murderer to kill him? NO! There was no forethought in the matter. Impulsively I had simply killed one of my father's murderers. Further, I had killed part of the slave-driving monster known as the Roman army. Perhaps I had done a just deed. Perhaps a noble deed. At least these hands would not add to the history of human torture. If I had disobeyed the Roman soldier and refused his offer, certainly he would have tortured and crucified me. Yes, eventually a new image of my self was presented--an image of which I was proud. With this pride came a new sort of strength, a strength which was not completely good and not completely evil. I began to feel that I was above the human race. I did not need other humans. I ate very little. There were enough fresh springs for water in the hill country. I could find honey and wild grain to eat. But when I say that I did not need other humans, I should also say that I secretly still feared the Romans and what they would do to me. I resolved not to cut my hair and beard. Then no one would know who I was. This fear coupled with the pride of my own self image kept me away from everyone for ten years.

Thomas: To hear you tell it, you really had no need of Jesus in the first place. I remember you quite differently. I remember you as a man-beast howling at the entrance of your cave. No one could approach you, give you anything, or in any way help. If you were so pleased with yourself and your image of yourself, why did you display such an outward show of madness? You would throw offered food at the giver. You even threw food, sticks, and rocks at Jesus Himself. Why didn't you simply hide in the cave when we were in the region of the Gerasenes?

The Beast-Man: I will tell you why. I grew arrogantly proud of my ability to live apart from the world. I had convinced myself that I could live without the wretched creature comforts which most people burn up their lives to acquire. I didn't need the animal warmth of the herd which flocks together like cattle waiting for the slaughterer's axe. I had seen death. I had buried the dead. I would howl at the entrance of my cave, "Kill me if you dare!" No one came near me! Once I was so wild that I manacled my own hands with two bracelets and a chain I had found in the hill country. Standing before my caves, I shouted at the swine herders passing by, "Look what I do to the bondage of this world!" I then smashed and smashed the chain with a rock until it broke. I saw my hands filled with blood and gore, but it seemed to make little difference to the pig keepers. They knew I was mad. They simply waited until the chain broke. Some shrugged. Some felt sorry for me. Some laughed.

It was at that time that a horrible conflict came forth in me. I watched the herdsmen walk away. I said to myself, "Where can they be going?" and I knew all too well. They were going home to their wives, their children, their suppers, and I was going back to my caves. At first I laughed hysterically. I was justified to myself. I had overcome this world. They would slop hogs in the morning. I would rejoice in my pride in the morning. I was superior, and that was all. Yet that evening, alone in the darkness, I gazed out at the star-strewn sky, and for once I thought of the future. I would have my self-image, my caves, and nothing else. I also thought of the herdsmen before the fire with their wives, children, and hot food.

Now the real conflict began. I could not give up my thoughts of so many years which had in a sense justified me. I had become superior. I had really overcome the world. But what was left? Every normal human need had been rooted out of me, or so I thought. But human needs appeared again and again. Hermits call such needs "temptations." I can only call them human needs. Yet this need to be justified for being born without my consent, for seeing my mother and father destroyed, for being forced to dig graves, for living ten years as a beast--that need of justification was always there to mock any normal and accepted human needs.

I had once heard that when armies are in a long and vicious war, both sides are almost destroyed and every battlefield is a scene in hell. My inward conflict was like such a war. The superhuman need of justification battling the genuine normal human needs were the armies at war. I was the battlefield or hell itself. Each combatant in the war also became horribly distorted. When isolation and loneliness began to succeed, I told myself I was a "god" capable of bearing any suffering. When my image of myself as a justified god began to succeed, I would ask myself what good that was since I was an isolated god unable to change anything in the world. I would then envy the lives of the pigs themselves. They were at least unconscious of such conflicts. So I was a "god" envying swine. That's how confused I became. The conflict went on with horrible distortions, images, howlings, and ravings all in solitary, self-imposed isolation.

Finally Jesus of Nazareth came to the caves. By then I did not want to hear another word or see another human face. I was sure I would scream myself to death for being human and wanting to be God.

Thomas [sadly]: Perhaps what you are saying first attracted me to Jesus of Nazareth. Perhaps in your caves you have discovered what is in all of us. So many crowds followed that man. He was able to bring to light the deepest human desires. He was able to overcome this world, to overcome death's fear, and He was still able to do so much good for His time on earth. You mentioned your overpowering desire for justification: justification for being born without one's consent. While He lived, I believed that somehow in the end He would justify our lives and make all things possible. Now that He is dead, everything seems hopeless and impossible.

The Beast-Man: Then you believed in Him for only as long as you could actually see Him. That is quite unfair.

Thomas [annoyed]: What is unfair about it?

The Beast-Man: What is unfair about it is that you wish to disregard the generations which will come. The generations which will also seek justification! Sure, you live in Galilee for a period of years. You meet a person like no other. One who can work miracles, draw crowds to Himself, overcome established legalistic religious traditions by Himself. One who could even draw a skeptic like yourself to follow Him. Well, what can I say, is it only you? You who happened to be "fortunate" enough to be in a particular place at a particular time. You say that the man was from God. What does that mean? Is God "fate" or "fortune" or something else that smiles on you for a while until the dice are thrown again, and then you are in misery? What do you mean when you say Jesus of Nazareth was from God?

Thomas [drinking]: I don't know what I mean. I suppose what I mean is that whatever was high, true, good, right and powerful was in Jesus of Nazareth including the justification for our being born without our consent.

The Beast-Man: So then fate or fortune or chance is not your God.

Thomas: Fortune is either good or bad. Fate justifies no one. Chance gives nothing of itself. Fortune does not sacrifice itself. No, neither fortune nor fate nor chance is God. I suppose fortune or fate or chance is just another human imagining which gives an untrustworthy and indefinite hope to desperate human beings.

The Beast-Man: Yet you imply that you were "fortunate" enough to meet Jesus of Nazareth, feel justified for a time, and now that Jesus has been "unfortunate" enough to die;

you are in despair. Think of what you are saying. If you say that He was from God then you yourself have defined God. You say that God justifies human life; you say that God gives of Himself; you say that God will sacrifice Himself for desperate human beings. In short, you say that God is like Jesus of Nazareth.

Thomas [quietly]: Yes, God is like Him.

The Beast-Man: And luck or fate or fortune is not God.

Thomas: No.

The Beast-Man: Then do you not somehow feel that Jesus had some purpose in asking you to be His apostle? We agree that it was not a chance occurrence that happened to pick you.

Thomas: He instructed me and the other eleven to aid Him in bringing forth God's kingdom. We all thought we knew what that meant. Now I'm not so sure.

The Beast-Man: Well, I know what it means. It, means that a powerful Light has come into this world. A Light that has and will overcome the darkness of confusion, conflict, and death. Perhaps I believe more in this Light than you because I was so long in the caves.

Thomas [listening intently]: Perhaps.

The Beast-Man: Do you remember the evening you landed the boat on the beach near the region of the Gerasenes?

Thomas: I vaguely remember it.

The Beast-Man: I looked down upon your group and laughed. I yelled down at Jesus from my high country, "It's the prince of fools with his band of clowns!" I don't know why I said it. I just wanted to challenge anyone who lived beyond my caves. I hated everyone and loved to sneer at the world. Then I watched Jesus talk to some swineherders about me. I could see them shake their heads and point at me. Then Jesus began to climb the rocky path to the caves. One of the pig watchers tried to hold Him back with warnings. Jesus simply smiled at him and kept climbing the rocky path.

Thomas: I remember now. We were all afraid for His life. When He got to your cave we saw rocks, sticks, and pieces of food come careening down the face of the cliffs. At the same time we heard your insane and bestial howling echo in the caves. The howling lasted a short time, and then there was an unbearable silence.

The Beast-Man: What happened was that He let me throw things at Him and howl until I was exhausted. In fact, I could barely lift my arms. My voice after a short time could only make a hoarse rasping sound. It's amazing what noises humans can make for a short time. But then their energy is spent and there is a type of peaceful exhaustion. He let me yell until I could yell no more, then I broke down and started crying. Why that was I do not know. Perhaps I was only glad to have a human being visit me. Perhaps it was total emotional exhaustion. I do not know. He waited until the crying stopped. He then asked me if I wanted Him to leave. Again, why He asked me such a question I don't know. Perhaps it was to give me back my dignity; perhaps it was just His way. I said nothing, and He stayed.

Thomas: It was His way. I mean He usually let someone respond before He acted. I believe He greatly loved the freedom of everyone. Many people told Him to leave and He did so. But sometimes He stayed regardless of what they said.

The Beast-Man [not listening but remembering]: Something in me told Him to go, and yet I fought that response in myself. I told Him to go and then immediately I told him to stay. At this time He said to me, "I know that you are a man split in two. All that you have is the type of freedom of a madman: a wild, uncompromising assertion of the sufferings you have had to bear. For this, I have compassion for you. What you are is not unknown to me or to the One who sent Me. But I have chosen you and your suffering to manifest real freedom to this world, a freedom quite contrary to that of a madman." To this I wanted to respond, "And who sent you, and who are you?" but something stopped me...I seemed to inwardly know Who sent Him and Who He was. He continued to speak,

"I said you are a man split in two. You love your life in the cave because it secures for yourself your image of yourself. You see yourself as one who is 'god.' No one can attack you or your image here. You are safe in the wondrous image of yourself. Yet at the same time you hate this cave. Your very nature cries out against it. The reason is you love freedom too much to see your own share of freedom wasted year after year. You know that if you remain here you will never change another human being's life. You will do no good for another. Your place in the world will be no different than the huge proud rocks which surround your cave."

At this point I began to rage. "If you are the Son of God, and that is Who I think you are, what would you have me do? Would you have me go back down amongst wretched and murderous humans who would kill me? I am not like you. People seek my death! Romans seek my death!"

Hearing this, He quietly and mournfully said, "Soon they will seek my life also. And although I am afraid like you are, I know there is a higher and truer Power than the powers of this world. It is faith in that Power which will give me courage when my time has come."

If He had not said this I would have not listened to Him any longer. I then said, "Tell me of this power." He responded, "If I told you, you would not believe. But do this: come down from this cave with me and I will show you throughout your life Who that Power is. Believe in me and you will know Who the Power is, and, very soon, you will fear no more." To this I said, "And what if I die?"

He said, "Follow me. I am to die for you and for everyone. After it is proven through me that the Power of God cannot die, you will not fear anything. You will know that you cannot die."

Puzzled, confused, doubting but trying to understand Him, I said, "I will try to come down the mountain with you. I am afraid, but I am horribly tired of life among the caves. But please have pity on me as we descend. I do not want to leave here, but I must." Saying nothing, He walked outside the cave. I tried to look back at my darkened home but could not. We walked to the ridge in front of the caves and a dense fog had covered the mountain. I said, "Perhaps we should wait until morning."

He responded, "No. Follow me. Have courage." We descended the mountain. Earth and rocks fell out from under our feet. When I doubted, although I said nothing, He would say, "Believe! Have courage!" Several times I thought I would slide down the mountain and be mangled, but always the words resounded, "Believe! Have courage!" In the dense fog it took us a long time to descend the mountain. I never thought we would make it. At the bottom, I was exhausted. The swineherders and you with the other disciples were waiting for us. I sat down ever so quietly. All of you thought I was in my right mind. I think I was, but I was also so extremely confused, tired and at peace.

[A few seconds of silence pass. Thomas, not knowing what to do, looks at the Beast-Man cautiously.]

Thomas: Do you have anymore wine?

The Beast-Man [as though waking from a dream]: Of course. [He goes into the back, and Thomas stares at his own glass.] Here we are. The best I have in memory of the best thing that ever happened to me. [The Beast-Man pours Thomas's glass full until it overflows. The Beast-Man laughs.] Sorry, but that's what happens with good memories. Good memories overflow whenever you have them.

Thomas [For the first time, he laughs.]: I know. He was the Good!

The Beast-Man [filling his own glass until it overflows]: He certainly was!

[They both drink a full glass. The glasses are refilled and remain on the table.]

Thomas: What did you do after that?

The Beast-Man: After an evening's rest, a rest and peace which was like nothing I had known before, I asked Him if I could follow Him as the other disciples did. His response was, "These men have much to learn. They must learn things you yourself know. You will follow me long after I have gone to my Father, because I will be with you. Go now and tell others what I have done for you. You do not need my physical presence as these men now do. From your sufferings, you have learned faith. You know that I can and will be with you always!" I believe He understood that I again wanted to be among people. Immediately that day I spoke to many of the swineherders. At first they were afraid of me, but soon, from a distance, they listened. As you will remember, they asked Him to depart from their lands. He did as they asked.. But I was left to talk to them about Him. From there I went to the neighboring towns and spoke of Jesus, The Son and Light of God. Although some laughed at me, although some threatened me, and although some ignored me; a few listened. Now and then I meet those who listened and we rejoice in the Good that God has given us. [Pushing his wine glass away.] I had heard that they have crucified Him, but I do not believe that they have killed Him.

Thomas: Oh, that I were you!!!!

The Beast-Man: Your doubt and suffering has brought you to the inward caves. If I were you, I would go back and seek the few who listened.

Thomas [rising]: I had best go. Morning grows near and the fog has set in. It is a difficult way down the hill.

The Beast-Man [blowing out one of the two candles]: I will go part way with you. [Now only one candle is burning on the center table. The Beast-Man smiles gently.] As has been said to me, "Believe...have courage..." [The final candle is extinguished by the Beast-Man.]

SOREN KIERKEGAARD

CHARACTERS

PROFESSOR
CONSTANTINE CONSTANTIUS
SOREN KIERKEGAARD'S FATHER
SOREN KIERKEGAARD
MANASSEH
SIMON
SEA CAPTAIN
GENTLEMAN
MARGARET
SONJA
ERIK
NEBUCHADNEZZAR
2 SERVANTS

PROLOGUE

[A churchyard located somewhere in the reflective imagination. The entire background of the stage is presented in black and grays. The tombstones are at all angles. The cemetery is unkempt and in a very deteriorated condition. A professor, approximately 55 years old, is seen walking about and attempting to read the tombstones. He is not able to find what he seeks and becomes frustrated. Constantine Constantius* enters with a book under his arm. Unseen by the professor, Constantine, approximately 25 years old, watches him until the professor sees him.]

Professor: The cemetery seems unused.

Constantine Constantius [ironically]: Look again.

Professor: I mean it doesn't seem as if anyone is maintaining the graves.

Constantine Constantius: One of the few signs of wisdom of those still living.

Professor: That's rather disrespectful.

Constantine Constantius: I'm sure the inhabitants will forgive us. [brief pause]

Professor: You wouldn't be able to show me the grave of Soren Kierkegaard would you?

---

* One of Kierkegaard's pseudonyms. Soren Kirekegaard, Repetition, trans. with intro. and notes by Walter Lowrie, Harper and Row, 1941.

Constantine Constantius: You merely have to go to a library. I suggest you look under "K" and forget about the commentaries, anthologies, and all the rest.

Professor: No, what I meant was the actual place where his body was buried.

Constantine Constantius: But that isn't Soren Kierkegaard.

Professor: You know what I mean.

Constantine Constantius: I'm sorry, but we are not speaking about the same person. [brief silence. The professor becomes impatient.]

Professor: Look, I have only a short time. After this I must go to Germany and visit the grave of Nietzsche, and then to Rome to visit the grave of Shelley, and then...

Constantine Constantius [interrupting him]: You're something of a demoniac, aren't you?

Professor: I resent that [He is not sure that he has been insulted.]...What do you mean?

Constantine Constantius: You seem to be gnashing your thoughts about the graves of the illustrious dead.

Professor [with dignity]: Young man, I'll have you know that I am not a demoniac at all....Why, I'm a professor of systematic, dogmatic, historical, philosophical, and Biblical theology.

Constantine Constantius: Who romps around tombstones.

Professor [pontificating]: I resent that. I really do. I am simply taking my vacation between my professorship and my...<u>ahem</u>...other duties.

Constantine Constantius: What are your...<u>ahem</u>...other duties.

Professor [pompously]: When I am not teaching, I am an official gamewarden for The United States Department of Parks and Recreation.

Constantine Constantius [cautiously]: You mean whether you teach or whether you don't teach, you keep others from catching the fish.

Professor [infuriated]: If you are referring to Our Blessed Lord and my dutiful service in catching men...if you dare to insinuate in your guttersnipe way that I am not a responsible teacher bound to His Holy Service...Why, I'll...I'll...

Constantine Constantius [blandly interested: You'll what?

Professor [gulping and then piously]: I'll...well...I'll excuse your lack of manners and overlook the offense this time.

Constantine Constantius [impishly]: ...and still stop the catching of the fish.

Professor [becoming irate]: Now listen...

Constantine Constantius: Okay...okay. But this simply brings us to your problem of finding Kierkegaard's grave.

Professor: How so?

Constantine Constantius: Every time his name is mentioned there should be a violent conflict over what it means to be a Christian. His life is a complete reflection of his striving to become a Christian. Yet you want to give a pious nod over a few feet of earth and go home raving about "The Grave of Kierkegaard," but you don't want to crawl in after him.

Professor: And how will I do that since I am still alive?

Constantine Constantius: Yes you're alive in the sense that you "live" in your official and objective capacities. You cannot find Kierkegaard that way.

Professor [annoyed]: All right...I've read his books....How do I "crawl in after him" as you say.

Constantine Constantius: That's up to you.

Professor: Look, you stand here as some kind of pinnacle of wisdom...what you have to say--say. After all, everything can be communicated.

Constantine Constantius [austerely]: Everything?

Professor [self-righteously]: EVERYTHING!!

Constantine Constantius: How much time do you have?

Professor: I have enough time to listen to a rational statement.

Constantine Constantius: That is only partial time.

Professor: Look, say what you have to say. I'll listen.

Constantine Constantius [opening his book]:

Gethsemane has cried out for blood
and found its violent call fulfilled.
The mob itself has called for death
and still is not contented.
Nature, man--
man--nature...
Both pull, drive, denounce...
head down--spirit crushed.
Both crack, break, split...
soul down--spirit crushed--

Ah, to will--Ah, the drive
inward through it all:
Through desires' flames
and laws' constrictions...
Through to WILL: the pulling together of self
and then to strike out
against it all.

To will--yes.
To will one's self in The Power of God Himself.

To despair and then to despair of despairing.

Into God--
Into God.

spirit/will
WILLING SPIRIT.
The lonely, solitary decision
for the Power
in the Power--
Christ, Christ Himself.

Through beauty's dreams,

Through decisions' screams,
Through "religious" speculation,
Through the world's ensnaring...
...spirit willing...
WILLING SPIRIT
  through life's stages
 to Christ, to Christ Himself.

[The professor's face becomes filled with anxiety. He looks at Constantine who appears to be quite serene.]

ACT ONE

[This act is based on the fragment "The Quiet Despair" in Kierkegaard's Stages on Life's Way, translated by Walter Lowrie, 1940, Schocken Books, p. 191 ff. The scene is an upper-class living room in a Danish home. The year is 1826. It is early morning. A young frail boy of thirteen is sitting idly watching his father.]

Father [His age should be about 65.]: Soren, would you like to go outside and play?

Soren: No, thank you.

Father: Would you rather we went for a ride in the carriage?

Soren: No, thank you, father.

Father: All my business affairs have been completed and there is time for a free day. What shall we do?

Soren: May we do the same as always?

Father: Yes...yes, of course. Let's go to Spain and see the king's court.

Soren [enthusiastically]: Yes...yes. The king's castles and the knights.

Father [smiling]: And the ladies.

Soren: Yes, the beautiful Spanish ladies.

Father: The king has declared war. The knights on horseback have assembled.

Soren: And the knights are riding from all sides of the regiments to give the notice "All ready!" to their lords.

Father: And alone, a knight cries in sorrow.

Soren: For he has left his love and may meet his God.

Father [sorrowfully]: We must all meet our God, Soren.

Soren [more intent on his describing what he sees]: In armor shining in the Spanish sun, he sits upon his horse. No one can see his tears for his face is hidden behind his helmet's visor. Only the red scarf of his lady's colors can be seen around his neck. How bright and courageous and immaculate he looks to his page and squire! How devotedly his lieutenants fear and admire him! And no one sees him cry. No...not one.

Father: The battle must start, Soren. The battle must start!

Soren: Father, why must there always be battle!

Father: Because there is always struggle: struggle against sin and loss and death.

Soren: And so the knight must weep.

Father: And must do battlė, Soren. He must do battle.

Soren: With sin, father?

Father: With sin and man. With both at once.

Soren: And now the knight and his legions ride forth. The cannons explode. The bullets fly. The knight falls wounded.

Father: But he gets up, Soren, as Our Lord did when He bore His cross. He fell, but He got up. We must all do the same.

Soren [concentrating]: And he gets up.

Father: And he gets up, and...

Soren [holding his ears with both of his palms]: And he curses man, and he curses God, and he curses sin, and he curses the devil. He curses. He screams, "Why have you made me?"...And there is no reply.

Father: I once cursed God and everything. I had nothing. I was hungry. It was on the barren heath of Jutland. I am no longer hungry, but I hunger to be at peace with the God I cursed.*

Soren [concentrating]: But father, the enemy is thrown back! The enemies' lines are broken, father! Look! See! He conquers--the enemy retreats!

Father: Look hard, Soren--does he still weep?

Soren [disturbed]: Yes, but why father? Why?

Father: Look once more.

Soren: The knight is very weak now; his armor weighs him down. He tries to get up again but falls. He has lost all his strength.

Father: Where are his men?

Soren: They have left him to pursue the enemy.

Father: Is he still alive?

Soren: Yes, but he is dying, father. He is dying and clutching his red scarf.

Father: And there is no one there?

Soren: No. No one.

[A servant enters the room.]

Servant [addressing the father]: Sir, the parson is here.

Father [in a trance]: Send him away. He is dying. [to himself] What good is a parson?

Servant: But, sir...

Father [irate]: GET OUT! And don't disturb us for the rest of the day.

Servant: Yes, sir. [The servant exists.]

Father [resuming the conversation as one in a trance]: Soren, does he remember the lady of the red scarf?

Soren: Yes, father, he dreams of her for a moment and then...

Father [delirious]: And then...

See Walter Lowrie's Kierkegaard New York: Harper and Brothers, 1962, vol. 1, p. 22.

Soren: He is no more.

Father [shaken]: No more?

Soren: He is dead. [a few seconds of silence.]

Father: And he did not have time to repent for his sin?

Soren: He could not repent, father. All was too sudden.

Father: Then it is over.

Soren [frightened]: Or it has just begun.

Father [filled with anxiety]: Stop it, Soren. Stop it.

Soren: But where is he, father?

Father [shuddering]: He is before the living God.

[Both look down in a melancholic and desperate way as the lights fall.]

ACT TWO

[The scene is a cemetery in Jerusalem during the first century C.E. It should appear more barren than the cemetery in The Prologue. This act is based on "A Leper's Soliloquy" in Kierkegaard's Stages of Life's Way, same edition as stated in Act One, pp. 220-222. Simon the leper is seen standing surrounded by tombstones. His right forearm has withered away. He is dressed in rags and bandages. His entire face is contorted my immense sores and swellings. What can be seen of his body through the rags shows brown patches where the blood has coagulated in scabs amidst his reddened sores and swellings. Manasseh, another leper, is with him. Manasseh's leprosy is only in its initial stage. Only a few small sores can be seen on his face, his arms, and his hands. His rags are not as tattered as Simon's.]

Manasseh: How long, Oh God? How long?

Simon: We've just begun.

Manasseh: I feel the disease crawling like lice under my skin. The marrow of my bones is alive with disease. The crawling, the eternal crawling of insects devouring my flesh....Is there no cure? Is there none?

Simon: It is not eternal. We only suffer once although it be seventy years.*

Manasseh: Seventy years?

---

* See Kierkegaard's Christian Discources. "The Joy of It-That We Suffer Only Once, But Triumph Eternally." London: Oxford University Press, 1940, pp. 101-110.

Simon [radiant]: The joy of it! That you only suffer once...and then eternity.

Manasseh: But time...this torture.

Simon: Once! Only once! And then eternity!

Manasseh: There must be some salve, some ointment for this bodily torment.

Simon: There is an ointment, but it drives the leprosy into the soul and then the soul becomes infected. It is better that the body be sick and not the soul.

Manasseh: Quick! The ointment! Where is it?

Simon: It is only for the moment, this torture. Should we not endure it?

Manasseh: The ointment! I must have the ointment.

Simon: If I tell you of the ointment you will never be cured.

Manasseh: Will I find relief?

Simon: Only for this life, but then...

Manasseh: But then...Who knows about "then"? Give me the ointment!

Simon: I cannot give it to you. Go to the towns and be humanly meek, look dejected; go to the temple and cry out in pain. You will have a temporal, false cure. But the inward, eternal cry will rend you. It will destroy you.

Manasseh: So then there is relief.

Simon: Yes, but such a poor relief which costs the wealthy priests nothing and salves <u>their</u> consciences. It heals the priest as much as the priest's victim, yet both live in inward despair. It costs the priest nothing, and thus the sufferer receives nothing.

Manasseh: I must know its name.

Simon: Oh, you will know it. Go and cry out. Scream in their ears. They will give it to you and try to hide their own internal leprosy.

Manasseh: I...I do not know what to do. I am held here with the dead, yet I want to go to the town...to life...

Simon: Would you call the city life? Go to the city! Find out for yourself! [Simon lies down on one of the graves. He appears to have fallen asleep. Manasseh walks back and forth among the graves. He looks closely into Simon's face. He shudders. He looks at his own sores and in anguish leaves the stage. Simon slumbers for a few moments more and then awakes. He attempts to scratch his face with his right withered arm. His right arm is too short to reach his face. He stops and then scratches his face with his left hand. In a tortured, mad voice he cries out as he stands up.]

Simon: Who is there? Who is speaking? Is it I? "It is you." Who is speaking to me? "It is yourself." Is it not the dead, my companions? "No, far worse, it is yourself among the dead." It is I. It is I, the one led to the graves of burning sand. The one drawn here awaiting a saving lotion. [He stops speaking for a few moments.] Where is Manasseh? He has not left! Oh, no! Oh, no! He has gone to the temple. He has gone to receive what not even the dogs who once licked Lazarus' sores would accept. The dogs could at least snap at those who would pretend to be their masters. He has gone to receive "priestly" compassion--a compassion changing with the winds--a compassion which relieves the giver of his guilt--a compassion like the rancid food which the rich man once threw to stray dogs. The compassion which costs nothing and is worth less. Oh, God, I once used such an ointment. When one suffers, one seeks any relief. But you have led me away from the living dead to the dead who live with Thee. Abraham, Isaac, Jacob--through suffering they came to know Thy Compassion which I seek, seek upon the graves. Oh God, help Manasseh! Lead him away from illusory peace! Do not let him fall a lost victim to the world's grunting, emotive solace, and cheap contentment. If need be drive him back to the graves so that he will know death's truth and seek Thy Compassion. Manasseh is no different from the simple and downtrodden, the lame, the insane, and the persecuted. He is like all of these who truly need Thy Compassion. Help them all and help me. Help me to believe in the place where a table is set and Abraham and

Isaac and Jacob await the leper's entrance to fulfill their joy.

[Simon becomes silent. He turns his back to the audience and sits down behind a gravestone so that the gravestone is between himself and the audience. The lights fall.]

[There should be an intermission with silence and darkness for a few seconds.. When the lights come up the cemetery scene of The Prologue is again in view. The professor is becoming irritated and begins to scold Constantine Constantius.]

Professor: Now wait just a minute. Just a minute. I am failing to grasp what you are trying to say. This entire treatment is both undisciplined and defies the prescribed canons of truly religious and truly human art.

Constantine Constantius: You mean that the "treatment" of the theme does not meet your systematic standards of philosophical-theological investigation. Further, the form lacks the essential criteria of modern drama stemming from what is currently accepted.

Professor [pompously]: Precisely.

Constantine Constantius: Precisely. We have just at this moment said "precisely" nothing to each other.

Professor [pedantically]: Precisely...ah, I mean...I mean...

Constantine Constantius: Precisely!

Professor [becoming frustrated]: No, that isn't what I mean.

Constantine Constantius: What do you mean?

Professor: It does seem that we can have a rational, systematic, disciplined interpretation of Soren Kierkegaard. You are presenting something else.

Constantine Constantius: Perhaps you would like a commentary on Kierkegaard or a biographical drama.

Professor: Precisely. A biographical drama would be in order. I have already written two commentaries on modern theology and Kierkegaard's basic theses have been covered.

Constantine Constantius: Then it's true.

Professor: What is true?

Constantine Constantius: What Kierkegaard said about his work being used by parasitical priests and professors to gain worldly reputation.*

Professor [not used to such comments]: You're rather ill-tempered and bellicose, do you know that? However, that is not the point. What the point is...

Constantine Constantius: Is that you are a professor because Someone was crucified.**

Professor: Now I resent that. Do you here me? I resent that.

Constantine Constantius: I thought we were discussing Kierkegaard and not your resentments. I was simply presenting Kierkegaard's attitude towards resentful or unresentful professors.

Professor: Well, yes, but...after all...

Constantine Constantius: But after all...nothing! We are discussing Kierkegaard, aren't we?

Professor: Yes...but...

Constantine Constantius: But you want some edifying thoughts about the man, some edifying prattle to discuss with your wife and students over coffee and crumpets.

Professor [trying to be cute]: Actually, I prefer tea.

Constantine Constantius [becoming irritated]: Fine. Anyway you don't want Who Kierkegaard wanted--Christ Himself!

Professor: Now just a minute. That is a philosophical-theological problem subsumed under the categories of Biblical, Historical, and Systematic theology.

Constantine Constantius: But what about yourself?

Professor [confused]: What? About whom? Look! I don't have to be insulted.

Constantine Constantius [bored]: I know...you're a professor.

---

* Soren Kierkegaard, The Last Years, translated by R. G. Smith. New York: Harper & Row, 1965, p. 310.
** Walter Lowrie, Kierkegaard, vol. 2, p. 507.

Professor [irate]: Look, you're supposed to be presenting a play. What does all this nonsense about an old man and a boy and a leper have to do with the matter at hand?

Constantine Constantius: Just that Kierkegaard drew religious reflection from himself. What transpires in this work are the most secret and enigmatic statements he recorded about himself during the varied stages of his coming to his goal. This goal was to become contemporaneous with Jesus Christ.

Professor: But there is no viable statement about the Christian community in all of this.

Constantine Constantius: Soren Kierkegaard was only interested in one thing--realizing that God is love. That someone says that God is love or that everyone says that God is love, and <u>you do not know</u> that God is love demands that you yourself decide whether some men or all men are liars.

Professor: Yes, of course...I know, but...

Constantine Constantius: Well, either God is love or He is not. What is transpiring is the struggle to uncover the nature of such love and what is required of the individual to make the statement to herself or himself, "I know God is love."

Professor: All right...okay...existentialism...I know...

Constantine Constantius: No, not existentialism, I know; but God is love, that I <u>inwardly</u> know.

Professor [mumbling]: Yes...yes, the strangeness of our being, our doubt, our...

Constantine Constantius: No, let's not make it all that complicated. Let's remain with the questions: "Is God Love?"

Professor [mumbling again]: Well, the anxiety of estrangement could symbolically point to the need for redemption and...

Constantine Constantius: Oh nonsense. The anxiety of estrangement could symbolically point to the statement "God is Evil." Regardless, one must <u>struggle</u> for light; one must find whatever light there is in one's self and seek The Source of that light everyday.

Professor [becoming confused]: But our finitude...and the historical process...and the historical Jesus...and ecumenism,...and, I...and the relation of all this to form criticism...and neo-orthodoxy...and...

Constantine Constantius: May I continue?

Professor [as the personification of The Tower of Babel]: ...and secularism in a world come of age...and oh, yes,...and the social gospel in the age of pluralism...and the god is dead movement...and the Dead Sea Scrolls in relation to Vatican II...

Constantine Constantius: Say, are you all right?

Professor [starting to recover]: Yes, it is very easy to lose one's self in theology. There is so much to examine scholarly, that I think I have forgotten to examine my own self.*

Constantine Constantius: I cannot see how it will profit anyone to lose her or his soul in the idol palace of theological slogans. I think Kierkegaard's major thesis has always been neglected: each individual should at all times struggle to become a believer, and by believing, become contemporaneous with Jesus Christ Himself!

Professor: Can we leave it at that?

Constantine Constantius: No!

Professor: Why not?

Constantine Constantius: Because of what one must endure in order to believe!

---

* See Kierkegaard's For Self-Examination, trans. by Walter Lowrie, Princeton University Press, 1941.

ACT THREE

[The same Danish living room as Act One. This act is based on "Solomon's Dream" in Kierkegaard's Stages on Life's Way, same edition as cited in Act One, p. 236.]

Soren: Father...

Father: Yes, Soren?

Soren: Father, shall we never be happy?

Father [sadly]: It is not our place to be happy in this life.

Soren: Can no one be happy? Surely wisdom must lead to happiness. Surely wisdom and wealth must lead to happiness. Was not Solomon happy? Surely Solomon must have been happy and at peace.

Father: How do you see Solomon?

Soren: I see Solomon sitting amidst his scrolls, finding pleasure and peace in knowledge and wisdom. I see him gathered amongst his colorful thoughts which are all bright red and green and purple--beautiful and edifying thoughts.

Father [smiling]: But amongst these thoughts does he not think now and then of his father?

Soren [delighted that his father, is engaged seriously in the same thoughts]: Oh yes! The mighty king David! How proud Solomon is! His father has conquered all their enemies and rules the land. David is also the elect of God. To have David as a father! No one could have a better father! Solomon and David--wisdom and strength! David and Solomon--kingship and knowledge! They must have been happy!

Father [sadly]: Yes, but Solomon must rest from his happiness and his many colored thoughts, must he not?

Soren [startled]: Yes, he must.

Father: And so he goes to his chambers one evening and, being the king's son, his chambers adjoin his father's.

Soren: Of course, yes, of course, father.

Father [darkly]: And he begins to doze and to sleep and he is not sure whether he is sleeping or awake....He hears moans and cries from his father's room....

Soren: Moans and cries?

Father: Yes, Soren. His father is kneeling and weeping. His father is repenting, Soren. He is repenting that he has cursed God by disobeying the prophet Nathan--that he has killed a good man to have that good man's wife. He has disobeyed God, Soren, and he despairs.

Soren: Despairs, father?

Father: His soul is shaken and broken and he cries out in torture to God. He cries out for forgiveness, for some hope. And David is alone, Soren, he is dreadfully alone.

Soren [quietly]: Alone.

Father: Yes, all alone. And Solomon who has always seen David as the most powerful of men, now sees him as a wretched cripple. He sees David as one beneath a crushing burden, the burden of his guilt before God; and for once Solomon does not understand.

Soren: But he is wise, father.

Father: Yes, he is wise after the fashion of our professors and our pastors. He is wise in that way. Indeed, Solomon shines in a worldly glory. But he is not in the darkness of God. He has not come to know sin and its wretched power which inwardly corrupts the soul. He has not despaired of himself and become strong through the inward knowledge of his own weakness and God's strength.

Soren: I do not understand.

Father: You cannot understand everything at once, Soren. You, too, must live and be broken.

Soren: ...and be broken...

Father: Yes.

Soren [anxiously]: Can no one escape this breaking?

Father: Yes, some do. Perhaps Solomon did. Solomon continued in his worldly wisdom, but he did not know God's foolishness. And Solomon always had a place of honor in the temple, but he did not become a man of prayer. And Solomon was praised by men but oh, what trouble there was within him, for he could really only value the praise which came from David. But David was broken and divided and only upheld by the living God. And so Solomon walked in his brightly colored realm of beauty, exquisite thoughts, and desires. What is more, Solomon inherited his father's earthly kingdom, but Solomon was troubled, Soren, so infinitely troubled for he never approached that <u>other kingdom</u> where David only wished to be a slave!

Soren [anxiously]: And what happens, father? How then does Solomon live and die?

Father [sadly]: In vexation of spirit because his colored thoughts give him no rest, he returns to his harem. To escape his troubles with pleasure he cries out to all the women, "Strike the tambourines, dance before me!" But his inward restlessness permits him no lasting consolation, and drifting in this realm of desire upon desire, he awaits his end in disquiet dreams. Finally the Queen of Sheba visited him in her magnificence with her false gods. She sought his worldly wisdom, and Solomon, for diversion's sake, spoke of exotic earthly ecstasy. Thus the queen and the spending of great fortunes amused Solomon until his death.

Soren [terrified]: And how did he die, father?

Father: He died with his final prayer being a confused intermingling of his own worldly wisdom and the strange prayer of David.

[Both look at each other as though recognizing a mysterious truth from their conversation. Then both stare at the floor.]

ACT FOUR

[This act is based on Kierkegaard's fragment "A Possibility" in Stages on Life's Way, pp. 258-268. The stage is set in such a manner as to place the entrance of a longbridge to the left of the stage as the audience sees the set. In the center of the stage is a small garden with chairs and a bench. The entire sky is black and dreary. A man with white hair, age 40, is sitting in such a way as to expose his hunched back. He is dressed in the fashionable attire of Danish gentleman of the 1840's. A robust, heavily bearded sea captain in uniform enters.]

Sea Captain: My friend, how is it that you are not pacing? [jovially] After all, this is your sacred hour for the march, is it not? [He takes out a watch from his vest pocket.] Yes, ten-thirty. This is not like you. No, not like you at all.

Gentleman [somewhat startled]: Yes...I mean no it is not like me [recovering himself] Heinrich! Have you just arrived? Where have you come from?

Sea Captain: We just docked yesterday evening. Came in from The West Indies. What a storm! One man overboard in the middle of the Atlantic. I had to fight both God and the devil to turn our tub around and rescue him. But we got him back. By God, we got him back.

Gentleman [smiling]: And how long will you be staying?

Sea Captain: Until the weather improves or until I get sick of the rum in Copenhagen. But, you, why is it that you are not pacing? I knew I could find you here with your restless thoughts, marching back and forth, just like I've found you for the past twenty years pacing and fretting before the longbridge...I'm glad I found you...But this isn't quite like you. Are you well?

Gentleman: I'm marvelously well. Yes, I feel better than I have felt in a long time.

Sea Captain: Well what happened, man? I never seen you resting in dry dock at this hour.

Gentleman: A certainty that was uncertain became certain.

Sea Captain [perplexed]: Well, that's too much for me. The only thing that is certain is a last voyage. It's there. Someday I will take it, and it will be the last. But that's a long way off...I hope.

Gentleman [musing to himself]: Yes, the last voyage, that is certain. Say how would you like some rum?

Sea Captain: Well, it's for certain that I would. [Both laugh.] But first tell me, before we talk about anything else, do you have any of your drawings left?

Gentleman: Drawings?

Sea Captain: You know, those fine things you do in your spare time. The children's faces.

Gentleman: You mean the drawings I have displayed in my rooms.

Sea Captain: Yes, those drawings. I'd like to have one of them. The face of the little girl with the big eyes and the wide mouth. Do you remember?

Gentleman [recollecting]: No, I don't remember. There are so many drawings. I... [He begins to pace absentmindedly.] I had almost forgotten the drawings. [He recollects something and then sits down. There is a brief pause.] The drawings...yes, you can have whichever one you want.

Sea Captain: Are you sure you're feeling well?

Gentleman: Oh yes. Yes. Is there any reason you want that particular one?

Sea Captain: The little girl reminds me of my sister's daughter who died of consumption while I was at sea. The resemblance is quite remarkable. I thought I would give it to my sister to try and console her. [A ragged beggar woman with two children, a boy age ten and a girl age eight, appears at the side of the stage. The little girl wishes to rush to the gentleman, but the mother constrains her.]

Girl [Her name is Sonja.]: But mother...

Mother [Her name is Margaret.]: Sonja. Be still!

[The Sea Captain and the Gentleman turn to discover the source of the noise. They both go and greet their visitors.]

Gentleman: Margaret, how are you? Sonja, my little princess...and who is this?

Sonja: This is Eric.

Gentleman: Eric, well, well. Sonja, is Eric a new friend?

Sonja: Of course he is, but he has trouble saying things.

Eric [Eric is partially retarded]: I...I...I...aaam glaaaaad...to...to [He strikes his head with his fists and begins crying.]

Margaret [going to Eric]: Now that's all right, Eric. That's okay. You're with a kind and good man--a very kind and good man. [to the Gentleman and Sea Captain] Eric finds it hard to talk to strangers. It took Sonja and me two days before he would trust us. We found him four days ago at dawn walking about the streets and crying.

Sonja [to the Gentleman]: Do you remember the dawn four days ago?

Gentleman [attempting to reflect but gives up the attempt]: No, I seem to have forgotten it.

Sonja: Oh, you must remember it! You must! The sun came up and everything was like gold. All the streets glowed in a quiet splendor, and the morning light made Copenhagen look like a dream--a white-gold dream. Yes, a peaceful, quiet, beautiful dream. [sadly] And there was Eric in the midst of it...and there was Eric in the midst of the white-gold dream reminding mother and me that we were awake.

Gentleman: So Eric has no home.

Sonja: Oh yes he does...with mother and me. [Shyly, for the first time, she looks at the Sea Captain.] Who is the man with the beard and the beautiful uniform?

Gentleman [smiling]: He is a great wanderer--a sea captain who visits enchanted lands and fights dragons and pirates and knows more stories than anyone else.

Sonja: Will he tell Eric and me a story? [The gentleman looks at the Sea Captain.]

Sea Captain [drying his eyes]: Of course...of course. But no captain can remember well or speak with his mates without first putting in for supplies, so to speak...[Since the Captain is used to speaking in a tavern, he becomes a little confused.]...at a bakery and a candy store. [He looks relieved especially after seeing Margaret's look of approval.] Will you be my mates and come with me? [Still hesitating, he turns to Margaret.] Is that all right, ma'am?

Margaret: Oh, of course it is.

Gentleman: Heinrich, you take Sonja and Eric for a...how did you put it?...a "putting in for supplies" [with good-natured mockery to the Sea Captain] ...yes, that was it..."a putting in for supplies"...not bad, Heinrich, not bad at all...and Margaret and I will see you soon. [Sonja takes Eric by the hand and they both skip off together before the Sea Captain to the right of stage as the audience sees the set.]

Gentleman: Margaret, please sit down.

Margaret: Why, thank you, sir. Thank you.

Gentleman [sitting down next to her]: And what brings you to see me on such a miserable day?

Margaret: More misery, unfortunately. I had almost figured out how to support Sonja and myself by taking in laundry and occasional cleaning jobs. But then we found Eric in the streets. Neither Sonja nor I could turn away from him and so...

[The Gentleman expressionlessly and almost mechanically reaches for his wallet in his coat pocket. Without looking at the bills, he hands all his money to her.]

Margaret [her eyes widening]: No, sir! No! This is too much! You won't have anything for your yourself or for the other people.

Gentleman [laughing]: Oh, please take it. [looking at the longbridge] I won't need it where I will be going and...yes, and for the others I must make some arrangements...for them, and for you and Sonja and Eric...

Margaret: Sir... [troubled and embarrassed, not knowing what to say] Sir, I did not see you pacing today....Was it because the Sea Captain is here?

Gentleman: No. Despite Heinrich's arrival I was not pacing at all today. It's funny Heinrich also asked me why I wasn't pacing. I must have a reputation like that of a caged animal which paces incessantly back and forth over its limited space and time. [sensing Margaret's embarrassment] But this is all too complicated. The truth is simple. Today, you see, I discovered that I must take a long and awesome journey across a dreadful bridge, yes...a very long and dreadful bridge...[attempting with difficulty to clarify his own statements] You see, you see in my youth when I was working very hard to succeed in my business, I lived alone. I had few friends and I had no wife. [staring at the longbridge] One evening...one evening long ago in my youth I had dinner with a few of my business acquaintances...and drinking too much and filled with youth's fire, we visited one of the houses down the street from here. I only remember in my drunkenness being lifted through the threshold into the house, and the unhappy women who were forced to work there with false smiles on their bizarrely painted faces. That is all that I remember. What I never forgot was the next morning. That next morning it occurred to me that it was now possible that someone in this world could be carrying my child. I was too ashamed to go back to the house even if I could have found it. I was so drunk I doubt that I could have found it. Besides, the women would have only thought I was crazy. Still, the possibility that I might be a father, that I might be responsible for someone besides myself began to grow and feed itself within me. The thought overcame me. I became obsessed with trying to fulfill my potential responsibility and be done with it...but it was not that easy. I did not know where to begin. Then I thought of scientifically attempting to solve my problem by studying the faces of children and comparing their faces to my own.

Margaret: So that is why all these years you've studied the faces of the poor children hereabouts.

Gentleman: Yes...that is so. One can never be sure--no, never. My doubts and worries increased. I studied books on physiology and anatomy. I made drawings in my leisure time. I did all of this in the hope of being certain--of somehow deriving a system by which I could be certain what my child would look like. All of this only to know for certain and then pay for my evil and be free...I never reached such certainty.

Margaret: And your pacing?

Gentleman: Yes, each day I would pace back and forth. My problem took everything from me. From, ten to eleven each morning I would walk back and forth hoping to discover certainty. For twenty-five years I searched for certainty and now...

Margaret: Now...

Gentleman: Now. Today, I have discovered that I have no more than a short time to live, and my search for certainty has fallen away to another certainty which all the pacing in the world will not resolve. [a brief silence.] I will be crossing over a long and dreadful bridge from this world to the next. [again, a silence]

Margaret [She begins to speak slowly and deliberately.]: Sir, I...I am not very smart and I do not understand everything you have said....But I know this for certain: within a short time you will not cross the longbridge alone. Perhaps your worries have blinded you to one thing--the most important thing to God. All the poor women and children you have taken care of for all these years have never stopped worrying and praying for you. We have watched you from a distance and we did not understand, but we watched and prayed. And so, sir, it is impossible for you to cross that longbridge alone. The prayers of the poor outrun you. They are before God right now. And when you die the poor will meet you and you will be carried across that bridge; you will be carried! We could not have survived without your kindness; and God, well, He can forget sin, but He cannot forget goodness. And so we go with you, sir, we go with you. [There is a brief silience.]

Gentleman [quietly]: Then you believe that I am not alone.

Margaret [smiling]: No, sir; you can't be. I and the other woman and children won't permit it. And God, well, He always listens to the poor, I know He does. So you're surrounded and might as well accept defeat.

Gentleman [smiling]: But such a defeat! [Both laugh.]

[Off stage the Sea Captain can be heard speaking.]

Margaret [anxiously]: Does your friend, the captain, know about...

Gentleman: No, not yet, and please don't mention it. I will tell him later. We shouldn't spoil the day for the children.

Margaret: The day, sir?

Gentleman: Yes, the day. We're going to the amusement park in Copenhagen.

Margaret: But do you feel well enough?

Gentleman: I feel wonderful and, thanks to you, I feel like having some fun... [reflecting to himself] a word I almost forgot, yes, an excellent word "fun."

Margaret: Oh, Sonja and Eric will love this!

Gentleman [laughing]: But you will have to loan us some money! [Both laugh. The Sea Captain enters with Sonja and Eric.]

Sea Captain [continuing his story]: So there I was off the southwest coast of Africa, and a pirate with a beard reaching to his belt, boards our ship! It was him or me! I grabbed him by his beard. [to a wide-eyed Sonja and Eric] You should have heard him scream! He sounded like a pinched Gypsy dancer! [He notices Margaret and he becomes embarrassed.] Pardon me, ma'am. Anyway, so I threw the pirate overboard. But his smell was so bad that not even the sharks would touch him. So I fished him out, gave him a shave, and made him my first mate. And then...

Gentleman [laughing]: I don't want to interrupt such a story, but we have an appointment.

Sea Captain [confused]: A what?

Gentleman: An appointment at the amusement park.

Sonja: Hooray!!

Eric: At the what?

Sonja: Eric's speaking like everyone else. I think it's because he likes the Sea Captain and the captain's uniform. I know he likes cookies and candy. [All laugh except for Eric who is a little puzzled.]

Margaret: We'll show you what an amusement park is, Eric.

Gentleman: We certainly will! Let's cross the longbridge!

[Eric and Sonja skip across the longbridge. Margaret follows them. The Sea Captain places his arm around the Gentleman's shoulders, and they walk across the longbridge after Margaret. However, as the Gentleman and the Sea Captain cross the bridge, the Sea Captain continues his story.]

Sea Captain: You should have seen that pirate's beard. Thick as a whale's head and twice as strong... [The Gentleman listens and is thoroughly amused.]

[There should again be a few seconds of darkness. There is the same scene as The Prologue.]

Professor: Okay...okay. Realized eschatology and all of that.... God "here and now" and the rest of it. We've all seen the development of Kierkegaard's thought through Twentieth Century existentialism. The "infinite qualitative difference between God and man" has been scholarly investigated, as well as the "leap of faith" and Kierkegaard's relation to Hegel. I think the scholars have done a fine job...I just wish I could find his grave and get out of here.

Constantine Constantius [smiling]: Well, if you must know, Kierkegaard is buried next to his father. On the day he was buried a quarrel began between the students and the professors,* a quarrel, I might add, which I intend to perpetuate.

Professor: Well, you certainly are adept at quarreling. Now, where is Kierkegaard's father's grave?

Constantine Constantius: I don't know.

Professor: What?

Constantine Constantius: It would be superfluous knowledge and not the knowledge of "faith." Since Kierkegaard's entire life's work is simply an attempt to come to faith, a noble and lonely attempt, I don't think he should be thought of as a rotting carcass occupying six feet of turf. As I said before, if you want to know where Kierkegaard is, go to a library. If you want anymore information ask the gravedigger; there are plenty of them in this world.

Professor [confused]: Well, yes. [regaining professorial control] I want to thank you for the ah...stuff you were reading to me. However, I don't think that's the way to approach the writing a scholarly work. After all, the Kierkegaard corpus, [laughing to himself] I don't mean his physical body, is being analyzed by a legion of Danish, German, English, and American scholars. They will no doubt give us all the truth we need to know about Kierkegaard's thought, style, language, and life. [He looks at his watch.] Now I must be gong. I still have to find the gravedigger, and then I have a luncheon appointment. Thank you for your time and your...

Constantine Constantius: My "stuff."

Professor: Yes, you're reading of your writings.

Constantine Constantius: Yes, good-bye.

[The professor leaves. Constantine Constantius looks at the graves surrounding him. He opens his book and continues reading.]

---

* See Walter Lowrie's Kierkegaard, vol. 2, pp. 586-588.

ACT FIVE

[This act is based on "A School Exercise: Periander" in Stages on Life's Way, pp. 298-302. The scene is Kierkegaard's father's bedroom. The father is sitting in bed supported by pillows. Soren, now age 25, is sitting in a chair next to him. Soren is extremely well dressed having almost the appearance of a dandy. He gives every impression of being a sophisticated man of the world.]

Soren: Father, do you feel as weak as you did yesterday?

Father: No. I think some of my strength is returning. I think I have the strength...yes, I do...if you are willing.

Soren: Strength to do what, father?

Father: When you were younger do you remember how we would walk all about the world by imagining things.

Soren: Yes, father.

Father: If you do not feel that you are too old, perhaps we could do that today.

Soren: No, I am not too old, father. Where shall we go? That is, if you feel well enough.

Father: I am well enough. First, I wanted to tell you before I...became any weaker, the reasons for our past visits to different places in history and in the world.

Soren: Yes, father.

Father: I only wanted you to come to properly believe in Jesus Christ. That is what the individual must do in this life.

Soren [stricken with anxiety]: That is a heavy task, father.

Father: Our Lord says that although we must bear our cross, yet His burden is light. I have never completely understood that, but perhaps you will.

Soren: Father, you know I have lost interest in such matters.

Father [becoming annoyed]: Soren, you are still quite young. Frivolous interest in artistic reveries and chasing the ladies will not save anyone. Now I am sorry that I will probably not have the time to speak more about this with you. [He begins coughing again. Soren stands up to look for assistance.] Sit down! Sit down! I am fine. Please listen to what I have to say and see if in any way it does not remind you of many of the stories which we used to tell each another. Perhaps you've read about Periander, the tyrant of Corinth.

Soren: Why, yes. Not long ago I read something about him in Diogenes Laertius.

Father: Fine.? What did you learn from Diogenes' account?

Soren [melancholically]: Only that he spoke like a wise man and acted like a madman.

Father: Yes, he was a man totally split in half. That is to say, he was a monster. His reign was characterized by equitable leniency and a consuming passion. However, these two characteristics were never drawn together, solidified, and purified within the man. He would pay homage to the gods, defend the poor, and conduct himself with wisdom among men of understanding. Yet the same man had sexual relations with his mother, kicked his wife to death, and tried to murder his own sons. His madness ended in an elaborate plot of suicide in which seven other men were killed as well as himself.

Soren: Yes, father, the story comes back to me now.

Father: Have you discovered in your experiences or in your studies a way in which to reconcile the conflicts of an individual like Periander?

Soren [anxiously recognizing himself as another Periander]: What do you mean?

Father [begins coughing]: I only mean. [coughing] Learn to love and serve Jesus Christ; He is the Way...[The coughing continues. Soren Kierkegaard leaves the room in order to get a servant.]

ACT SIX

[This is based on "Nebuchadnezzar" in Kierkegaard's Stages on Life's Way, pp. 330-333. The scene is Nebuchadnezzar's bed chamber in his palace at Babel. He is seated in bed. Around him are strewn rolled and unrolled scrolls. His servant is apprehensively watching him.]

Nebuchadnezzar [impatiently]: Daniel...where is Daniel?

Servant: My lord, I will get him

Nebuchadnezzar [raging]: I am not your lord!! Call Daniel. No, wait. Perhaps Daniel will not speak to me. Here, quickly, find something on which to write. Quickly, quickly. [The servant nervously rushes out about the room in confusion.] Here, take this. [He hands him an unraveled scroll.] Write on this.

Servant: But, my lord.

Nebuchadnezzar [excitedly]: I said don't call me that. Write! I, Nebuchadnezzar, once king of Babel, proud and sure in conquest and defiant in rage, placed all hope in my glory and majesty. My kingdom reached to all the ends of the earth; my power and wrath caused all mortals to tremble.

And then THE WORD came to me.

THE WORD shrouded itself in darkness and gave me a secret dream that I would be like a beast which eats grass until seven seasons passed.

I then jumped to my feet, girded on my sword, and assembled my legions. I told them to warn me when the enemy approached. My general said, "No army can attack proud

Babel and survive!" My captain said, "He who even entertains evil thoughts against Nebuchadnezzar will breathe no more." My servant said, "My lord, I would strike my son dead if he offended thee!" Then my general, my captain, and my servant led me to a high mountain and showed me that the earth was mine. In secured comfort, I mocked my fears and smirked before the dream.

But THE WORD!

THE WORD came in a voice and, more quickly that does a woman change her thoughts, I was transformed! Grass was my food, its dew added to my tears, and no one knew me for whom I was.

But I knew Babel, and was I not Babel's king? On all fours I cried out, "I am king of Babel; more so, I am king of the universe!" But no one listened and everything that I said sounded like the grunting and the bellowing of a beast.

My thoughts terrified me. Like an implacable legion they assembled against me and reminded me of my great arrogance. They cried out against me; they howled like victims near death; the thoughts were against me and my own voice was silenced. Like a muzzled dog who is burned alive, so was I to myself.

Amongst the legions of thoughts and my silent screams
I wondered and finally said to myself. "Who really is
The Mighty One? The Lord, The True Lord whose wisdom
brings itself to the deepest, secret and darkest dream.
Who aids Him in the interpretation of my dream, and who
will force Him to allow interpretation if He does not
so wish?
Where is my general? Where is my captain? Where is
my servant?
How am I to ride into The Lord's kingdom?
Where is such a chariot?
Who makes the spear with which to strike against Him?
Who can even guide me to the place of surrender?
What need does He have of human power?
What need does He have of spies to watch His realm?
The Lord cannot be found, nor harnessed, nor put off.
He does not wait for tomorrow but perpetually He says,

'Today!'
In His own inward counsels He says do it, and it is done.
He says now and it is not later.
He says seven years an animal, an animal will be the king of Babel, and for seven years I ate grass!"

At the end of the seven years I again became Nebuchadnezzar. I called together my wise men who were not wise in The Wisdom of the Lord. I asked them to explain the why and the how of That Power by which I became a beast of the field. Surrounded by their scrolls, they laughed and smirked and said, "Great Nebuchadnezzar, this is but an evil dream, an imagination. Who could do that to thee?"

And my wrath was kindled against these "wise" men. My blood ran hot, hotter than the flames which devoured the muzzled dog. My blood called out for theirs and I saw their blood run like the overflow from a cask of wine split by an axe. For The Lord possesses all might, wisdom and truth. He needs not such "wise men." Nor does He need the city of Babel and its king.

Henceforth I decree that every seventh year a feast will be held in Babel. It will be called "The Feast of the Transformation." On that day the lepers, the poor, the orphans, the widows, and all those spiritually and physically crippled are to be praised as God's beloved. The transformation of Nebuchadnezzar is to recited; all are to be told how Nebuchadnezzar became a beast and was no longer king. They are to be told how he spent his last years thanking The True God for having made him a beast and for having known The True God's might.

And, if during The Feast of the Transformation, a false "wise" man is found, he is to be led through the streets clad like a beast. He is to carry his writings with him. His writings, however, are to be torn to shreds and bound like a torch of hay. As he is pushed through the streets, let everyone cry, "The Lord, The Lord is the Mighty one. His actions are swift and powerful. His secrets no man knows, no, not one."

And now I will wait for soon The Fashioner of Kings and Beasts will again transform me. I do not know if this mere trifle of a testimony to His power will find favor in His eyes. I only know that there is in the distance an invisible land where The Almighty One's favor and peace turn nightmare into joy.

Thus have I, I--Nebuchadnezzar made known to all people the power of The True God. Great Babel is humbled. It has One True Lord and should seek no other.

EGMONT AND THE THEOLOGIAN

A Vision in the Dialectic of Hope

CHARACTERS

CLOWN
THE CHORUS IS SPOKEN BY A CHILD
EGMONT
DIETRICH BONHOEFFER
CHILDREN, WOMEN, AND MEN OF THE
    CONCENTRATION CAMP
1ST SOLDIER
2ND SOLDIER
STOCKBROKER
INVESTOR
RINGMASTER
POPCORN SELLER
LION TAMER
SWORDSWALLOWER
WOMEN AND CHILDREN OF THE CIRCUS

Stage Directions

Beethoven's "Incidental Music to Goethe's Egmont" should be playing as the people enter the theater and as they leave at the end of the fourth act. If one wishes to read the play alone or with others, the same music should also be played.

The Prologue and quotation from Goethe should be read in that order by the clown.

The Chorus should be read by a child.

PROLOGUE

[Both the Prologue and the quote from Goethe are to be read by a clown on a darkened stage with half-light on the clown.]

Count Egmont of Flanders was executed by the Spanish Catholic forces of Phillip II in 1568. Dietrich Bonhoeffer, a Christian theologian, was hanged by the Nazis in 1945. Both men died trying to safeguard the human right of freedom of conscience.

Yet each of these individuals acted from different reasons and motives. Egmont was a nobleman by birth and resented foreign invaders in his country. Bonhoeffer believed it was a Christian's duty to remove from authority any leader like Adolph Hitler who would take the place of God. Bonhoeffer was also actively involved in the plot to kill Hitler.

Thus we have different individuals acting from different motives. Yet both are adamantly opposed to tyranny and dictatorial power. It is lamentable that two such individuals could not meet. It is lamentable because the interchange of thought between the two would be illuminating and instructive to most of us.

Be that as it may, lamentations do not instruct us. Consequently the author has seen fit to bring Egmont and Bonhoeffer together. This has been done primarily to juxtaposition the highest form of romantic humanism with an active form of Christian witness.

Egmont remains a man of his century, but he is summoned to Bonhoeffer's era through the power of our reflective imaginations.

And that God, whom in their rage they have insulted, sends down his angel from on high; at the hallowed touch of the messenger bolts and bars fly back; he pours around our friend a flood of splendor, and leads him gently through the night to liberty.

Goethe, EGMONT, Act V.

ACT ONE

Scene One

CHORUS [This is spoken by a child on a darkened stage with full light being on the child.]:

Egmont--
Thou, the thunder crash
and earth's resounding
shudder.
Nobility arising before
wantonness,
and the standing of one of scorn
in mockery of the Spanish born--

Thy spirit again upon us.
Thy blessing again to us.
As now we talk,
as now we balk--
no defiance now
where once thy challenging brow.

Is defiance no more?
Does striving for the highest
fall by the wayside of rhetoric?
And will all-too-clever men always
march forward in their wanton procession
as those satisfied with another's transgression?

Do not forget us, Egmont.
Do not scorn too much
this shallow, blighted
world.

It does not seem as it once did then,
when courage cried out for action.
Now a mechanized civilization
belittles the glory of individual
struggle.
Now the "fearless" press their buttons,
and children's lives are the food of gluttons.

Egmont, where thou once wept for a country
now beweep the world,
and seek again within the heart of hearts
another man of thy persuasion,
who mocks the tyrant
and claims our liberty!

Scene Two

[As the lights come up slightly, a prison cell is seen. For a few seconds the stage is dimly lit. Dietrich Bonhoeffer is a heavy set man of medium height in his late thirties. He is partially bald and wears wire glasses. He is attired in gray prison garb. Egmont is in his mid-forties and attired in the dress of a nobleman of the 16th century. He has greying hair and a refined attractive appearance. The bars in the background display a rope with a hangman's loop on the other side of the bars. There is a table, a chair, a Bible, notes, letters, and writing materials. There is a copy of Albrecht Durer's "Apocalypse" on the wall. Bonhoeffer has his head cradled in his arms upon the table. The stage is dimly lit. Egmont places his hand on Bonhoeffer's shoulder. As Egmont speaks the lights gradually increase.]

EGMONT [gradual tempo and force increasing in strength]:
I know, I know this world is but a show.
Seek thy harbored glory first.
And if there be a tyrant's gloom
that defies thy will and proclaims thy country's doom,
then stand as I and shout thy fierceness.
No one, no power shall endure
the spirit we rebellious men procure.

No wealth, no lady, no art, and no religion
stand before freedom's decision:
    to die in the quest of all,
    to defy and thus affirm,
    to denounce that infringement.
        which leads to imprisonment.
They cannot kill thy spirit!
They cannot touch thy life!
What is matter if it does not matter?

Up my friend--climb the scaffold floor
and let those in eternity sing thy hymns.
The stars are the symphony.
Thy death--a theophany.

What did it offer the, this life
of finitude and strife?
What was its meaning
while now they heart is beating?
For thy glory is for thy nation,
and thy life is a proclamation
of man beyond himself.

Mock their hanging rope!
Decry their sentence!
Show them not repentance!
Thou hast made sublimity.
Thou hast scorned servility.
Thou hast denounced the manacle
of invader, plunderer, and betrayer.
Heaven's gate becomes thy harbor--
Thee--a shipwrecked vessel ever looking starward.
Look up, eternity's thy mother,
and I--thy brother!

BONHOEFFER:
Your thoughts rise beyond the stars,
but they speak of an honor which is not ours.
The world of churches and men of scrolls
often times fail freedom to extol.
Their interpretations and sacred rites
often denounce the sphere of valor's might.

Still, I do not die for honor's title.
I do not face the rope of condemnation
for solely a wordly proclamation.
It is true I am your brother,
but we are one beneath an Other.
It is for Him; I go.
It is for Him; I defy the tyrant.
It is not for heroic edification.
Rather, it is a witness to His Proclamation.

EGMONT:
But the struggle for the right beckons me here.
It has always been history's denunciation I fear.

BONHOEFFER:
I do not denounce right.
I do not denounce courage.
I do not denounce honor.
That which you have scorned; I have scorned.
Yet there is great mystery in that you
and I were born
Life is significant in all its aspects.
I have believed in the depths of things
I have cared; I and He have shared
the many thoughts of time and distance.
We have known each other.
We have lived each instant.

EGMONT:
Then thou hast found meaning beyond the forces of history?
There is more than the history of man's noble repertory of deeds and feats of wonder?

BONHOEFFER:
Yes, far more...far more.
What it all is, I cannot say.
And if I could then only language
would have its day.
But you are correct in a belief in wonder.
One came who tore false gods asunder.
He showed me that the world was good,

but nothing was so good as
His coming.
He showed me the meaning of faith
through the preaching of His word.
He unfurled meaning more than you and
I,
and yet without us what He showed
would be a lie.

EGMONT:
That is fine; I suppose...
Regardless, I see the military movements
of a tyrant,
necessary rebellion,
and man-willed resurrection.

BONHOEFFER:
Many of the things you see;
I see.
Yet I still hope for things I cannot see.

EGMONT:
What are we discussing?
There is justice, and there is injustice.
One must choose justice.
It is that simple.

BONHOEFFER:
Yes, but there is still time in
other dimensions.
Time to weigh the fine points
of argument,
time to see again the reasons
which move with the ages,
time to recount again the
endless pages.
Let us not hurry.
Soon enough we meet death surely.

EGMONT [somberly]:
Unfortunately the lovers of
justice have too little time.

BONHOEFFER:
Regardless, there is no need to
hurry if one only believes.
Many have thought and argued about the
place of God in history and men who
would make themselves "gods" of history.
I would show you that history's
meaning begins with Jesus Christ as
history's center.
It is through Him that death is
conquered.
It is through Him that we hope
not only for life eternal,
but we also hope
for a better world for
future generations.
I have believed and taught this.
And without a belief in such things
my life would have been so much
theological play.
What I am discussing is not merely a
topic for scholarly contemplation
logic and recitation.
It is not merely a question for
sharp-witted assessors
and
quick-tongued professors.
It is a question of all time:
whether there is a meaning in each breath;
whether life itself is more than death.

EGMONT:
But history could be just so many
recurring events before the void.
I have never worried about such things.
In my time the hero was as God.
Courage said all. Each day looked forward to
grandeur.
Nobility rode the wind of thought.
Heroism was what we sought.
I do not understand these times

of cheap wealth and a lack of verse.
I do not comprehend the growing
mechanisms of the earth.
Regardless, let me for one week watch
men in action,
and see if my times were so very different.
[Egmont exits.]

BONHOEFFER:
Such a spirit as Egmont's comes to me!
I who am bound to this cell's confinement.
I who often wonder if my thoughts for assassination
were to God an abomination.
Egmont, Egmont, the man of total independence
comes to praise me and announce my greatness.
I, I the one of dependence--
yet to be dependent on God....
It is difficult to explain to Egmont
life's need for its Center.
It is difficult to discuss the ends
of sin.
To him this makes no difference.
What matters in his eyes is resistance.
However, the consequences of man-willed
resurrection
he will surely come to know.
[The lights fall.]

ACT TWO
Scene One

[Concentration camp. Stage right are eight to ten Jewish men, women, and children dressed in rags, with the Star of David on the left breast. Stage center are two Nazi SS men watching the Jews proceeding off the stage. Between them the control lever for the poisonous gas is situated. Egmont, stage left, is barely visible. There is a low chant among the Jews as they march off the stage.]

FIRST SOLDIER:
Is this the nobility of the Reich?
We hurl its people from our sight.
We deceive them; we do not tell them
that their singing breath
is the last before the face of death.

SECOND SOLDIER:
Silence! You know better than to question
our orders and High Command decisions.
What they have said is absolute
it admits of no revisions.

FIRST SOLDIER:
Then with the throwing of the lever
you and I have ceased to be,
and it will matter little
what we're forced to see....
Yet they all have lives.
Each one with his own
beliefs and sudden yearnings. [He hesitates a moment.]
<u>It is we ourselves we're</u>
<u>búrning!</u>
Are we men to stand and let pass by
commands through which a leader lies?

Let them go, we cannot pass judgment.
They were born to be;
it's for us to set them free.

SECOND SOLDIER:
And what is it that we free them to?
A life in the market, a time
for amusement, a few children?
Surely that will not alter the world.
It is now our sacred mission
to rid the world of its division.
There must be only Germany.
All else is infamy.
We must destroy; we must destroy!
There is no concern for girls and boys!
We cannot take account
of common lives of no account.
We give them death and their God.

[He moves to the lever.]

FIRST SOLDIER:
Wait!
What then had you and I?
We've lived.
We've watched the passing of the seasons.
We've talked of war and wives and reasons.
It was something to us both.
And now because of black uniforms
and the blind uniformity of new regime,
have we only become the servants
of a death machine?

SECOND SOLDIER:
Enough of this!
Because I have been commanded;
I obey.

[The switch is thrown. Light is now on Egmont. All other lights are extinguished.]

EGMONT:
What has become of thee, oh world?
There is no longer passion in death.
These people die like flies.
Death, oh wonder and enchantment,
somehow, somewhere your significance was lost.
Wholesale slaughter--to trick a people
and swindle life from them...
And the swindler would blame the "High Command."
Well, the "High Command" is
no command at all.
And "obedience" to a madman
is madness itself.

And once the Germans were
a tortured people.
Ravaged by "civilized"
invaders not so long ago.
Burdened, trying to survive,
they willed themselves back
upon history's stage.

Men resurrected a country.
and threw off the yoke
of foreign tribute.
How fine!
How noble!
Only to be besmirched
with death camps.
Senseless death camps.

Is it then that human power unchecked
and without limitation
resurrects more evil than good?
Is it under the thoughts of lofty
struggle,
that the monster quietly
enters to torture,
burn, and kill?

[The lights fall.]

Scene Two

[The same prison cell as Act One.]

PRISON GUARD [cheerfully and with admiration.]:
Letters, Doctor. I hope that your confinement will
soon be over.

BONHOEFFER [smiling]:
Thank you. I hope and pray
your hopes are heard.

[The guard exits. Bonhoeffer picks up the Bible, ponders and reads aloud slowly.]

BONHOEFFER:
Behold what I have built I am breaking down, and what I have planted I am plucking up....And do you seek great things for yourself? Seek them not...but I will give your life as a prize of war! [slowly]
Jeremiah...Jeremiah, no matter what I do or say
I know the prophet will have his day....
O God, who does call and to whom we respond,
if Thou would answer to the living
tell me now of Thy merciful giving! [He moves to the back of the stage.]
Still, I know that I must wait in turn.
I must wait and have patience.
Yet my spirit has called out in question
the oldest thought of our dimension:

Who am I?* They often tell me
that I walk from my cell
deliberately, calmly, firmly,
like a nobleman from his castle.

Who am I? They often tell me

---

* Dietrich Bonhoeffer. Widerstand und Ergbung. München: Chr. Kaiser Verlag, 1959; pp. 242-243. This translation as well as the others that will appear in this play are my own.

that I speak with the jailers
freely, friendly, clearly,
as if I were the one in command.

Who am I? They also tell me
that I bear the days of misfortune
quietly, cheerfully, proudly,
as one who has lived for victories.

[Egmont returns and is barely visible. Bonhoeffer does not notice him.]

Who am I really? What the others tell me?
Or am I only that which I know of myself?
turbulent, longing, sick, like a bird in a cage,
grappling with life's breath as it strangles me,
hungry for colors, for flowers, for the
singing of birds,
thirsting for kind words, for human surroundings,
trembling with rage over both despotism
and paltry insult,
spun 'round in expectation of great events,
powerlessly fearing for friends at an infinite distance;
exhausted and empty at praying, thinking, and creating,
lifeless; and ready for the final leave-taking.

Who am I? This or the other?
Am I this one today and tomorrow the other?
Am I both together? Before men--a hypocrite
and before myself--a scorned and wretched weakling?
Or yet, is there still something within me resembling a beaten army,
which is already retreating from hard-won victory?

Who am I? They mock me, these lonely questions of mine.
Whoever I am, Thou knowest me, O God, I am Thine.

[Silence. Bonhoeffer turns and sees Egmont. Egmont is melancholic.]

EGMONT:
Who we are at this time, I am afraid to say.

I have tried to understand this world
and I have been lost to sorrow
that this world has learned to live
on the price of the lives it borrows.
Let us quickly pass away from this to another place,
Any other time or space.

BONHOEFFER [fiercely]:
This is no answer!
We cannot forsake this world
for another.
We cannot say that we are chosen
and must not bother
with those who will be
left and torn and scarred
by this, our generation.

EGMONT:
What else can be done?
You are powerless and
are living in a world gone mad.

BONHOEFFER:
Regardless, did you find,
since last we met,
the daring thoughts of
<u>man-willed resurrection?</u>
Did you come to know the
demonic tortures
of such "resurrected men"?

EGMONT:
I saw...I saw what I fear
can only add to the world's despair.

BONHOEFFER:
Speak! What is it that you have come to know?
Does this world still seem “a show”?

EGMONT:
I went to the concentration camps.
I saw the children

being paraded to a cleansing
which was itself their ending.
And the guards spoke to one another
in an argument concerning death's lever
of who was to blame
for the horrid shame
as that which man has done.
And in those deaths there was
no passion.
They were tricked and swindled.
They were treated as so much meat
before the butcher.
I felt the guilt in that I am
man.
I see no hope of expiation now
that I have come again.
Let us quickly go; a week here
is a week too long.
Let us both depart; for me my
world is forever gone.

BONHOEFFER [slowly]:
It is now the other lives that we must treasure,
and weep for as we watch
the motions of the clock.
And know that we have become
helpless but have tried.
We have attempted to unmask evil,
but it has not stopped the
brutal onrushing
of man's Satanic plunging
into a formless world.
And I have said that man was
coming of age,
that he was turning a final page
for his own fulfillment.
But now he has become so strong
that he will not accept any
limitations of life.
He has made so much and he has
solved so much that
his strength becomes his weakness.

He forgets the gentle thoughts of meekness.

EGMONT:
It is true...,Still, I must go out
again and attempt to find
the noble thoughts of daring
which once bespoke a higher life
than evil acts and strife.
It cannot all have passed away
since last I met the day. [Egmont exits.]

BONHOEFFER:
I am afraid he seeks again a noble aristocracy
and will find more readily a cheap hypocrisy.
I am afraid he seeks a romantic sensitivity
and will only discover a feverish activity.

[The lights fall.]

ACT THREE
Scene One

[Stockbrokerage office. Tickertapes. Desk stage right with investor and stockbroker. Entire American bourgeois atmosphere. Egmont, stage left, is barely visible.]

STOCKBROKER:
The war, ah, the war, it has relieved our oppression.
Thanks to it we've conquered the depression.
Our investments in armaments and supplies
have aided the administration
and made sound again the nation.

INVESTOR:
Yes, we prosper
on what becomes machine-gun fodder.
We sit and take our coffee.
We speak of our investments.
Still, there is something shocking
in how I make my profits.
Something sudden grips me
each time I touch my pocket.

STOCKBROKER:
What is that to us?
If you want to make a killing,
and you want the dollar-safety
then support the war and country.
ACT NOW.
Surely the war is soon to end.
Best make money now and
leave your conscience to attend.

INVESTOR:
Certainly we make a killing,

each penny buys a round
each cent another bullet
each dollar fills the mud
with gallons of another's blood.

STOCKBROKER [irritated]:
Look, my time is filled.
Do you want to invest or debate?
I cannot force the war's conclusion.
I can only offer you a taste for action,
for quick wealth and security.

INVESTOR:
I invest; I invest.
I am no different than the rest.

[Stage darkened. Light only on Egmont.]

EGMONT:
In my time there was more time
to discuss in a market place
the movings of our race.
Today this present market
of symbols and usury,
of points and investments,
gives man no time for reassessment
of whom he has come to be
of how he measures to his measure.
He only measures wealth
and his soul hangs on a
figure's dance.

I used to ride at full gallop
to the place of commerce
and stop and listen and parley for a while.
Yes, then transactions seemed worthwhile.
Persons met and persons listened
of whom was born or died or christened.
Now, there's only a mechanical watching
of a board of gain or losing.
Man and world have moved so fast;
there's little left that's meant to last.

Scene Two

[The same prison cell as in Act One.]

BONHOEFFER [recollecting]:
Egmont, the romantic Count Egmont.
Once, before his execution,
he loved Clara.
He would know the heaviness of my
sorrow that I must lose
Marie.
Oh, that again she and I walked
the fields and the long, lush
grass played its melody
in the winds.
The freshness of my memory of those
times,
when earth and Thou and she were one
and mine...

[Stricken with the gravity of knowing life's depths and the possible loss of everything. Bonhoeffer speaks anxiously.]

Egmont, hasten quickly!
Egmont, you are courage:
the hope for all the living and the greatness
of the race
which will live
which will last.

[Egmont is again seen by the audience. Half-light is on him. He is not seen by Bonhoeffer.]

Egmont knows this tale of loneliness,
of the staleness of the prison,
of the thoughts once born
which have risen giving voice
to Freedom;
and Freedom listens but will
not respond.

[He notices Egmont.]

EGMONT:
Listen, thou knowest there is never
one side without the other.
If there is misfortune then there is also fortune.
One never was without the other.
Thou knowest these matters well.
Listen to me, express thy thoughts on the matter;
bring forth thy spirit, unbind thyself.
Speak of Occurrence and despair.
Speak of the spinning and The Care.

BONHOEFFER:
Fortune and misfortune*
vanquishing they overcome us;
and, like heat and frost
at first contact,
they can scarcely be distinguished.

As meteors
hurled from unearthly heights,
shining and threatening they mold
their path above us.

Confounded and afflicted we stand
before the wreckage
of our dull, commonplace lives.

Huge and ominous,
devastating, destroying,
are fortune and misfortune
--requested or unrequested
they add to
the convulsions of men
changing and re-making
the wreckage
with severity and dedication.

---

* Ibid., pp. 223-224.

Fortune has its terror
Misfortune has a sweetness,
Indistinguishable they shine forth from eternity
and come to all.
Both are great and terrifying.

Men, far and near,
rush hither and look,
and gape
half envious, half terrified
into the Vortex
where the Eternal
creates and destroys,
confusing and entangling
this earthly drama.
What is fortune? What is
misfortune?

Only time decides between the two.
When the incomprehensible excitement
of sudden Occurrence
changes our exhausting and torturing tedium,
when the weary, insidious hour of day
first discloses misfortune's true appearance,
then do most of us,
disillusioned and bored,
turn away from the
weariness of lifeless unhappiness.
[Bonhoeffer hesitates and catches his meaning.]
But that is the hour of truth,
the hour of the mother and her children,
the hour of friends and brothers--
the true hour which illuminates
all misfortune
and gently hides it
in a quiet,
unearthly splendor.

EGMONT [after a few moments]:
"The hour of truth...
and unearthly splendor..."
It is to that hour the world

must be recalled.
I say this because I have been
to the market in America.
There I have seen a
sophisticated bandit culture.
It is a place where
all is permitted
provided investments are successful
and MAMMON is the judge of success.
It is a place where
they also steal
the daily "hour of truth"
from themselves.

BONHOEFFER:
To strive to succeed is
always necessary, yet
too much is always
made of it.
And as for sophistication,
it practically rules the world.
And from sophistication
come the sophists with their
"gods"--
"gods" which are far too human
to be in any sense divine.

EGMONT:
Yes, iconoclasts have destroyed some gods,
but the most important one that they forgot
is the one which has brought this world to naught.
The one of public admiration;
the one which is called "sophistication."
There is only insipid tedium
in the shallow world
of what we are to wear,
where we are to eat,
what is "the thing to do"
and whom we are to meet.
Most have forgotten heaven's oldest remittance.

BONHOEFFER [highly amused]:
Which is?

EGMONT:
The principle of indifference!
Each moves too fast before the clock
and spends his life in idle talk.
Each looks and fails to see
that he has forgotten first to be.

BONHOEFFER:
Then you've seen the fall of dignity
and the laughing at nobility
which now adulterates the world.

EGMONT:
Yes, but dignity and nobility
and the love of the good
must still survive.

BONHOEFFER:
It is precisely the love of dignity,
nobility, and the goodness which must be
sought, found, and nurtured.

EGMONT:
But where to look?

BONHOEFFER:
Seek the single one striving
for the highest.
Seek the one who knows his
own time must end.
He will be your guide
to cross to Freedom's side.

[The lights fall.]

ACT FOUR
Scene One

[Circus trailer. Posters of the circus cover the walls. There is a bed on which a clown is lying. Egmont is barely visible. Solemn attitudes on the faces of the ringmaster, lion tamer, swordswallower and other performers. Children and women who are a part of the circus are also seen. A popcorn seller who is new to the circus is scanning the ceiling.]

RINGMASTER [hastening popcorn seller, lion tamer and swordswallower to the clown's bed]:
Quickly! A clown is dying.

POPCORN SELLER:
Only a clown?

LION TAMER [fiercely raising his whip to the popcorn seller]:
Back off!

SWORDSWALLOWER [irritated with popcorn seller]:
Keep silence!

[Ringmaster, popcorn seller, swordswallower, lion tamer, women and children move towards the bed. The women and children are weeping softly.]

CLOWN:
Be not sorry brothers;
I have destroyed the fears
--if only for an instant--
of those who came and watched
with the passing of the years.
For those who came to laugh awhile,
I brushed away their tears.
I have conquered death and loss

through my pranks and foolish wit.
I have sanctified our laughing
much more than those of Sacred Writ!
And the children! Yes! The children!
They always beckoned near--
what more could I or God Himself
ask of life throughout the years?

I am not worth a great amount
In the ages that will pass.
I do not have a legacy that
shall be counted as very much
in the eyes of those who pass
on very little.
My name is not one for history
and this is always good
for history has never recorded
precisely what it should.
Yet I came to know in my own time
the weeping and the laughing,
the jeering laughter,
the sighs,
the cries,
and the why's of why
I was put here.
It was only for an instant
to dance awhile, to sing,
and pace upon the ground.
Yet before me now the children all
are laughing,
and many hands are clapping,
and...and...

[Lights fade gradually on the clown. Now there is only half-light on Egmont.]

EGMONT [sadly but with strength]:
For this sudden passing
the circus is something less
--more so--
the world is a great deal less.
Those who had gathered saw

the passing on of goodness.
Other clowns will come it is true.
But none will be as he.
None again will have his touch of wonder
and his laughing spirit.
And few will say as he did
to the inner command which
calls all clowns, "Yes, I'll be it!
I will continue!
I will continue despite the laughter
of the cynics
for it was I who willed to even
make the cynics laugh!
It was I who stopped the hopeless
from their plunging if only for
an instant!
It is I who have come to know
THE ETERNITY OF THE MOMENT
for all laughed, yes, for a second!"

[Egmont ponders his thought. Then he speaks slowly and deliberately.]

So then it is not just "the few"
who receive
God's call
or "the great men" only.
It comes to all.
But none so well respond
as the laughing jokings of clowns.
Nothing greater rises to God's ear
than the buffoon's mockery of fear!

Scene Two

[Same prison cell as in Act One.]

BONHOEFFER:
Soon enough surely my life is fulfilled.
And what have I come to know
since now I will be set free from this prison's odor?

Is it that there are stations
on Freedom's road?
Yes, but no one can speak for all.
Each one must discover for one's self
the holy meaning of The Other.
Yet there are stations on
Freedom's road.
Discipline, Action, Suffering
and Death
are for us
guides.

Discipline*

If you go out to seek Freedom, then learn
at the beginning
to discipline your perceptions and your mind, so that
the wild desires of your body do no lead you
into bondage.
Your mind and body must be undefiled
and totally under your control,
so that obediently they will seek after the
goal which is set for them.
No one ever learned the secret of Freedom
except through discipline.

Action

Not what is pleasing.
but what is right you must
dare to do.
Not by soaring on the wings of possibility,
but by boldly grasping the actual,
not in the flight of thought
but only in action is there Freedom.
Turn from your doubts and go out
to the storm of Occurrence,
sustained only by God's command and your faith;
and Freedom, rejoicing will receive your spirit.

---

* Ibid., pp. 250-251.

Suffering

There is a sudden transformation.
Your strong, effective hands are bound.
Powerless and alone you see the end of
your activity.
Still, you hope, laying your cause
in Stronger Hands which comfort and console.
Only for an instant you touched upon Freedom,
then you gave it over to God
in order that He would will its perfection.

[Egmont again returns.]

Death

Come now, highest feast on the road
to Eternal Freedom.
Death -- destroy the base bondage of
chain and wall,
destroy our ephemeral bodies and
out deluded senses
that we may finally behold what
temporally we are unable to see.
FREEDOM, we have sought thee
in discipline, in action; in suffering;
dying we now know Thee as THE PRESENCE OF GOD!

[There is a silence for a few seconds.]

EGMONT:
The hour hastens to the FINAL FREEDOM.

BONHOEFFER [smiling]:
Yes, but will "the striving for the highest" continue?

EGMONT:
It will. I am sure that it will.
After the struggle for the highest
has been attempted,
and we have done what we could,
I am sure that God draws near.

BONHOEFFER:
Acceptance, yes, acceptance
for what it is, for what is was
that we have done in honesty,
of whom we've come to be--
of what we now call free.
And still there is always dignity
despite our place or what we face
in the hour which will come.
[There is a knock at the prison door.]
Let us go in silence. [solemnly]
Stay with me as I walk
those final steps to heaven's door.
Let us not rush nor be too far behind.
Patiently I've lived and patiently I'll die.
No sound they'll hear nor complaint.
[He turns to Egmont.]
And now we've said what must be said
for those who will live on after--
that nations which forget Mystery
must meet their own disaster,
that "sophisticated" investment killing
will have its henchmen willing,
that still for all there's hope
despite the swinging rope.
[The light is now only on Bonhoeffer. He stares at the audience and then seems to see something above the people.]
O God,
Who punishes sin and willingly forgives,
I have loved this people.
I have born its disgrace and its oppression
and seen its Redemption -- that is enough.
Hold me, contain me! My staff is sinking.
O faithful God, prepare my grave.

[The lights fall.]

REMEMBER TORRES!

CHARACTERS

GOMEZ

GONZALES

CARDINAL

ELENA

ISABELLA

CAMILO TORRES

PEDRO

MIGUEL

COMMUNIST

NIHILIST

SOCIALIST

CARDINAL'S SECRETARY

STUDENTS

SOLDIERS AND PEOPLE OF THE REVOLUTION

ACT ONE

[The setting is a living room in a Colombian hacienda. There are protective bars on the windows. The entire room is extravagantly decorated with elegant Spanish furniture and silver candle fixtures. Persian carpets, glass bookcases of polished wood, and expensive art objects are to be seen. A portable bar is situated in front of the large and comfortable sofa in the middle of the room. The sofa is directly facing the audience. To the right and left of the sofa are individual, expensive, large, soft chairs. Gomez is sitting in one chair, and Gonzales is lounging on the sofa. They are both overweight, greasy men in their mid-fifties. Their hands look like small soft pillows. Both appear remarkably identical in their pampered dress and bearing. As the act begins both are drinking whiskey.]

Gomez: Would you like some more whiskey?

Gonzales: Yes, I would! It is excellent. Where did you get it?

Gomez [going to the bar in front of the sofa]: I had it imported from the United States. It is from Kentucky.

Gonzales: Yes, Kentucky is a great country.

Gomez: I believe they call Kentucky a state.

Gonzales: Yes, you're right: a state part of the United States. That great land of beauty, industry, war, and...

Gomez: ...and gold!

Gonzales: Yes, and gold.

Gomez: Besides, it is an aristocratic country. Their symbol is the eagle.

Gonzales: From what I have heard recently, it should be the buzzard.

Gomez: Why do you say that?

Gonzales: Because the Americans have a tendency to live off dead countries.

Gomez: No...no. That is not true. The eagle is the right symbol because the Americans swoop down, give us money, and secure our power.

Gonzales: Yes, but then we buy their whiskey, guns, and machinery. However, I will agree to the symbol of the eagle. Nevertheless they should take the olive branch out of its mouth and replace it with a silver dollar.

Gomez [laughing]: Very good. And they should find a way for the eagle to bite the dollar to see if it is still good.

Gonzales [laughing]: But why are we complaining?

Gomez: I don't know.

Gonzales: Why should we discuss this matter so lightly? Have not the Americans done us a lot of good?

Gomez: They have! They have!

Gonzales: Still, one should be sensitive to world problems if only for the feeling of nobility.

Gomez: Yes, we must have all the luxuries. [Both laugh. Elena, the attractive twenty year old daughter of Gomez, enters the room.]

Elena: Father, the Cardinal is here and would like to see you.

Gomez: Show him in. [Elena exits.]

Gonzales: I had better go. I am in too good of a mood to give my confession...or hear the Cardinal's.

Gomez: Don't leave me with him...I...[The Cardinal enters, he is extremely fat and bears a striking resemblance to Gomez and Gonzales. He is dressed in a scarlet cape and wears the pectoral crucifix which is attached to an elaborate gold chain. One expensive ring is seen on each hand.] Your Eminence! How wonderful it is to see you. [Gomez bows and kisses the Cardinal's ring.]

Gonzales [greeting the Cardinal and kissing his ring]: Your Eminence! A pleasure to see you. Excuse me, but I must return to my hacienda.

Cardinal: Could it wait a few moments? This is rather important. I would like to speak to the two of you together.

Gonzales [obsequiously]: Why certainly, your Eminence, certainly.

Cardinal: I trust that both of you are well.

Gomez: Yes, your Eminence, I never felt better.

Gonzales: Yes, your Eminence, but I have missed our past conversations concerning <u>our</u> infallibility. [All three laugh.]

Cardinal: Yes, yes of course.

Gomez: And how are you, your Eminence?

Cardinal: Well, I feel fine I must say. [glancing at the bar] Ah...do you have any...

Gonzales [taunting him]: Ah...any altar wine, your Eminence?

Cardinal [annoyed at first]: That's enough...[But he reconsiders.] or on second thought [smiling] that really isn't quite enough.

Gomez: Perhaps some American whiskey?

Cardinal: Since you offer it. [Gomez goes and gets a drink for the Cardinal. Gonzales also gets a healthy drink for himself. By now Gonzales is starting to slip into a very euphoric state.]

Gonzales: And what brings you to the Gomez hacienda?

Cardinal [sipping the whiskey]: Excellent...excellent.

Gonzales [smiling with the slack-jawed look of an imbecile]: It's not just another hacienda, your Eminence.

Cardinal: No, I mean the whiskey.

Gomez: But that goes along with the hacienda.

Cardinal [putting down his glass]: Which brings me to the reason for my visit. Do both of you like things the way they are?

Gomez: They were never better.

Gonzales [He has been drinking steadily and is now almost completely drunk. He laughs.]: Of course we need your blessing now and then to take care of us both in this world and the next. But then...

Cardinal [He is now quite serious.]: I know...I know. But listen...if things are to remain as they are, we are going to have problems.

Gomez [startled]: Certainly you don't advise a change?

Cardinal: Hardly, but a young priest does.

Gonzales: Simple. Excommunicate him.

Gomez: Exactly.

Cardinal: Not quite so simple. If I excommunicate him, the common people will look upon him as a martyr for the cause of social justice, and then we will really have a problem on our hands.

Gonzales: Who is the priest?

Cardinal: Father Camilo Torres.

Gomez: Can he be bribed?

Cardinal: Not this one.

Gonzales: Can he be threatened?

Cardinal: No.

Gomez: Is his mother living? She is probably able to influence him. If you as a Cardinal got in touch with her, perhaps...

Cardinal: No...no, it wouldn't work.

Gonzales [boisterously drunk]: There have been radical priests before. Let him have his say. Things will die down, and we will be sitting here a year from now calm and secure again.

Cardinal: I hope you are right. However, this one is educated. He has a degree from the University of Louvain in sociology. He is brilliant and has already begun to effectively organize segments of the population against us.

Gomez: What are we supposed to do?

Gonzales: Yes, what could we possibly do anyway?

Cardinal: I was thinking that you and the fifteen other major land owners could make a gesture.

Gonzales [drunk and enraged]: You don't mean give up something?

Cardinal: It would only be a small gesture. It would not be lasting. If you gave some extra money to your workers periodically, things would calm down. I and the bishops as well as some trusted priests could turn the people away from Torres and lead them back to our way of thinking.

Gonzales: Impossible! Impossible! Your Eminence, I barely have enough for the necessities of life.

Gomez: I must send my daughter to a foreign university, preferably in the United States. She must have a British sports car and all the luxuries. If she does not have these things how will she find a husband who suits me! No, it is impossible to give anything at this time.

Gonzales: Impossible!

Cardinal: But...

Gonzales: But if we give our workers more money now, they will only demand more in the future. No, leave things as they are.

Cardinal: You don't understand. If you don't give them something now you may have nothing to give them in the future. That is a definite possibility.

Gomez: There may be some other way. You say this Father Torres is educated. What kind of degree does he have in...what was it? Socio...

Cardinal: Sociology.

Gonzales: What's that?

Cardinal: A study that could aid Torres and his people in destroying us.

Gonzales: Oh...well...why, he shouldn't have been allowed to study that in the first place.

Gomez [irritated]: Gonzales, would you shut up!

Gonzales [totally drunk and slurring his words]: All right, but I don't see...

Cardinal: Gentlemen, gentlemen, let us not argue among ourselves. We have a common enemy to be gotten rid of.

Gomez: You're right, your Eminence. What kind of a degree does this young priest have?

Cardinal: A master of arts degree.

Gomez: And are there higher degrees?

Cardinal: Yes, the University of Louvain offers a doctorate.

Gomez: Ah-ha!

Cardinal: What are you saying?

Gomez: And where is this university?

Cardinal: In Europe...Belgium.

Gomez: Perfect!

Cardinal: I think I see what you're getting at.

Gonzales [helplessly drunk]: What? What? See what?

Gomez [ignoring Gonzales]: It's simple. Agree with Father Torres.

Gonzales: What? What are you saying?

Gomez [still ignoring Gonzales]: Listen, your Eminence, tell Father Torres that you agree with his program of social reform. However, ask him if he would not like to study a little longer at Louvain in order to get a "higher" degree. After he has completed his education he can return to Colombia and continue his work with the people. While he is away we can work out a new strategy for ourselves.

Cardinal [reflecting]: It might work. Yes, [smiling] yes, it might work. I could...so to speak...use my power for his best interests.

Gomez [smiling]: I should think, your Eminence, that your power would not only work for his best interests but also for our own.

Gonzales [slurring his words]: Excellent...excellent!

Cardinal [thinking out loud]: Yes, I could touch his vanity in the name of God.

Gomez: What was that?

Cardinal: Why, I could say to him that the Church might more readily delegate greater authority to him if he had a doctorate in his field.

Gomez: Precisely.

Gonzales [by now unaware of everything]: Precisely!

Cardinal [finishing his drink]: Well, I had best be going. Thank you for the whiskey and...the advice. [Gonzales and Gomez stand. Gomez has to help steady Gonzales.]

Gomez: Good-bye, your Eminence, and good luck.

Gonzales [really not knowing what he is doing]: Good luck, your Eminence, and say some Masses for the patron saint of Kentucky. Bill me at your convenience. [The Cardinal tries to understand him, but Gonzales falls back into his chair and shuts his eyes with his head leaning to one side.]

Cardinal [to Gomez]: Take good care of our friend. [The Cardinal exits. Gomez studies Gonzales for a few seconds.]

Gomez: Gonzales...Gonzales, you ass, wake up.

Gonzales [half-groggy]: How much did it cost us?

Gomez [laughing]: Nothing. Not even an extra glass of whiskey.

Gonzales: Really. Well...well...

Gomez: I'll get you some coffee. [calling off stage] Elena...Elena. [Elena enters.]

Elena: Yes, father?

Gomez [Looking at Gonzales, Gomez begins laughing.]: Elena, please tell one of the servants to get Gonzales some coffee.

Elena: Yes, father. Oh father, may I use one of the cars today?

Gomez: Yes, of course, where are you going?

Elena: Into Bogota to do some shopping.

Gomez: Speak to the servants and then you may go. Oh, wait a minute.

Elena: Yes, father?

Gomez: Could you give Gonzales a ride to his hacienda on your way to the city? I don't believe that he will be able to drive.

Elena: Yes, father. [Elena exits.]

Gomez [looking at Gonzales]: Ah, excellent. All is as it should be...just as it should be.

[The lights fall.]

ACT TWO

Scene One

[A shack in Colombia. The entire atmosphere portrays extreme poverty. Newspapers cover the windows. A bed with a ragged cover is situated in the center of the stage. A young but exhausted woman is in the bed. She is moaning quietly. Her husband, Pedro, is standing near her. His appearance is shabby. Camilo Torres, a young priest, has just entered. Camilo Torres is thirty-five, intense, and relatively handsome.]

Torres: Pedro, what has happened? What has happened?

Pedro: Not long ago she started screaming that something exploded in the lower part of her stomach. She has grown weaker and paler.

Torres: Did you send for the doctor?

Pedro: I sent for the doctor, but he would not come. [weeping] I have no money...and he would not come. [becoming frightened] Father, what is going to happen?

Torres: She is going to die, Pedro.

Pedro: But she cannot die, Father...

Torres: God will welcome her. Pedro, He will welcome her. I will hear her confession...and give her the sacrament.

Pedro [weeping and anxious]: But she is too weak to speak.

Torres: God will hear her. He will hear her. [He takes a small black case from his coat. From the case he takes out a white wafer.] Isabella, accept Our Lord.

[Camilo Torres tries to give her the wafer but sees that it is useless. He slowly places the wafer back in its case.]

Pedro [anxiously]: She is too weak, Father, and you have not heard her confession.

Torres: It is all right, Pedro, it is all right. She has nothing to be sorry for. She has already paid for everything. You stay with her, and I will find a doctor to see if anything can yet be done. [Pedro moves next to Isabella and takes her hand. He looks at the priest with horror.]

Pedro [weeping with rage]: There is no need for a doctor!

[Camilo Torres starts to come to Pedro. He stops realizing the futility of present consolation. He leaves. The lights fall.]

Scene Two

[A city street in the slums of Colombia. It is the same day. There are shabby buildings, garbage, and general trash about the place. There is also a bench for those awaiting the bus. Camilo Torres is sitting alone on the bench. His head is bent down in thought. Miguel, a young student who is about nineteen years old, enters. He sees Camilo Torres and approaches him.]

Miguel: Father Torres, how are you?

Torres: Hello, Miguel. I am well, and yourself?

Miguel: I am fine. Are you going to the meeting today?

Torres: The meeting...oh yes, I almost forgot. Yes, I will be there.

Miguel: You must come, Father. The communists and socialists have been trying to gain control at each past meeting. They are each defending a purely ideological thesis which often times sounds inhuman.

Torres: What do you mean?

Miguel: I mean they are arguing more for blood than for bread.

Torres [pleased with Miguel's criticism]: I see. Yes, that is certainly the case. The radicals have become too heated with their own thoughts to see beyond themselves. At times I do not blame them.

Miguel [scanning the scene]: Yes, you only have to look around.

Torres: Yes, you only have to look around. [placing his head in his own hands] Do you know Pedro's wife, Isabella?

Miguel: Yes.

Torres: She died not more than an hour ago. I tried to give her the last sacrament, but she was too weak to receive it. [reflecting] Besides what good would that have done? She died of a burst appendix. She would have lived if a doctor, any doctor, would have come to her a few days ago. It is a very simple operation, Miguel, a very simple operation. But no one would help her because her husband had no money! After seeing such things over and over again I, too, become more and more enraged. Of course I will meet the radicals today.

Miguel: And what will you say to them?

Torres [reflecting]: Not a great deal.

Miguel: But I thought...

Torres: I know, I know. You thought I would come down on them and accuse them of only being radicals.

Miguel: Yes.

Torres: The time is not ripe for that. The radicals must still be used when and where they can be effective.

Miguel: I see.

Torres: Although I believe that we are all children of God and therefore should be housed, fed, and clothed in accordance with Christ's teachings; I do not expect our fellow revolutionaries to accept all my beliefs.

Miguel: Father, you had better be careful that they do not use you for their own ends.

Torres: That is true; I must be careful. But I must only take care to the extent the primary objective is achieved. The people must have doctors, food, and adequate housing. That is the teaching of Christ, and I am His priest.

Miguel: The communists wish to accomplish the same objective. So do the rest of the radicals.

Torres: Yes. But without reference to Christ. I am afraid if only the radicals gain power there will only be more slavery.

Miguel: What kind of slavery?

Torres: The kind of slavery people impose upon themselves in the name of an ideal. Sooner or later the ideal becomes the devil since people cannot tolerate the reality that they are human in the face of their own ideal. The ideal can make people incompassionate and mad with their own power. The ideal can become hard, cold and dead; and those under the ideal lose a living reality which is the true and the good basis of this world.

Miguel [confused]: What is that reality?

Torres: The reality and the power is the same reality and power that was in Jesus Christ.

Miguel: But the Church has done little to help the poor.

Torres [with quiet bitterness]: The Church is not always Christ!

Miguel: Be careful, Father. You are right, but the hot blood of our people often forces them to forget all perspective.

Torres: At times my own hot blood clouds my own theological perspective. However I am not allowed the luxury of being only a radical. I am a priest and must always place before me and above me the thought and compassion demanded by Jesus Christ.

Miguel: I do not know if the people can measure themselves as well.

Torres: They must or else hot blood and destruction will work against us. The rich will crush everyone in the name of law and order. [Miguel and Torres stand up. They begin to walk.]

Miguel: Step carefully, Father...carefully.

Torres [smiling and taking a light skip]: But we need not be that careful. Have a little faith, Miguel...just a little faith.

[The lights fall.]

Scene Three

[A closed room in a tavern. Three radicals are speaking. There is a communist, age 45; a socialist, age 32; and a nihilist, age 21.]

Communist: Colombia is a key to the world revolution!

Nihilist: Yes, but before the revolution can succeed we must destroy! We must bomb the haciendas of the rich aristocrats. At the same time we must bomb the Cardinal's residence. If we can steal the gold and jewels from the Church, buy guns, and then completely destroy the power of this feudal society, the people will have to turn to us and then we...

Socialist: Wait a minute...wait a minute! We must have change but gradual change. The people must have power not us!

Nihilist [raging]: But how will the people have power if we do not destroy the present power structure? We must tear everything down and then begin to build!

Communist: Yes, we can be helped afterward by the other communistic countries of the world. They will help us in restructuring a people's government. First the aristocratic and bourgeois swine must be slaughtered.

Nihilist [to socialist]: And the people will live off the bacon! [Communist and Nihilist begin laughing.]

Socialist: All right, but we must keep destruction to a minimum otherwise the people will have nothing on which to build.

Nihilist: We must have <u>maximum</u> destruction or else we will not root out all the diseases of the present system!

Socialist [confused but holding his position]: No.

Nihilist [sure of his position]: Yes!

Communist: Let us destroy it all and then we can appeal to my comrades who will help us rebuild.

Nihilist [raging]: But let us destroy! Let us destroy!

Communist: If we keep anything of the present structure it will only again be subsidized by the United States as it presently is.

Socialist: But we could use the money to hold free elections and aid the people.

Communist: But the purity of the revolution would be marred. No...a total overturn of power is needed!

Nihilist: And that means total destruction!

Socialist: No.

Communist: Yes!

Nihilist: Yes!

Socialist: But...

Nihilist [waving off the socialist]: Nonsense, that is all there is to it.

Socialist: I am leaving. Both of you want blood and power more than you want reform.

Communist [hedging and trying to contain the socialist]: Wait. We, too, want reform. Not just for Colombia but for the world.

Nihilist [going insane with the thought]: The world! The world! We must destroy!

Socialist [about to leave again]: I am going.

Communist: Stop...wait. The priest is supposed to come any moment now. We need him. The people trust him. He is a necessary instrument in bringing forth <u>our</u> plans.

Nihilist [reflecting and calming himself]: Please wait. If we are not united, he will lose confidence in us.

Socialist: I cannot unite with you.

Communist: Wait! [The socialist is in the process of leaving.] Wait! [There is a knock at the door. Torres and Miguel enter.]

Socialist: Father, there is no possibility of...

Communist [interrupting him]: There is no possibility of coming to an agreement without you. We need your help, Father.

Torres [sensing that he is about to be played into their hands]: What is the difficulty?

Communist: We cannot find a unifying theme.

Torres: What is the trouble?

Communist: I am afraid we have among us a moderate who wishes to betray the revolution.

Socialist: Not at all. I only wish that the power remains in the hands of the Colombian people and that the country does not become so ravaged that the people will only be governing a desert.

Nihilist: Ha! Half measures and too much wind. Let's do all or nothing. We must destroy before we can rebuild.

Torres [with authority]: That is enough! Look, do you want to overthrow the powers which make our people live like diseased animals, or do you want to argue forever among yourselves? Nothing is going to happen without a united front.

Nihilist: But we must destroy the present government.

Socialist: Not in the way you want it destroyed.

Communist: You see, Father, we have a moderate and thus a traitor.

Socialist: A traitor! At least I do not want a foreign power to control my people.

Communist: Neither do I.

Socialist: But you just said before Father Torres arrived that a foreign communistic power would have control of Colombia. I only want the Colombian people to be able to govern themselves and raise their standard of living.

Communist: By a foreign power I meant a power controlled by the workers...that is, a power forging to the present system.

Socialist: You're lying.

Nihilist [to Torres]: No, he isn't.

Torres: Look, if we cannot work for a united front among ourselves, I am leaving.

Communist: The Father is right. Let us work together.

Socialist: All right...against the present power system.

Torres: Exactly.

Nihilist: Against the privileged class and their indifference to the people.

Torres: Exactly. But we must use effective and measured tactics. We must remember that the prime objective is to get power into the hands of our people.

Communist: Exactly.

Torres: This means that more pamphlets and speeches must be made so that the revolution will come from the people. If enough pressure is exerted by them, the present regime will fall. This is the present concern. Let us trim all our ideologies to fit the immediacy of the hour. Only in this way can we unite for the present.

Socialist: And the future?

Torres: A socialistic government established through free elections will be the new life of the Colombian people.

Nihilist: But the present feudal regime will be destroyed.

Torres: Of course.

Nihilist: Bravo! Let us continue our work.

Communist: Precisely!

Torres: Remember that the people must be united. I will do what I can at the university and through the Church. You must all start to mobilize your groups for the final overthrow, but move carefully. The secret police and the army are ruthless. They could destroy the entire movement before we could gain a satisfactory foothold. Keep things directed toward the people. If enough pressures can be exerted by present social needs, and our showing a way to alleviate such needs, the revolution will succeed.

Socialist: Long live the revolution!

Communist: Long live the revolution!

Miguel and Nihilist: Long live the revolution!

Torres: But first let us make sure that it is given a satisfactory birth.

Communist: I must be going.

Nihilist: I will come with you.

Communist: Good-bye, Father. We will continue our work. [The communist and nihilist leave.]

Socialist: Thank you, Father. I agree with what you have said. I will tell my friends of your proposal. [He exits.]

Miguel [after a few moments]: Well done, Father, but...

Torres: I know...but we cannot really trust any of them.

Miguel: Yes, that is true.

Torres: But we need them for the present.

Miguel: And afterwards?

Torres: We must have unity now. If we cannot have unity, we will only fight among ourselves. Once the people have been united and mobilized and the revolution has succeeded, then we will be in a better position to discover what is best for the people. Until then we must use our friends.

Miguel: Do you think if the revolution succeeds the people will trust you?

Torres: We must have some faith in the goodness of the people. I must believe that they trust me now and that they will trust me in the future. We are fighting for them, Miguel, and the people are not ungrateful.

[The lights fall.]

ACT THREE

Scene One

[A city street.]

Torres: Miguel, it is time we parted company. I have an appointment with the Cardinal for which I am already late.

Miguel: I will see you tomorrow, Father.

Torres: Fine. Speak with your friends. Get together four or five of those you can trust. I will speak with them soon. [Torres leaves. Miguel waits a few seconds and starts to leave in the opposite direction. A girl's voice is heard.]

Elena: Miguel...Miguel. [Elena enters.] There you are. I have been looking for you.

Miguel: Elena. [They kiss each other.] Does your father know where you are?

Elena: Of course not. I told him I was going shopping. Where have you been all day?

Miguel: I have been with Father Torres.

Elena: The radical priest?

Miguel, Yes, and a real priest.

Elena: And what have you been saying?

Miguel: Very little. I should have been speaking to him about us, and our wedding.

Elena: But my father would never permit that.

Miguel [smiling]: I know and that is why I often participate with a radical priest for reasons closer to me than politics.

Elena: Do you think he would really marry us without my father's consent?

Miguel [laughing] I am sure he would. It would be part of the revolution.

Elena: The revolution?

Miguel [There is a brief silence. He then speaks with helpless bitterness.]: The revolution which will destroy the shame of being poor. [brief silence]

Elena [concerned]: You should not feel shame. It is the rich who deserve the shame. [brief silence] Do you know Gonzales, the landowner?

Miguel [bitterly]: No, but I know of him.

Elena: This afternoon he became drunk again at our hacienda. Father asked me to drive him home. Gonzales, between periods when we had to stop so that he could vomit, kept mumbling something about your friend, Father Torres. Something about education as bribery.

Miguel: Education as bribery?

Elena: Apparently they want to get Father Torres out of the country. The Cardinal was also at the hacienda today. Apparently my father, Gonzales, and the Cardinal are going to send Father Torres to Europe for more education.

Miguel: And frustrate his work?

Elena: I suppose that is their plan.

Miguel: Then everyone is against him...everyone.

[The lights fall.]

Scene Two

[The Cardinal's office. His "Eminence," is seated at a large desk in a swivel chair. A huge Bible is on the desk. His office is elaborately decorated. A gold crucifix hangs on the wall. There are polished wood bookcases. Behind the desk is a Renaissance painting in which a plump and smiling Christ is depicted changing water into wine. On either side of the painting is a picture of John XXIII and Pius XII. The room exudes elegance, having the same type of rugs and candle fixtures as Gomez's hacienda in Act One. The Cardinal is seated and is looking at his official papers. His secretary, an overweight and puffy priest, enters.]

Secretary: Your Eminence, Father Torres is here. [The Cardinal stands up and straightens his robes and pectoral cross.]

Cardinal: Show him in. [The Cardinal remains standing. Torres enters.]

Torres: Good afternoon, your Eminence.

Cardinal: Father...Father, how good it is to see you. How good it is to see you. Please sit down. [The Cardinal escorts Torres to a seat at the left of the desk. The Cardinal picks up a cigar box and goes to Torres.] A cigar?

Torres: No thank you, your Eminence.

Cardinal [Sitting behind his desk and leaning back in his swivel chair, he lights and puffs on his cigar.]: Well, Father, what have you been doing since we last saw each other?

Torres: Your Eminence, you know that I have been teaching and serving the Church as a priest.

Cardinal [narrowing his snake-like eyes]: And what else?

Torres [blandly]: That is more than enough for anyone.

Cardinal: There have been many reports that you have been engaging in revolutionary activities.

Torres: Those activities have not been so much revolutionary as Christian.

Cardinal: But they have not been done through Holy Mother Church's authority.

Torres: That is true in some cases.

Cardinal: However, the Church has begun to admire your zeal in these pursuits.

Torres [surprised in a guarded fashion]: Really?

Cardinal: Yes, Father, yes indeed.

Torres: Would the Church be willing to aid me with finances to help the poor?

Cardinal [thinking and puffing smoke]: It would.

Torres: Excellent. Then the Church should begin by building more hospitals, homes for orphans and the aged. It should sell its gold chalices, emerald rings, and immense land holdings. It should use the proceeds to help the poor. We should all work for a living like everyone else. Now priests are supported financially by the people. We should be helping the people with our financial contributions to them. No poor man should ever be asked for money!

Cardinal [taken aback but remaining the negotiator]: You are very progressive, Father, very progressive. However, you realize that it will take Holy Mother Church time to adjust to such changes.

Torres [annoyed]: The people cannot wait for the Church to "adjust." Every day people are dying from the needs of bare necessities. The rings on your hands could buy enough food to feed an entire village for a month. Yet the rings will remain on your hands just as the Church will remain speaking the word "adjustment."

Cardinal [resenting the attack]: Now just a minute, Father. Just a minute. I agree that changes should come. However, the Church is not ready for such drastic changes as you are advocating. And I, as one of the Church's leaders, do not believe that you are, yourself, prepared to take the responsibility for the consequences of such changes.

Torres: Whether I am prepared or not, the people are prepared to undertake such action and be responsible for the consequences.

Cardinal: But who will control the people if not leaders like ourselves?

Torres [cringing at the last statement]: Your Eminence, the people do not need to be controlled. They need to be freed from poverty and disease.

Cardinal [conciliatory]: I agree, Father, and you are one of those who must help to free them. However, I do not know if you are sufficiently prepared to do so.

Torres: What do you mean?

Cardinal: Simply this. I have been sufficiently impressed by your efforts thus far to place more power in your hands. However, Father, you are very young. You have not completed your education. I have decided that it would be for your own best interests, Colombia's best interests, and the Church's best interests, if you returned to the University of Louvain and earned your doctorate in sociology. Then we could both see more clearly what would be the best attitude to assume for both Colombia and the Church.

Torres: And how long should I stay at Louvain?

Cardinal: Until your studies are completed.

Torres: That would take at least three years! All that I have done thus far would be ruined.

Cardinal [putting down his cigar and looking heavenward]: Father, you have no faith in me and your fellow priests. You as a priest should know that the Church's care of souls is an absolute spiritual responsibility. All our power is from God and is based upon our beloved Lord's statement; "Thou art Peter and upon this rock I will build my Church, and the gates of Hell shall not prevail against it." You know this, Father, and you also know that all right, all power, all charisma, as well as all spiritual and all temporal gifts both in heaven above and on earth below are delegated to that Holy Catholic and Apostolic Church and Her divinely ordered structure.

Torres [becoming infuriated]: I know, your Eminence, and this is all that I know: I cannot go up to the altar of God as a priest when my brothers and my sisters are dying from hunger, from disease, and from statements like you have just made!

Cardinal [taken aback, but measuring himself]: Father, certainly you cannot go against our beloved Lord's statement to the founder of the true, holy, and apostolic Church.

Torres [furious]: The Church is that place where the poor are fed and justice is enacted on behalf of the needy. There and only there is Christ's Church! I can't find anywhere in the Bible where Jesus said to Peter: "We'll live off the poor until we're so fat and weak that we'll be forced to look at the sky since we'll be unable to see over the top of our bellies."

Cardinal [becoming enraged]: I suppose you're making a reference to me.

Torres [with mockery]: So the snake of conscience can even strike at a Cardinal!

Cardinal: [trying to control himself]: All right, Father, all right. Perhaps I am overweight.

Torres [laughing out loud]: That's not the point.

Cardinal [red in the face and blurting out the question]: Father, will you go to Louvain or won't you?

Torres [knowing when to stop but unable to control himself entirely]: Your Eminence, I must have time to consider your request.

Cardinal: Please take a few days to consider my proposal. I trust you will complete your studies or else.

Torres: Or else what?

Cardinal: Or else severe measures must be taken.

Torres: Oh, I see. [He pauses for a few moments and then stands up.] Good day, your Eminence. [Torres goes to the door. The Cardinal bows but looks up and realizes that no one is there to acknowledge his bow. As Torres opens the door the secretary, who has been listening at the door unseen by the audience and who has had his weight pressed up against the door, falls on the floor. Torres turns to the Cardinal and points to the secretary on the floor.] Your Eminence...your servant. [Torres leaves laughing.]

Cardinal [furious and raging at his secretary]: Get up, you fool.

Secretary: But, your Eminence...

Cardinal: I said get up! [He picks up his cigar, takes a puff and begins choking. The lights fall.]

Scene Three

[A university classroom. Torres has just completed a lecture. He is standing near a table with a few books on it. The students have surrounded him.]

1st Student: Father, when will we move?

2nd Student: Next month or at the end of the year?

3rd Student: Yes, Father, when?

Torres: We need more people before we can act as a united front. Go to the villages and speak with the farmers. Go to the factories and speak with the workers. The time is growing ripe for an all-out revolution. But we need more people. Be careful. You must all use discretion. More and more I am forced to speak in public. But each of you can be effective by speaking to workers and farmers. You can also be effective by listening to their sufferings and their questions. Be gentle with the people. Explain yourselves clearly and show them that you are sincerely trying to bring about a better life for them and for their families.

1st Student: Long live the revolution!

2nd and 3rd Students: La Revolucion!!! [The students leave. Torres sits down on the table and Miguel enters.]

Miguel: The students look as though they are ready.

Torres [sternly]: They are not ready yet. We need more people behind us. The students will need more patience and will have to become more acquainted with the people. [Miguel reflects a moment.]

Miguel: Father, I have some news for you.

Torres: Oh?

Miguel: I was speaking with Elena, the daughter of Senor Gomez. She mentioned that the Cardinal was at her father's hacienda and was speaking about bribing you with more education. Does that make any sense to you?

Torres: Oh yes, yes it makes a great deal of sense. Yes, everything is much clearer now. [He picks up his books and begins to leave.]

Miguel: What is it, Father?

Torres: I have an appointment with the Cardinal.

Miguel: May I walk with you?

Torres: Certainly, come along. [stopping] Miguel, do you know what they are trying to do? They are trying to take my work away from me by holding out some abstract degree and many false promises. I realize exactly what they are trying to do. Perhaps I should be quiet and let them toy with me a little longer. However, I am sick of their sordid, cheap, and underhanded maneuvers. It is time I confronted them directly.

Miguel: If you do that, they will not allow you to speak at the university.

Torres: They will also deny me the privilege of saying Mass and other rites which a priest may use to comfort the poor. Still, I have waited too long. Soon they will begin to tell lies about me. They will invent lies to try and destroy the people's trust in me and the revolution. [Torres notices that Miguel has become quite anxious.]

Miguel: But if they silence you, what can you do against them?

Torres [attempting to sort out many thoughts at once]: Miguel, whatever will happen in the future I do no know. I only know that whatever means are available I will use to crush the evil that is all about us. You and the others must carry on the work that we have begun at the university. Try to understand that many students at the university mean well but they, too, are of the privileged class. Many simply want to rebel for purely psychological reasons. Their rebellion is therefore unstructured and very temporary. It is simply a type of non-conformism which offends the workers and the farmers. You must work to unite the students with all segments of the population.

Miguel: I will try, Father. But what will you do?

Torres: I will meet with the Cardinal first. After I have spoken with him, I will then know which course to take. I will probably join the army of liberation in the mountains. That will be the only effective means left for me to aid the revolution.

Miguel [terrified]: But, Father...

Torres: Shh, Miguel. We are friends now. Call me Camilo before we part for I will not be a priest in the eyes of this world much longer.

Miguel: But what if you are killed? And what if I fail? And what if the army of liberation is destroyed?

Torres [quietly and with simple dignity]: We shall not fail. Whether the revolution succeeds completely now or later is not so important. And Miguel, remember this: even if both of us are killed and many armies of liberation are destroyed, others will rise up again to attack the indifference of the privileged classes. Many need only look at the people's suffering and their consciences as well as the consciences of many others as yet unborn will rise up to demand justice. The High Spirit of Christ Himself will aid them in their struggle just as It has aided me. [He stops for a few seconds and tries to control his emotions.] Miguel, have faith in Jesus Christ and in the revolution; that is all you need. And now we must part. [They stand up, shake hands, and embrace each other.]

Miguel [on the verge of tears]: But, Father...

Torres [smiling]: Shh, Miguel. Remember...Camilio. [He leaves quickly. Miguel starts to follow him but stops. He looks around the classroom as the lights fall.]

Scene Four

[The Cardinal's office. The secretary is now occupying the chair next to the desk formerly occupied by Camilo Torres. The Cardinal is seated behind the desk.]

Cardinal [furiously]: Write a letter to Senor Gomez. Tell him that the plan is not working. Tell him also that if Father Torres does not go to Louvain, I will deprive him of the right to say Mass. I will also forbid him to lecture at the university or speak in public. Gomez must use his influence with the secret police to see that my commands are enforced. [sounding more and more like a dictator] Tell Gomez that Torres's insubordination will not be tolerated! [There is a knock at the door. The Cardinal yells at the door.] Come in!

Torres: Your Eminence.

Cardinal [trying to control himself]: Come in, Father. [turning to his secretary] Get out of here!

Secretary: Yes, your Eminence...Yes, your Eminence. [Grabbing his papers, he hurries out.]

Cardinal: Would you like a drink?

Torres [smiling]: No, thank you, your Eminence, but please help yourself.

Cardinal: I believe I will. [The Cardinal looks puzzled for a moment as though he had misplaced something. He then remembers what he was looking for. He opens the large Bible on his desk which is actually hollow. He takes out a large bottle of Kentucky whiskey, the same brand of whiskey used by Gomez and Gonzales in Act One. Torres begins chuckling.] I see that you are in a good mood.

Torres [baiting a trap]: Oh, I am, your Eminence. I am.

Cardinal: And have you reached a decision? [The Cardinal leans back in his plush swivel-chair, holding his drink.]

Torres: I have. [a brief silence]

Cardinal [imperiously]: And what is it? [He leans forward looking intently at Torres.]

Torres [smiling]: I have decided to agree with you.

Cardinal [leaning back again]: Oh, excellent, excellent. And when do you plan to leave for Louvain? [He takes a sip of his drink.]

Torres: Oh, in about five years. [The Cardinal chokes on his whiskey. He spills half of his glass on his scarlet cape. He stands up and begins coughing. Torres stands up and goes over to assist him. He slaps the Cardinal on the back with great enthusiasm.] There, there, your Eminence. Something went down the wrong way, didn't it?

Cardinal: It certainly did. Thank you...thank you. [The Cardinal is puzzled. He realizes that something has gone wrong. He slowly remembers.] Why is it that you have decided to wait five years?

Torres [realizing that the fun is over]: Because in that way I could better study our Colombian problem. In that way I would be better prepared to make the most of my studies at Louvain.

Cardinal [desperate--changing to a more hostile tone]: But you are prepared well enough now. If you left now your most important work could begin sooner. [imploringly] Please go to Louvain now, Father. Let us not make things difficult for each other.

Torres [realizing that the end has come]: Your Eminence, I cannot see how things will be made difficult by my staying here.

Cardinal [fiercely]: You know what I mean.

Torres [matching him in fierceness]: No, your Eminence, what do you mean?

Cardinal [He takes a sip from his glass and puts it down. He folds his hands on his desk. During these gestures he is trying to gain control of himself and the situation.]: Look, Father, you are backing a revolution. You as a priest have no business doing such a thing. You should mellow in mind and spirit, yourself, before you try to change such an ancient society as this.

Torres [sarcastically]: Very good, your Eminence, but when some men mellow, they rot!

Cardinal [slowly]: Father, if you remain in Colombia for another month, I will have to deprive you of the privileges of saying Mass, preaching and lecturing. I am sorry, but my hands are tied.

Torres [staring at the whiskey bottle]: By the rich!

Cardinal [jumping to his feet]: What? I'll...we'll...

Torres [He also stands. He speaks with total passion.]: All right, your Eminence, you'll stand there and lie over the top of that crucifix which lies on your chest. Well, I am tired of listening to you and your petty threats. You sound like a dying man who has sold his soul for a soft chair and a glass of whiskey. [He rips his own Roman Catholic collar off and throws it at the Cardinal.] Here, take your "official" symbol. Before I ever again go up to the altar of God, I will be sure my brothers and my sisters are fed first. That is Christ's teaching and I am His priest. I need neither your threats nor your consent to serve God and my neighbor. [He starts to leave.]

Cardinal [shocked and seeking any phrase]: It will hurt you to fight against the Church of God.

Torres [turns and stops]: I will not be fighting against "the Church of God." I will only be fighting against a few lazy rich men who live off the labor and the misery of the poor. [He leaves. The Cardinal is left standing. The lights fall.]

ACT FOUR

Scene One

[A jungle camp of the army of liberation. Four soldiers are dressed with bandoliers and are holding rifles. Torres is with them. He has a bandolier of bullets across his chest and his rifle is lying close to him. The general mood is one of brief relaxation between battles.]

1st Soldier: It looks like it's going to be brutal.

2nd Soldier: How many men did we lose last night?

3rd Soldier: Fifteen.

4th Soldier: And the night before?

1st Soldier: Five.

3rd Soldier: It is not good. The army of the rich has plenty of supplies, better guns, and the chance of sleeping.

2nd Soldier: Yes, they have everything but honor.

1st Soldier [laughing and slapping his own neck]: And mosquitos. Say Camilo, you look a little sad. Still praying, eh?

Torres [good naturedly]: No...not praying--thinking.

1st Soldier: I would think a little more myself before I ran back and forth across the front lines as you did yesterday.

3rd Soldier: Yes, Camilo. If we lose you how shall we explain it to God? Not that He'll listen to me anyway. But you know, if I commit many more sins He will put me in the same place with the rich people.

Torres [smiling]: And then God will have another revolution. [They all laugh and then stop. There is a brief silence.]

1st Soldier: I wonder where our friends are who died.

3rd Soldier [somberly]: What do you say, Camilo?

Torres: They are with God and yet they are still with us. So let us bring God's kingdom to earth! Let us continue the fight for which our friends have died!

1st Soldier: Viva la Revolucion! [The rest chant, "Viva La Revolucion!"]

2nd Soldier: We had better join the rest of the troops. [He leaves.]

1st Soldier: Let us go. [3rd and 4th soldiers leave.] Camilo are you coming?

Torres: I will be with you in a moment. I want to watch the stars in the heavens for just a little while. Then I will join you.

1st Soldier: As you wish, but don't spend too much time. We are soon to fight again. [He leaves.]

Torres [alone and looking at the sky]: It is a strange thing the way seven stars seem to dance upon one another. [He looks about him.] They are saying something to me. Ah, I know. [He looks at his rifle and then picks it up. He stops.] Something pulls me backward and forward at once. [He looks around and then at the sky.] Life would hold me here. Yet it is a higher life for all that calls me onward. Soon we must fight again. [He takes seven bullets from his bandolier. He smiles. Immediately his smile changes to a fierce seriousness.] And I must dedicate each bullet:

One--for Isabella who died unaided. [A bullet is placed in the rifle after each number is announced.]

Two--for Pedro's sorrow!

Three--for Miguel and the united front!

Four--to destroy the rich and give all to the people!

Five--for the Revolution!

Six--for Christ!

Seven--for Christ and the Revolution!

[He places the seventh bullet in his gun and begins yelling with a mad happiness.] Christ and the Revolution! [Facing the audience he moves to the back of the stage with his rifle. He starts shouting wildly.] La Revolucion!!! La Revolucion!!! [His shouts are answered from all the corners of the stage. The other soldiers join him. All are on the stage shouting "La Revolucion" waving their rifles and shouting as they leave the stage. Shots are heard. The lights fall quickly.]

Scene Two

[Two days later. The same closed room in a tavern as Act Two, Scene Three. Elena and Miguel are seated at a table.]

Miguel: This place is very lonely.

Elena: But I am here.

Miguel: Yes, but Father Torres's presence seems to inhabit the room from the last meeting we had here.

Elena: Have you heard from him lately?

Miguel: No. He said he was gong to fight with the army of liberation. Since then I have not heard from him. [The socialist from Act Two, Scene Three enters.]

Socialist: Father Torres is dead.

Miguel [gripping himself]: Let me see. [He takes a newspaper from the socialist and studies it for a moment. He then reads aloud.]

"Camilo Torres, renegade priest and communist, was justly killed by the National Army on Friday. His body and the bodies of other traitors have been buried in a lime pit. This is a just and fitting end for an animal who wished to subvert the peace and security of Colombia. Let this be a warning to all those who wish in any way to attack the sacred truth of our blessed protectress, Holy Mother Church, or in any way change unlawfully the established policies of state."

[Miguel stands up and begins to laugh out loud. He stops. Fiercely, he speaks] What do the other newspapers say?

Socialist: Two other papers describe him as an anarchist and as a traitor. Another paper is not sure whether he ever existed.

Miguel: I thought so. Look, there is no time to lose. Quickly. Mobilize all the factions you can find in the city square.

Elena: But Father Torres is dead.

Miguel [laughing]: No he isn't. Quickly. We must act before the rich and the Church publish any more reports like this one. [At once the lights fall.]

Scene Three

[As soon as possible the lights come up again. Miguel is standing on crates in the public square. Pedro, nihilist, communist, socialist, and other people surround the crates. By now the impact of Camilo Torres's death begins to show its effect. He begins speaking slowly. He attempts to choose the right words.]

Miguel: Some of you have read the newspapers and you are confused about Camilo Torres and what he has done for you. The Church and the government have already begun to defile his name. Already they are trying to make you forget him. [He hesitates for a few seconds. His voice breaks into a passionate eloquence. He is no longer concerned with precisely the right words. Rather he wishes to present the images of the priest as they present themselves to his mind. The more he speaks, the greater becomes the force and eloquence of his plea.]

But do not forget, rather remember...

Remember Torres
when they shall tell you that God
can be controlled,
and that His men are false.
Remember Torres
when time and man
will tell you to forget him.
Remember Torres's spirit.
Remember that his spirit
is now one with The Spirit of God.
But also remember that
prophets die alone and deserted
so that a child
may have bread.

Did he die in
the Church?
Do not ask such questions.
You know that as the
stars present themselves in the heavens
Torres presents himself to God!
Let the Church fall to perdition
With its articles of retribution.

Torres lives--
his name to thousands.
Torres strives
in Holy Passion.
Will you have him lessened
by the hypocrites who will question?
Damn them!
To the battle against tyranny!
To the altar of justice!
If we are to see God,
then let us feed His children!

Church and State erect
the scaffold
of disease and starvation.
Church and State have made
all our sufferings.

Load the rifle!
Surmount the barricade!
And as the bullets fly
and the blood of innocence
flows--
Remember the cries of the oppressed!
Remember the Spirit against the flesh!
Remember the saint and not the devils!
Remember his sacrifice for our liberation!
Remember his death for our resurrection!
Remember Christ and His servant!
Remember Christ!
Remember Torres!

[There are multitudinous shouts all intermingled of "Christ!" "Torres!" "La Revolucion!" and "Viva la revolucion!" This frenzy continues for several seconds. Shouts are heard. A bomb explodes. The police appear. Workers, students, and police collide as the lights fall.]